THE POWER OF THE POSTER

EDITED BY
MARGARET TIMMERS

V&A PUBLICATIONS

To the memory of my mother who inspired me

M.W.T.

First published by V&A Publications, 1998

Reprinted 1998, 2003

V&A Publications
160 Brompton Road
London SW3 1HW

Photography by Christine Smith, V&A Photographic Studio

Designed by Janet James

ISBN 1 85177 2413

A catalogue record for this book is available from the British Library

Printed and bound in Great Britain by Butler & Tanner Ltd, Frome

Note: Every effort has been made to seek permission to reproduce those images whose copyright does not reside with the V&A, and we are grateful to the individuals and institutions who have assisted in this task. Any omissions are entirely unintentional, and the details should be addressed to the publishers. Copyright holders, where known, are listed on page 250

All posters are lithographs unless otherwise stated in the caption

Front of cover: Boris Bućan.
'The Fire Bird' and 'Petrushka',
Croatia, 1983.

Back of cover: Tom Purvis.
'East Coast by L.N.E.R.', UK, 1925.

Anon. 'Pax Sovietica', Poland c.1982.

Guerrilla Girls. 'Do women have to be naked to get into the Met. Museum?',
USA, 1989.

Half title: Roy Lichtenstein.
'Crak! Now, Mes Petits... Pour La France', USA, 1963.

Frontispiece: Tomoko Miho.
'65 bridges to new york', USA, 1968.

CONTENTS

ACKNOWLEDGEMENTS

The Board of Trustees of the Victoria and Albert Museum is most grateful to the exhibition sponsors: The Maiden Group, JC Decaux, Mills & Allen and The More Group.

The authors acknowledge with gratitude the enthusiasm, encouragement and expert guidance of all those who have helped with the preparation of this book. They would like to thank their friends and colleagues at the V&A, and above all Susan Lambert, Curator of Prints, Drawings and Paintings, for her generous and unwavering support. They are also grateful to Paul Greenhalgh and Malcolm Baker of the Research Department; Linda Lloyd-Jones, Juliette Foy, Suzanne Fagence and Alison Pearce of the Exhibitions Department; Andrew Bolton of Far Eastern; Divia Patel of Indian and South East Asian; Pauline Webber and Alison Norton of Paper Conservation; Martin Barnes, Shaun Cole, Mark Haworth-Booth, Rosemary Miles, Elizabeth Miller, Frances Rankine, Gill Saunders, Moira Thunder, Tim Travis and Pat West of the Prints, Drawings and Paintings Department; Ngozi Ikoku of Textiles and Dress; and Margaret Benton and Jim Fowler of the Theatre Museum.

They are also indebted to Jeremy Aynsley of the Royal College of Art and Susan Lambert for reading the texts, and to Moira Johnston for her sympathetic and meticulous copy-editing. The V&A Photo Studio, especially Ken Jackson and Christine Smith, triumphantly photographed large numbers of unwieldy posters, which the object handlers transported to and fro with skill. The V&A Archive & Registry produced quantities of files with great efficiency. As well as the V&A home team, the book was fortunate to have the devoted help of some wonderful volunteers: Harriet Comben, Maria Georgaki, Anna Gustavsson, Daan de Kuyper (for work both in London and in New York), Isobel Lowyck, Devorah Moritz, Emma Nicholson, Yasuko Suga and Fiona Tomlinson. The secretarial help by Clare Moore and translation of Russian by Susan Reid is gratefully acknowledged.

Expert guidance and sharing of information was given by many, including Will Birch; Nicky Bird; Jenny Bissett; Rodney Brangwyn; Dr Judith Bronkhurst of The Witt Library; Kenneth Burton; Craig Clunas; Diana de Vere Cole of The Jointure, Ditchling; Beverley Cole of the National Railway Museum, York; Michael Cudlipp of The History of Advertising Trust Archive; Pen Dalton; Krzysztof Dydo of Cracow; Edwin Embleton; Michael English; Eileen Evans; James H. Fraser of Madison, New Jersey; Elizabeth Greig; Professor Mitchell Hall of Central Michigan University; Leila Horvath; David Fraser Jenkins of the Tate Gallery; John Jenkins of Onslows; Bob King of De Wynters; Csaba Kozák of the Palace of Art, Budapest; Marius Kwint; Paul Liss; Jane Livingstone of the English National Opera; John Marriott; Holger Matthies; Elena Millie of The Library of Congress, Washington; Michael Moody of the Imperial War Museum; Péter Pócs; Maurice Rickards; Jonathan Riddell of the London Transport Museum; Katrina Royall; Jan Sawka; Rosemary Seligman; Michael Twyman of the University of Reading; James Whitehouse of Aerofilms; Michael Wilson.

The authors are extremely grateful to V&A Publications for having faith in the book, and especially to Mary Butler and Miranda Harrison for their encouragement and support.

INTRODUCTION

MARGARET TIMMERS

In an age of instant transmission and computerized technology, it is perhaps surprising that the poster continues to flourish as a significant art form and primary means of communication. Drawing on the extensive collections at the Victoria & Albert Museum, this book and the accompanying exhibition re-examine the nature of the poster, and the special qualities that have enabled it not merely to survive, but to evolve throughout its history as an effective medium of publicity and persuasion.

What is a poster? The current Oxford English Dictionary definition is 'placard posted or displayed in a public place as an announcement or advertisement'. The word 'poster' probably derives from the practice of placing public announcements on posts; subsequently the definition of the word (like that of the French 'l'affiche') was expanded to refer to a public notice that is posted or put up in a public place.

Attempting a precise definition is difficult, but broadly speaking a poster may be defined by its function and form. At the edges of the definition lie the exceptions and variants which help us to understand what we normally mean by the term. In its function, a poster is essentially a product of communication between an active force and a re-active one. Its originator (individual, institution, business or organization) has a message to sell; the recipient, its target audience, must be persuaded to buy the message. The interchange takes place in the public domain.

In its form, the poster is generally identified by characteristics of size, shape and materials, and by means of production and communication. Mass-produced posters have commonly been printed to standard formats (based on paper sizes) specific to intended sites; individually made posters do not necessarily follow this pattern. The materials used are usually ink on paper, the image having normally been reproduced by a printing process. There are, however, many examples of posters that are original one-off designs which use any variety of graphic materials. The form most frequently relies on a combination of text and imagery, but either text or image can be used in isolation.

How does the effective poster achieve its aim? By its nature, the poster has the ability to seize the immediate attention of the viewer, and then to retain it for what is usually a brief but intense period. During that span of attention, it can provoke and motivate its audience – it can make the viewer gasp, laugh, reflect, question, assent, protest, recoil or otherwise react. This is part of the process by which the message is conveyed and, in successful cases, ultimately acted upon. At its most effective, the poster is a dynamic force for change.

Since posters may be aimed at virtually any sector of society, the means by which their messages are conveyed are crucial to their effectiveness. Above all, they communicate through the accessibility and adaptability of their graphic vocabulary. Posters address us in everyday, contemporary language, and appeal to us with directly compelling imagery. Through the distillation process which is part of their creative form, they have the ability to embody complicated thoughts and messages with a concentration of imagery akin to poetry. They can have broad popular appeal, and yet specifically target the individual who is alert to decode their deeper meaning. Their voice can vary from plain announcement to emotional, moral or intellectual appeal, or to imperative advertisement. Also, being cast in a colloquial idiom, they can change their tone and vocabulary to express and reflect shifting cultural values and codes of behaviour.

Equally crucial in explaining the continuous popular appeal of the poster is the availability of the means of production. For the poster can be reproduced using any printing process, from state-of-the-art technology to simple duplication. In the beginning, it was the development by Jules Chéret of high-speed printing by colour lithography that brought the emerging art form to millions; nowadays, the majority of posters are printed by colour offset lithography. But the fact that they can also be produced by means of screen-print, lino-cut, line-block, letterpress, woodcut, simple lithography, etc., is of importance to individuals and organizations where money is not available for sophisticated, expensive productions.

A third factor in understanding the continued power and appeal of the poster is the accessibility of its physical deployment. From the beginning, it was present in the public spaces we all inhabit – streets (plate 1), trains and buses, Underground stations (plate 2), shops and factories, theatres and cinemas. In 1872, John Ruskin wrote from Florence that 'the fresco-painting of the bill-sticker is likely, so far as I see, to become the principal Fine Art of Modern Europe: here, at all

1. **Street Advertising. Photograph by John Thomson, c. 1876-77, from J. Thomson and A. Smith,** *Streetlife in London* **(London, 1878).** Ph. 985-1978

2. **Notting Hill Underground Station, London, with posters** *in situ*, **c. 1919. The London Transport Museum.**

events, it is now the principal source of street effect. Giotto's time is past...but the bill-poster succeeds'.[1] It has indeed had a marked effect on the urban, and in some cases, the rural landscape.

During the twentieth century, posters have become ever more inventive, with advertisements that light up, rotate and generally use all manner of optical and even aural and olfactory illusions. As well as the ubiquitous roadside hoardings (over 80,000 in the United Kingdom), there is a vast panoply of external and internal surfaces for the legal and illegal posting of bills. Posters are not limited to the static walls of architecture and

3. Shell-Mex and BP lorry with Curtis Moffat's 'Photographers Prefer Shell' 1934 bill on its side, UK.

fixed constructions; they are also to be seen on surfaces that move – lorries (such as those of Shell-Mex and BP which carried posters in the 1930s, plate 3); trains, buses and cabs; on human beings (demonstrators, sandwich-board men); even on animals (for example on beef cattle during the UK 1996 'mad cow disease' scare; plate 5). They are part of street theatre: the very action of pasting up posters is an event, and hoardings can create a dramatic setting for stunts (plate 6). Together, competing and jostling for position, they offer compelling showcases of public art – sometimes described as the art gallery of the street – vying for the attention of their captive audience.

4. George William Joy. 'The Bayswater Omnibus', UK, 1895.
Oil on canvas.
The Museum of London, no. 29-166.

This painting illustrates the use of small posters, and in particular shows Pears' *'Adeline Patti'* and *'Bubbles'* posters (plate 174, chapter 5).

5. Cows wearing advertising jackets in a field in Hockley Heath, near Birmingham, 27 May 1996. Photograph by Steve Hill.

6. Boase Massimi Pollitt: art director: Peter Gatley; copywriter: John Pallant. 'Imagine What London Will Be Like Run By Whitehall', UK, 1985. E.340-1985

Issued by The Greater London Council in protest against its proposed abolition.

For the purposes of this book and the V&A exhibition, posters have been grouped into three broad categories based on the 'products' they are selling. The first, entitled 'Pleasure and Leisure', has posters announcing performances and cultural events, including the physical culture of sport; a sub-section focuses on posters by artists, mainly those advertising exhibitions. The second, 'Protest and Propaganda', is for posters of challenge and commitment, promoting issues and ideas. The third, 'Commerce and Communication', includes posters advertising consumer products, and services such as the railways and postal communications. The three sections are explored by writers who approach their subjects from different perspectives, and therefore speak in a variety of voices. All are concerned to investigate the power and effectiveness of the poster, and to set it in an intellectual and physical context.

POSTER COLLECTIONS

Virtually all the posters illustrated in this book, and shown in the accompanying exhibition, are drawn from the national collection held by the Prints, Drawings and Paintings Department at the V&A. This important collection of about 10,000 is international in scope, about half are British and half come from other nationalities; it ranges from classic posters of the 1880s and 1890s to present-day acquisitions. A small proportion is on display in the Museum's galleries, while the remainder is easily accessible though the Department's Print Room. Further collections of posters are housed in the Theatre Museum, the Far Eastern Department, the Indian and South East Asian Department, and within the National Art Library's Museum Archive Section. With the specialist collections in the Imperial War Museum, the London Transport Museum and the National Railway Museum, the V&A's holdings are an essential resource for the study of poster design in Britain.

The idea that posters merited collection by a museum was first formulated by Roger Marx in the periodical *Les Maîtres de l'Affiche* in 1899: he proposed a 'Musée moderne de l'Affiche illustrée' as a testimony and document of the life and art of the times.[2] A discussion was subsequently conducted through the pages of *L'Estampe et l'Affiche*,[3] and while the principle itself was generally accepted, immediate questions were raised over the suitability of a museum as the setting for posters; over the mechanical difficulties of mounting changing displays; and over funding, selection procedure and criteria for acquisition. The debates sound familiar to this day. In France, Marx's proposition was eventually accepted when the Musée de l'Affiche opened in Paris in 1977. It is now re-christened the Musée de la Publicité and housed in the Louvre.

Posters have been preserved in the great collections of the world for different reasons. In the United States, for example, the nucleus of the 100,000 posters held by the Library of Congress was the result of legislation making the Library the first central agency for the registration and custody of copyright deposits. Other great poster collections of the world have come about as the result of personal initiative. One out of many is the collection held by the Deutsches Historisches Museum in Berlin, which is of particular interest to students of the poster. It derives substantially from the collection of Dr Hans Sachs, the enterprising founder in 1905 of the Verein der Plakatfreunde (Society for the Friends of the Poster) in Berlin and of its internationally influential periodical *Das Plakat* (1910-21). His own collection, which was international in scope, was formed largely between 1900 and 1922 and mainly through exchange and trade with Society members, as well as through contacts with artists and printers.[4]

At the V&A Museum, posters were actively sought from about 1910 onwards; retrospective collecting made up for absences from earlier periods. To some extent, therefore, the collections do reflect the history of the European and American poster and the extraordinary growth of publicity in the nineteenth and twentieth centuries, as well as the rise of the interconnected professions of poster artist/designer. As with other museums of decorative arts, posters were chosen for their significance in style, form and technique. The majority came as gifts, while others were bought either from individuals or institutions, including at auction.

A guiding light in the formation of the V&A's poster collection between the wars was the distinguished curator, etcher and watercolourist Martin Hardie.[5] He applied scholarship and energy to the task of acquiring posters, and his subsequent gleanings from the worlds of the arts, propaganda and commerce culminated in but did not abate with his organization of the Museum's important *Exhibition of British and Foreign Posters* in 1931 (further discussed below).

Hardie served as an officer in World War I, and it was appropriate that his first major work on the subject of the poster, with A. K. Sabin, was *War Posters issued by Belligerent and Neutral Nations* (1920). Its publication was prompted by the ephemeral character of posters:

> In its brief existence the poster is battered by the rain or faded by the sun, then pasted over with another message more urgent still. Save for the very limited number of copies that wise collectors have preserved, the actual posters of the Great War will be lost and forgotten in fifty years.[6]

The book was illustrated largely from the Museum's collection of several hundred war posters gathered from Germany, Austria, Hungary and other countries, as well as from Great Britain and her Allies – an important foundation for the Museum's fine holdings of propaganda posters.

Significantly, *War Posters* opened with a dedication to Frank Pick of the Underground Electric Railways Company of London 'in honour of his brave and successful effort to link art with commerce'. The authors praised Pick for his encouragement of posters as an art form in their own right, and for 'setting an example in poster work by securing the services of the best artists of the day'. Pick's enthusiasm for design, and visionary patronage of artists like the young Edward McKnight Kauffer, were of course crucial in the evolution of the twentieth-century poster.

A special personal link had developed between the entrepreneurial Pick and the Museum, from which the latter greatly benefited. Initially the Museum was slow to realize the value of the publicity that London Transport could offer: in connection with the State Opening of the Museum's new buildings in 1909, Frank Pick wrote to the Museum's Director, Cecil Harcourt Smith, to request that he be told the time when the King would open the new portion of the Museum, 'in order that we may advertise the event in connection with the District Railway'.[7] He received the somewhat disdainful response that 'As the Museum will...not be available to the public on the day of the opening, I should have supposed it was hardly worth your while to advertise the event, but, of course, I must leave that to your discretion'.[8] Undaunted, Pick renewed his contact in 1911: 'I have pleasure in sending you a roll containing a selection of posters which we have issued during the last two years as I understand that you keep a file of such things'.[9] From these beginnings, and through Pick's enterprise and interest in adding to the V&A's collections of contemporary holdings, the Museum laid down a rich seam of over 1,800 London Transport posters, a collection of great importance for the study of twentieth-century poster design.

Perhaps symbolically, at the beginning of Martin Hardie's tenure of keepership in 1921, the Museum had the good fortune to be offered by Mrs Agnes Clarke the magnificent collection of early posters assembled by her husband, Joseph Thacher Clarke, at the end of the nineteenth century (see plate 7). Clarke had been a pioneer of poster collecting, and was a member of the honorary committee that organized innovative exhibitions of posters at The Royal Aquarium, London, in 1894-95 and 1896. In his introduction to the catalogue of the first one, his enthusiasm directly communicated itself:

> A Collection of Posters! Saved or torn from the hoardings – posters plucked from the pasting,
>
> as it were!
>
> Nothing less than this.
>
> And this Collection of Posters exhibited at the Aquarium – of all places!

He expanded upon the historic and artistic significance of the poster:

7. F. Hugo d'Alési. 'Exposition du Centenaire de la Lithographie, Galerie Rapp', France, 1895. E.140-1921 Originally collected by J.T. Clarke and given to the V&A in 1921 by Mrs Agnes Clarke.

To those who study the tendencies of our modern modes of artistic expression it has for some years been evident that in no other branch of design do the most characteristic features of everyday life find clearer and more drastic utterance than in the art of pictorial and mural advertisements...

The finest posters are, indeed, not only exemplars of artistic originality, beauty, and excellence in technique, but actual records of the daily life and interests of the age. From these documents the future historian may derive the fullest information concerning our food (physical and intellectual), our clothing, our diseases, and our remedies therefor – in short, concerning our vocations, our amusements, and our morals. What would not the archaeologist be willing to give for a set of such documents, relating, let us say, to Pericleian Athens or to Augustan Rome?[10]

Lively accounts exist of the exhibitions at The Royal Aquarium, designed in 1876 as a place of Victorian entertainment, which by the 1890s had become a sort of glorified music hall. The reporter for *The Sketch* (7 November 1894) relished the surreal nature of the setting and paid wondering respect to the new art form on display:

At times a group of solemnly-occupied art critics would find a rope dancer in tights brushing past them; or a learned analysis of decorative art would be cut short by the report of a cannon close by. Mr. Edward Bella, the originator of the admirably-managed display, deserves the first word of praise, if only for the daintiest of catalogues, illustrated by a score of capital reproductions, and prefaced by a most admirable essay by Mr. J. T. Clarke. To the uninitiated, all this interest in the poster must be inexplicable; yet people now not merely observe posters, but collect them .... for all the world as if they were pictures, bronzes, or gems, and a collection of posters a distinguished proof of being a connoisseur of art.

Hardie endorsed the proposed gift of J.T. Clarke's collection to the Museum:

The collection was formed in the 'nineties – i.e. in the early days of the poster – and contains examples of the work of many of the leading British & French poster-designers, who were really the founders of the movement. The main part of the collection is by the pre-eminent Frenchmen, such as Steinlen, Chéret, Forain, Mucha etc .... [It] gives us just the material which I feared might always be lacking.[11]

The Clarke collection also included German, Italian and American posters.

It was at Hardie's request (the first made in 1921) that the Shell-Mex Company Ltd (later Shell-Mex and BP Ltd) gave important sequences of posters to the Museum during the 1930s. These gifts were sanctioned by Jack Beddington, publicity manager of Shell-Mex and BP, and the man who had the vision to commission designs by so many outstanding young British artists of the day – Rex Whistler, Paul Nash, Graham Sutherland, McKnight Kauffer, Ben Nicholson, John Armstrong and Duncan Grant, to name but a few.

Shell-Mex also made gifts to the travelling exhibitions organized by the Department of Circulation which lent to schools of art and secondary schools; the latter enthusiastically received these loans of exemplary advertising material – tangible evidence of contemporary trends in art and design – which were being constantly circulated around the country. As Eric Maclagan, Director of the Museum, acknowledged to Jack Beddington in 1938, '... it is in fact very rare for any Shell poster to remain in the Department for more than a few days'.[12]

The Railway Companies, prolific commissioners of the poster, were similarly approached by the Museum, beginning with the Great Western Railway in 1914, and followed by the Southern, London Midland & Scottish, and London & North Eastern Railways during the early 1920s. Series of gifts followed. Like Frank Pick, the LNER's advertising manager, William Teasdale, had a genius for spotting talent – Tom Purvis, Frank Newbould, Gregory Brown, Walter Spradbery, Frank Mason, Fred Taylor and Frank Brangwyn were among his protégés – and he recognized the educative role of the V&A in preserving and making accessible a record of the company's output: 'the whole purpose of Railway posters being included in your collection is to educate the public in what the different Railway Companies are doing to raise the standard of commercial art'.[13] The majority of posters acquired had landscapes or townscapes as their subjects.

Presses and publishers saw the Museum as a valued repository for their design work. R.G. Praill of The Avenue Press, which printed many of Frank Brangwyn's posters during and after World War I, gave many notable works by Brangwyn, including several which showed his involvement in the colour printing process. Sanders Phillips & Co. Ltd, printers at The Baynard Press, presented works by F.C. Herrick, Charles Paine, Charles Shepard and others, some of which entered the Museum's educational travelling exhibitions.

The editor of *The Studio*, Geoffrey Holme, offered from 1924-30 international posters received for possible publication not only in *The Studio* but also in such special numbers as *Posters and their Designers* (1924), and its offspring publications *Commercial Art* (1922-36) and *Posters and Publicity* (1927-29). Through *The Studio* connection, an outstanding gift of 94 American posters, including works by Louis Rhead, Will Bradley, Edward Penfield and Maxfield Parrish, was given by the great American collector H.L. Sparks in 1925. Further gifts from the world of commerce came during the 1910s and 1920s through approaches to such stores as Bobby & Co., Derry & Toms, Heal & Son and Marshall & Snelgrove.

8. Lucian Bernhard and Fritz Rosen.

'Reklameschau', Germany.

E.1335-1931

Poster for the 1929 Advertising

Exhibition in Berlin, bought from the

dealer Artur Wolf of Leipzig in 1931.

Martin Hardie also sought gifts from another outstanding patron of good poster design, the Empire Marketing Board, which 'aspired to secure the best from many of the most distinguished designers of the period ....The Board's attempt to harness aesthetic power for political and ideological purposes enhances the value of the posters as historical records.'[14] V&A acquisitions included magnificent designs by Gerald Spencer Pryse, McKnight Kauffer, John and Paul Nash, Mark Gertler, Clive Gardiner and Clare Leighton. Pryse was already represented by his 1910 general election posters (given by the Labour Party), and together with the earlier World War I posters by Pryse and Frank Brangwyn, these provide outstanding examples of auto-lithography and of political propaganda.

Political, as well as commercial and cultural graphics (plate 8), also came from Germany between 1926 to 1931, providing a fascinating record of German propaganda issued by parties of all political persuasions during that period. These, together with earlier World War I posters, gave context to later donations of Spanish Civil War and World War II material.

In 1931, an *Exhibition of British and Foreign Posters* was held in the Museum's North Court (plates 9 and 10). The 628 works shown were grouped under their countries of origin, and then arranged chronologically within each country. In his introduction to the accompanying catalogue, Martin Hardie set out the Museum's approach to the poster, and the *raison d'être* for the Exhibition:

> This Museum is concerned less with the economic aspect, the publicity value, of the poster than with its technical method and the artistic impulse which finds expression in the special means employed. From a Museum point of view, therefore this Exhibition of Posters might almost equally well be described as an exhibition of lithographs and of lithographic technique.

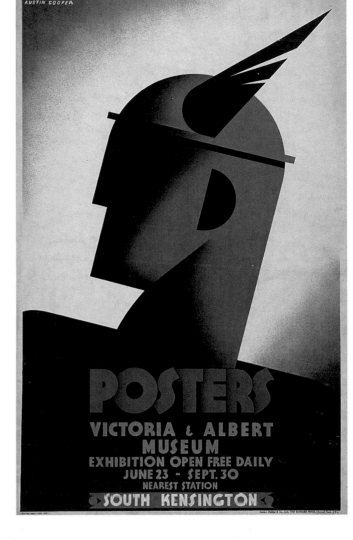

9. Austin Cooper. 'Posters. Victoria & Albert Museum Exhibition', UK, 1931. E.1837-1931

10. Preparations in the V&A's North Court for the Exhibition of British and Foreign Posters, 1931. Photographed by Emil Otto Hoppé. E.655-1996

Hardie debated the perception of the 'ideal' poster: for some it was the reproduction of a finished painting in oils (e.g. Millais' *Bubbles*; plate 174, chapter 5); for others it might be 'an image, entirely abstract, depending for its value on some arbitrarily chosen form, or a deliberate selective pattern of line or colour'. The Exhibition emphasized the technique and purpose of the poster and also aimed to illustrate its history. The range included early pictorial advertisements, 'artistic' posters of the 1880s and 1890s, and twentieth-century posters whose experimental treatment reflected new movements in painting. By the way it was arranged it also highlighted distinctions between the varying national styles: about half the exhibits were British, nearly half continental (by far the greatest number French and German), with a small proportion North American. After the large 1931 Exhibition, others, smaller in scale and more specialized in subject, followed in the post-World War II period. Their purpose has been to provide a shop-window for new acquisitions, a focus on different aspects of the collection, and a forum for publication and debate.

A culminating event marking the special relationship between London Transport and the Museum was the jointly organized exhibition *Art For All* held at the V&A and opened by Prime Minister Clement Attlee on 5 April 1949. Besides more than 100 London Transport posters from 1908 to 1949, it also included many original paintings for them, drawn both from London Transport's archives and from the collections of the V&A itself. This allowed comparison between the original designs and the finished posters, and a chance to see how art could be fostered by industry and thereby be made accessible to a widespread public. The exhibition was opportune. In the aftermath of World War II, as Harold F. Hutchison (Publicity Officer of the London Transport Executive) wrote:

> ...artists, art critics, educationists and the general public alike sighed for a lifting of restrictions so that once again Londoners could look forward to an everchanging public art gallery, whose pictures might challenge their criticism, but which nevertheless would again be an accepted and valued part of metropolitan life. In these early days of nationalization, it seems the right moment to review the poster art of these forty years in order that so distinguished a heritage may be neither lost nor disowned ...[15]

Good art (as Frank Pick believed) was good business; the best in poster design – and that included avant-garde as well as more traditionally acceptable design – would foster goodwill in the customer as well as pride in the service.

This spirit of optimism was not altogether matched by enterprise in the Museum's collection of posters in the post-war period of the late 1940s to the early 1960s, although new work commissioned by London Transport and Shell-Mex was acquired, as well as interesting material from other nationalities, notably Japanese (by Hiroshi Ohchi, Kenji Itoh and Yoshio Hayakawa, for example). The poster itself was coming under threat as commercial television and radio began to encroach on its patronage and position.

However, during the 1960s the poster went through one of its periods of regeneration, and two exhibitions at the V&A had an influence on poster design itself. In 1963 *Art Nouveau Designs and Posters by Alphonse Mucha* publicized for the first time Mucha's role as a leading exponent of the Art Nouveau style, and also contributed to the revival in popularity of the style itself. The characteristic swirling lines, organic forms and convoluted lettering of Art Nouveau (plate 11) found new expression in the decorative psychedelic posters and magazines of the Pop and Hippy era.

11. Alphonse Mucha. 'Bières de la Meuse', France, 1897. E.78-1956

People and institutions (including the V&A which acquired posters by such artists as Victor Moscoso, Martin Sharp, Nigel Waymouth and Michael English, and put on an exhibition *Posters Then and Now*, juxtaposing works from the 1890s with those from the 1960s) started to collect these posters. They were often used to decorate the walls of student bed-sits, alongside images of such cult heroes as Che Guevara, Karl Marx and Jimi Hendrix. Reviewing the Mucha exhibition in his article 'First Master of the Mass Media' in *The Listener*, 27 June 1963, Reyner Banham immediately discerned links between the revived popularity of Mucha and contemporary art trends:

> We are on a pop art kick and there could not be a dead painter better equipped than Mucha to benefit from the way opinion is running. Not only did he work with the mass media in such fields as posters, packaging, book-design and prints for home decoration, but the manner in which he worked these media is strikingly like the way some pop artists do today.

Three years later, in 1966, the *Aubrey Beardsley* exhibition at the V&A, then the most comprehensive ever held on Beardsley, reinforced the contemporary taste for the art of the 1890s, and also appealed to the emergent taste for hallucinogenic, sometimes 'decadently' erotic, imagery in vogue with contemporary underground culture. In a colour supplement of *The Observer* (3 December 1967) devoted to 'The New Society', the jazz critic George Melly introduced his article 'Poster Power' with these words:

> Sometime in the early summer of 1966 I went along to the Victoria and Albert Museum to look at the Beardsley exhibition and was rather surprised to find it packed with people....Many were clearly art students, some were beats, others could have been pop musicians; most of them were very young, but almost all of them gave the impression of belonging to a secret society which had not yet declared its aims and intentions. I believe now...that I had stumbled for the first time into the presence of the emerging Underground.
>
> That this confrontation should have taken place at an art exhibition is, again in retrospect, significant. The Underground is the first of the pop explosions to have evolved a specifically graphic means of expression, and Beardsley...was one of the earliest formative influences in this openly eclectic process.

The curator of the exhibition was Brian Reade, who wrote the standard monograph on Beardsley a year later.[16]

In 1973 the advertising firm of Ogilvy Benson & Mather Ltd gave 189 posters from the extensive and well-preserved archive of S.H. Benson, and 130 were shown in the exhibition *Posters of a Lifetime* held at Bethnal Green Museum the same year. The public could view as a single group the 70-year output of a single advertising agency (plate 12). The selection concentrated on the type

12. 'Posters of a Lifetime' exhibition at the Bethnal Green Museum, London, 1973, with posters from the archive of S.H. Benson given to the Museum by Ogilvy Benson & Mather Ltd in 1973.

of popular commercial poster, advertising household commodities such as Bovril, Guinness, Colman's Starch and Mustard and Rowntree's Chocolate, which had previously received less attention than the 'fine art' poster. Technically, they provided an outstanding illustration of the formats used in the British hoarding-size poster: they were largely in sheets of double-crown size (30 x 20 ins), designed to be pasted up singly, or together to make up 4-, 6-, 8-, 16-, or even 32-sheet posters; a 16-sheet, for example, thus measured 10 x 6 ft 8 ins.

13. Peter W. Branfield. 'E. McKnight Kauffer. Poster art 1915-40'.

E.2003-1973

Poster advertising the travelling exhibition arranged by the Circulation Department of the V&A, 1973.

Further commercial advertising material was given by successive editors of *Modern Publicity* from the 1950s to the 1980s, and commercial posters have been actively sought from various advertising agencies up to the present day. (Since many of these recent campaigns appeared in 48-sheet format, the Museum has normally opted to acquire small-scale proof versions.) Through such product advertisements, developments in advertising strategy can be traced, from the early Benson branding devices to the shock tactics of a Benetton campaign today.

Posters of a Lifetime subsequently travelled around the country as part of the work of the V&A's Circulation Department, which itself had assembled outstanding groups of material in order to collect and disseminate examples of modern graphic art and design. Other touring exhibitions in the 1970s included loans of the work of poster designers who had made outstanding contributions: Edward McKnight Kauffer (whose work is richly represented in the Museum; plate 13), Tom Eckersley, Abram Games, Ashley Havinden and F.H.K. Henrion.

The Museum's more recent acquisitions particularly voice the causes and concerns of our times, with propaganda posters on political, social and environmental issues. From the raw urgency of the French Atelier Populaire student protests of 1968, to the bitter American opposition to the war in Vietnam in the early 1970s, and to the outpouring of posters unleashed during the overthrow of Communism in 1989 and 1990, posters have fulfilled a need to communicate quite literally on the street. The Museum collected many of these now-historic images at the time of their production, and the exhibition *Political Posters from Eastern Europe and USSR* (1990), for example, followed hard on events. Powerful works by the Hungarian Péter Pócs and István Orosz, the Polish Tomasz Sarnecki and the German Holger Matthies were among those gathered in. The displays *Green Images: Posters and Printed Ephemera* (1992) showed the work of concerned institutions and pressure groups in evolving a new graphic vocabulary to meet the needs of environmental campaigns and issues, while *Graphic Responses to AIDS* (1996), explored artists' and designers' treatment of the subjects of AIDS and HIV

Posters, within the overall context of graphic design, remain a fascinating subject for debate. We hope that this book will stimulate further the already widespread interest in, and exploration of, their role and effectiveness.

PART I
PLEASURE AND LEISURE

1 POSTERS FOR PERFORMANCE

CATHERINE HAILL

'It is difficult to live up to one's posters,' commented the actor-manager Herbert Beerbohm Tree ruefully, looking at posters designed by Charles Buchel, advertising Tree's productions at His Majesty's Theatre in the 1890s and early 1900s. His audiences would not have been worried; illustrated entertainment posters had always promised delight and amazement, like the painted show cloths that earlier entrepreneurs had used to advertise menageries, freak shows and other forms of popular entertainment (plate 14). Although the actual marvels might not quite have matched up to their images, the advertisements had done their work once the product was sold and the entrance price paid. From the eighteenth century to the present day, the best examples of entertainment posters have often been the result of personal commitment, produced by artists who were involved with the events they were promoting, who knew the performers and went to the venues, whether the *café-chantant* haunts of Montmartre in the 1890s, the clubs of the 1960s underground culture in London or the contemporary music scene.

In England in 1881 *The Magazine of Art* published an article entitled 'The Street as Art Galleries'; it was an impassioned plea for established artists to produce 'pictorial advertisements' so that art could 'step out of the picture gallery' on to the streets. It bemoaned the abysmally low standard of contemporary posters and quoted the Royal Academician Hubert Herkomer in his condemnation of theatrical posters:

> The theatrical advertisements are intended to lure people into the best seats of the house. Now
> the hideousness and vulgarity of pictorial advertisements seem an insult to the understanding

14. Anonymous. Painted signs on a

shop front advertising curiosities on

display, UK, c. 1840. Engraving

cut from an unidentified periodical.

S.276-1997

of our thinking and educated classes – an insult hurled at them from every spare wall, scaffolding and conveyance.

One exception to the dire output of posters was singled out for praise – a poster by the Royal Academician Frederick Walker advertising *The Woman in White* at the Olympic Theatre, October 1871, of which Walker had written to the wood engraver W.H. Hooper, 'I am bent on doing all I can with a first

15. Frederick Walker. 'The Woman in

White', UK, 1871. Charcoal, black and

white gouache on buff paper.

Tate Gallery, London, no. 2080

attempt at what I consider *might develop into a most important branch of art*'.[1] This frequently quoted statement, and praise for the poster by *The Magazine of Art* and subsequent commentators, has assured Walker's place in the history of British poster art. His poster has been called 'the first high-art poster the world ever knew'[2] and 'the first work of any importance in the history of the pictorial poster',[3] its significance deriving from its audacious size as well as from Walker's acknowledged high standing as an artist.

Walker was primarily an illustrator and watercolourist, and since poster design was not regarded as a serious form of art in the 1870s, it was an unusual project for him to embark on. Nevertheless, Wilkie Collins's novel *The Woman in White* had been tremendously popular when it was first published in 1860, and Collins's 1871 dramatization was regarded as an important event. Walker had personal reasons for wanting to do the poster; he had theatrical contacts and was a close friend of Charles Collins, Wilkie's brother. On 6 September he wrote to the wood-engraver W.H. Hooper: '... I propose trying my hand at the thing itself – a dashing attempt in black and white.'[4] The resulting life-size cartoon in charcoal, chalk and black and white gouache (plate 15) was laid on to the wood to be pricked through for cutting by Hooper. Hooper also added the lettering which gave only the

name of the play above the image and the name of the theatre below. The huge poster would have been intriguing and original, and it even featured in a contemporary cartoon showing Wilkie Collins pasting up the poster himself (plate 16)! It had the effect of a modern 'teaser' campaign, fuller details of the production being provided in two smaller posters that the theatre also produced. Sadly, no copies of the large poster appear to have survived.

Although the size of Walker's poster for *The Woman in White* was remarkable for a purely pictorial poster in England in 1871, typographical theatre and music-hall posters in England had become dramatically larger during the first half of the nineteenth century, as revealed in a photograph showing music-hall posters on a Chelsea hoarding in 1865 (plate 239, Epilogue). William Smith, the advertising manager of the Adelphi Theatre, noted the increase when he compared the six-sheet posters (about 90 x 40 ins) he was ordering for the theatre in the 1860s with those measuring only about 12 x 8 ins half a century earlier.[5] As the size of playbills increased during the nineteenth century, images became increasingly important, and in Britain circus playbills led the way.

Phillip Astley, originator of the circus and founder of the first circus in London in 1772, was particularly astute at publicity. He spared no expense in his early newspaper advertisements which described his feats of horsemanship in great detail. Similarly, in his original handbills or posters of the 1780s, the acts were described in the text; but Astley soon discovered that images meant more than wordy descriptions, especially to the illiterate, and began to add illustrations produced from etched metal plates. By 1833, the year of the *Siege of Troy* poster (plate 17), colourful broadsides (so-called because the long, thin posters literally had 'broad sides'), illustrated with woodcut or wood-engraved images, had become a characteristic of Astley's circus, and were emulated by other managers with means to promote popular entertainment. Neither artist nor engraver is credited for the superb image of the towering Trojan horse, only the printer, who at this date would have increasingly called upon engravers to produce illustrations for playbills, ballads and broadsheets. As Astley's posters became longer and more colourful, he even took to using an advertising cart to display them (plate 235, Epilogue), influenced by the French custom of wheeling posters around city streets.

Perhaps as a reaction against popular entertainment, most theatres that specialized in drama clung tenaciously to their letterpress-only advertisements, the relative sizes of typefaces constantly concerning the thespians involved. The earliest theatre posters in Britain had been written announcements on hand-made paper, giving the briefest details about the performance, and measuring about 7 x 3 ins – small enough to be pasted on to posts. We know that some were

16. 'He wrote the "Woman in White"'.
Anonymous cartoon showing Wilkie
Collins as a billposter pasting up
Frederick Walker's life-size poster
advertising *The Woman in White*; from
an unidentified periodical, UK, c. 1871.

17. Anonymous. 'The Siege of Troy,
or, The Giant Horse of Sinon', UK,
1833. Advertising an equine spectacle
at Astley's Circus. Woodcut and
letterpress. S.2-1983

printed by 1587, the year that a licence for 'the only ympryntinge of all manner of bills for players' was granted to one John Charlewood by The Stationers' Company, and in his diary Samuel Pepys recorded looking for playbills on posts in London: '24 March 1662. I went to see if any play was acted, and I found none upon the post, it being Passion week.'

The introduction of iron printing presses in the early nineteenth century made it possible to print larger typefaces and new letter forms, changing the appearance of theatrical advertising – particularly for popular entertainment, which the flamboyant new lettering suited so well.

'Display' faces such as the 'fat face', used in the *Siege of Troy* poster, were introduced specifically for posters. Letter forms consisting of two or more units were designed for 'shaded' letters, which made the type seem to stand out from the page, and the imagination of talented letter-cutters ran riot in the creation of decorated letter forms, such as those used in the 1859 poster for the *Final Masquerade* at Vauxhall Gardens (plate 18). These were probably made for an earlier masquerade, but when printers had a set of letters as glorious as these, they used them at every opportunity. Large woodcut images were also employed, proving especially effective when hand coloured.

Nevertheless the most important technical development influencing poster production was the introduction of colour lithography, discovered in 1798 by a German playwright, Aloys Senefelder. Lithography – literally, drawing on stone – was a method of surface printing which could produce delicate tones and colours from an image prepared directly on the lithographic stone by the artist. In England colour lithography soon became the preferred medium for such publications as music-sheet covers, illustrated trade cards, souvenir brochures and novelty paper items. By the mid-1860s, artists such as Alfred Concanen and John Brandard, who specialized in music-sheet illustration, were also producing small posters and 'hanging cards' for the more affluent London theatres like Covent Garden.

Another graphic artist working in London in the 1860s was the French lithographer Jules Chéret, then designing book-covers for the publishers Cramer and producing posters for opera, circus and music-hall. His career was truly launched however by the innovative perfume manufacturer Eugène Rimmel, for whom he designed brochures, showcards and perfumed papers. In 1866 Rimmel financed the establishment of Chéret's own printing firm and lithographic studio in Paris, which Chéret equipped with large lithographic presses bought in London. At his first premises – J. Chéret, rue de la Tour des Dames – Chéret began his amazingly prolific output of colour lithograph posters which was to earn him the title: 'the father of the pictorial poster', or the 'Maître de l'Affiche'.

Chéret experimented with colour lithography as an exciting medium in its own right for producing commercial artwork. He was a craftsman who was fascinated with the artistic possibilities of colour and tone, and he worked on the lithographic stones himself, though preferring to leave the design and execution of the lettering to lettering artists. Although he produced drawings, pastels and oil paintings, it was as a lithographic poster artist that he gained official recognition. The exuberant lines and the feeling of movement in his work reveal his admiration for the eighteenth-century Rococo-style paintings of Tiepolo, Fragonard and Watteau, and all his posters have a sense of theatre, whether advertising cabaret or cough-drops.

Chéret was familiar with the world of circus, cabaret and Paris theatre, and during the 1870s and 1880s produced hundreds of posters for performances. The innately theatrical style of his work attracted the American dancer Loïe Fuller, who asked him to produce a poster for her 1893 Paris debut at the Folies-Bergère. Her 'abstract' dances, which had made her famous as an 'artistic, scientific and revolutionary spectacle' in New York, depended on the changing effects of coloured spotlights projected on to her flowing, diaphanous costumes which she manipulated by long batons attached to the fabric. She had not liked the photographic posters produced to advertise her performances in New York, and once in Paris realized that Chéret's ebullient, colourful style of posters would suit her performance. For her Folies-Bergère debut she performed the 'Serpent Dance', the 'Violet Dance', the 'Butterfly Dance' and the 'White Dance', and Chéret created his first poster for her in four versions, different colour combinations which reflected the spectacular lighting effects of each dance (plate 20).

Chéret's posters were a revelation when they were first seen in New York in 1894 for a revival of the popular musical *The Black Crook* which was advertised by Chéret posters taken to America by a Mr Eugène Thompkins. Writing in the magazine *The Poster* (June 1898) the impresario Charles Cochran commented that when he first visited America in 1891 he had been struck by 'the horrors that looked down from the hoardings', saying that the huge theatrical posters lacked taste in design and colour: 'The figures were tailors' dummies without life or movement, and the backgrounds were the old stereotyped German photographic reproductions of scenes from the plays advertised.'

American circus posters around 1900 could be lively and imaginative, such as that designed by Edward Potthast for the great Barnum & Bailey Circus (plate 19), but as late as 1913, in his book on posters, the American author Charles Matlock Price blamed the bulk of uninteresting contemporary American theatre posters on their production by commercial lithographic firms. He complained that they preferred images based on sketches or photographs of actors or actresses

20. Jules Chéret. 'La Loïe Fuller', France, 1893. E.112-1921

19. Edward Henry Potthast. 'The Barnum & Bailey Greatest Show on Earth', USA, 1895. E.448-1939

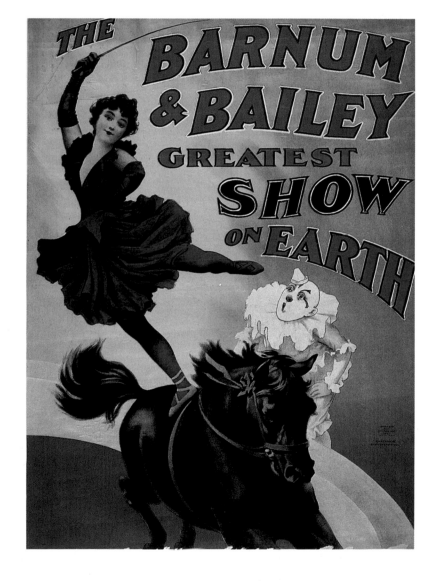

21. Anonymous. 'The Chronicles
of the Battle at Ichinotani',
Japan, c. 1900. Watercolour and
gouache. D.266-1903

'embraced in a composition of lines and circles, with interesting lettering'. In contrast to the homegrown lack of talent, Price praised Chéret's 'daring, sparkling sheets of flaming colour that have decorated the streets of Paris', credited France as the country in which poster making was first recognized as an art, and Jules Chéret as its leading exponent.[6]

In a long life, Chéret produced over 2,000 posters advertising a multitude of products and events. By contrast, his contemporary, Henri de Toulouse-Lautrec, produced few, but all were intensely dramatic. As Charles Hiatt wrote in *The Poster*, May 1899,

> If the placards of Chéret dance in disordered joy on the hoardings and thus arrest the attention,
>
> if those of Mucha catch the eye from sheer extravagance of decoration, those of Lautrec
>
> inevitably bring one to a standstill...

Toulouse-Lautrec became fascinated by posters in the 1890s. He liked the way they reached a vast audience, and many of the drawings and sketches he made were studies for posters. New and uncompromising, his posters reflected his admiration for Japanese woodcuts, which were recently to be seen in Paris. He studied and adapted the powerful Japanese line, the simple flat areas of colour and the often unusual viewpoints. These aspects are also apparent in late nineteenth-century Japanese theatre posters, such as the wonderfully energetic gouache poster advertising the Kabuki play *The Chronicles of the Battle at Ichinotani* (plate 21). Lautrec's posters stem from his wholehearted involvement with the cabaret, dance hall and *café-chantant* world of Montmartre in the 1890s. He was a regular patron of the Nouveau Cirque where the clowns Footit and Chocolat performed; a table was always reserved for him at the Moulin Rouge, and the performers he constantly sketched became his friends.

Lautrec's first posters advertising entertainment date from 1891 when the impresario of the Moulin Rouge, Charles Zidler, commissioned a poster for its re-launch. The opening of the Moulin Rouge in 1889 had been advertised by an acclaimed Chéret poster, a copy of which Lautrec had in his studio. By 1891 however, audiences were dwindling and Zidler wanted fresh publicity to reflect the new artistes he had engaged, including the ethereal dancer Jane Avril, 'as graceful and as pale as a narcissus', and Louise Weber, whose avaricious appetite for food and drink had earned her the nickname 'La Goulue' – 'the glutton'. La Goulue was to be the star of the new show dancing the famous 'naturalist quadrille' (the forerunner of the 'can-can') with Jane Avril. Two of Lautrec's paintings already hung over the bar at the Moulin Rouge, and he had sketched La Goulue many times. He could draw on the stone as freely as he could on paper, and he found the possibilities presented by the size of posters very liberating. Once the poster was displayed, Lautrec's name became famous. A contemporary wrote: 'This remarkable and highly original poster was, I remember, carried along the Avenue de l'Opéra on a kind of small cart, and I was so enchanted that I walked alongside it on the pavement'.[7]

Lautrec showed La Goulue performing on the dance floor, surrounded by silhouettes of the standing audience. The Bal Moulin Rouge, as its name indicated, was a dance hall and the audience sat at tables or stood for particularly exciting turns such as La Goulue's. In his poster Lautrec made her white petticoats and bloomers the focus, but featured in the foreground the comical shape of her partner, the contortionist dancer Valentin 'le Désossé' – literally 'the boneless' – who, as Yvette Guilbert recalled '...danced in a frock-coat and top-hat, but what a frock-coat and what a topper! He was the type of long, bony, cadaverous acrobats seen at village fairs'.[8]

The success of this poster ensured that the following year Lautrec was given a similar commission by the proprietor of the *café-concert* Le Divan Japonais. *Café-concerts*, where audiences could eat and drink and were encouraged to join in the singing, were immensely popular in Paris in the 1890s, and Le Divan Japonais (named after its oriental-style decor) was one of Lautrec's favourites. Yvette Guilbert remembered it as:

22. Henri de Toulouse-Lautrec. 'Divan Japonais', France, 1892. **CIRC** 272-1964

> ...a little hall such as you may see in a provincial café, with a low ceiling and where at a pinch a hundred and fifty or two hundred people might be got in....A platform perched about five feet above the floor made it necessary to remember that I musn't raise my arms incautiously or I should knock them against the ceiling. Oh, that ceiling, where the heat from the gas footlights was such that our heads swam in a suffocating furnace![9]

Much of its atmosphere came from the noisy but good-natured crowd, and in his poster (plate 22), Lautrec focuses attention on the audience as well as the shapes made by the instruments and the conductor's baton. The slender figure of Jane Avril is in the foreground with the music critic Edouard Dujardin, whilst the waif-like singer Yvette Guilbert performs on the tiny stage in the distance. She is lit ethereally by the foot-lights, recognizable by her characteristic long black gloves and pose, Lautrec's 'Japonesque' viewpoint sardonically eliminating her head.

23. Henri de
Toulouse-Lautrec.
'Ambassadeurs...Aristide
Bruant dans son cabaret',
France, 1892.
CIRC 551-1962

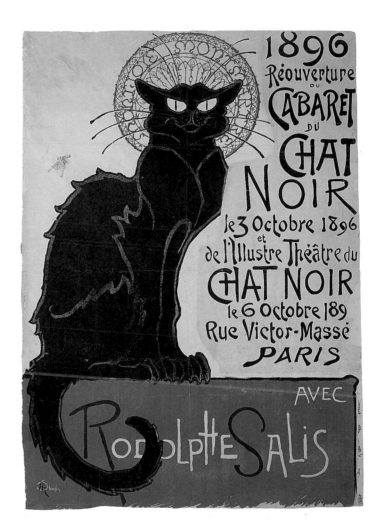

24. Théophile Steinlen. 'Cabaret du
Chat Noir'. Advertising the re-opening
of the Cabaret du Chat Noir and
Théâtre du Chat Noir on 3 and 6
October 1896. France. E.321-1978

Lautrec's friendships and interests inspired his work, and when the satirical singer Aristide Bruant became a star at the *café-concert* Les Ambassadeurs, he insisted that Lautrec did the poster. Lautrec's image of Bruant with his wide hat, black velvet jacket and red scarf was stark and arresting (plate 23), but it horrified Pierre Ducarre, the director of the Ambassadeurs, who insisted it was taken down. At Bruant's insistence it remained and the poster became a success, prompting *La Vie Parisienne* to comment, 'Who will relieve us of M Aristide Bruant's posters? One cannot take a step nowadays without coming face to face with him.'

Bruant was also a great friend of the Swiss illustrator Théophile Alexandre Steinlen who came to Paris in 1881 and soon became part of the artistic world of Montmartre. From 1883 until 1885 Bruant was a regular entertainer at Le Cabaret du Chat Noir, owned by Rudolphe Salis, and Steinlen's poster of 1896 for the *café-concert* (plate 24) balances the silhouette of the black cat on the left side of the poster against the decorative lettering on the right. The silhouette was a reference to shadow-theatre performances, a popular feature of the Chat Noir, where silhouettes of black cats were painted along the walls and above the stage. The treatment of the cat on the poster echoes the black cat that Manet depicted in his illustration for Champfleury's book *Les Chats* (1868), which was also seen on the hoardings, pasted on a larger typographical poster.

25. Eugène Grasset. 'Jeanne d'Arc',
France, 1889-90. E.189-1921

An interest in the decorative aspects of the poster was also the hallmark of two of Steinlen's contemporary poster artists working in Paris – Eugène Grasset and Alphonse Mucha. Originally from Switzerland, like Steinlen and Rudolphe Salis, Grasset was a versatile designer. He was one of the leading book-illustrators of the late nineteenth century, and his enthusiasm for the jewel-like qualities of medieval art and stained glass can be seen in his heroic poster advertising Sarah Bernhardt as Jeanne d'Arc in the title role of Jules Barbier's play at the Théâtre de la Porte St Martin, Paris, 1890 (plate 25). The Gothic-style lettering, an integral part of the design, incorporates medieval-style illumination. As Joan of Arc is shown standing resolute in a shower of arrows, Bernhardt is reminiscent of a martyr in stained glass.

'The divine Sarah', the red-haired actress Sarah Bernhardt, unwittingly provided the impetus for Alphonse Mucha's poster work that has come to be seen as the essence of Art Nouveau. He executed a lithograph of Sarah Bernhardt as Cleopatra in 1890, and in late December 1894 he was asked if he could produce a poster, within a week, to advertise her appearance as Gismonda at the Théâtre de la Renaissance in Paris. Mucha sketched Sarah at the theatre where she was starring in *Phèdre*, and executed a large preparatory watercolour before working the finished design on two stones. He did not have time to finish the background of the lower half of the poster to the standard of the top half, but the poster was on the hoardings by 1 January 1895, and reproduced in the *Courier Français* six days later. The elongated format of the poster was similar to Grasset's *Jeanne d'Arc* poster, but whereas Bernhardt never liked Grasset's poster, she loved Mucha's. His exotic vision of her matched her own, and for the next six years he designed her posters, costumes, sets, wigs and hairstyles, and even helped her to rehearse. His poster for her as Marguerite Gautier in Edmond Rostand's play *La Dame Aux Camélias* at the Théâtre de la Renaissance, Paris, 1896 (plate 26), is a romantic, pastel, mosaic-like image, incorporating a shower of silver stars, decorative lettering and an arc framing her head; its sinuous flowing line is typical of Art Nouveau. Sarah loved the poster and adapted it for her American tours, where its style was a revelation.

26. Alphonse Mucha. 'La Dame Aux Camélias', France, 1896. E.515-1939

"YES MOTHER, I COME! I COME!"

In England in the 1880s, printing firms increasingly commissioned designs for colour lithographic posters advertising entertainment. The work of many of the artists employed revealed a debt to the precursors of poster art in England – woodcut and engraved images on broadsheets, playbills, handbills, ballad sheets and music covers. Customarily, posters advertising melodramas depicted exciting or heart-rending scenes from plays, as in that for the stage version of Mrs Henry Wood's novel *East Lynne* (plate 27), where Little Willie is seen on his death-bed, his mother, Lady Isobel, at his bedside, known only to him as his governess Madame Vine. Narrative posters like this continued to be produced well into the twentieth century, unaffected by stylistic advances in graphic design, and were the direct precursors of the film poster.

In the early 1890s innovative French poster design began to influence English artists whose work included entertainment posters, especially Dudley Hardy, Aubrey Beardsley, John Hassall and the two artists who worked as The Beggarstaffs, the brothers-in-law James Pryde and William Nicholson. Dudley Hardy's work was splashed on the walls in London when, in 1893, the manager of the Prince of Wales' Theatre posted up a frieze of Hardy's large and effervescent *Gaiety Girl* posters (plates 28) outside his theatre. The effect of the silhouette on the hoardings ('a bold striking outline which will arrest the eye of the passer-by')[10] is powerful, and the decorative treatment of her unfurling hat ribbons evokes the ebullience of Chéret's poster work.

Dudley Hardy's *Gaiety Girl* poster was exhibited in Britain's first exhibition of posters, organized by the businessman Edward Bella, with the French section under the supervision of Toulouse-Lautrec. It opened in October 1894 at The Royal Aquarium, London, a palace of entertainment which by the 1890s specialized in variety, acrobatics and aquatic displays. The critic of *The Sketch* (7 November 1894) reflected on the unusual nature of both the exhibits and the venue:

> The huge, insistent exhibits, with their daring experiments in patterns and colours, attracted
> the eye, but the rival attraction of the music and noise of the daily show in the arena below made
> it hard to devote all one's attention to them. Indeed, at moments, even the most ardent devotees
> of the 'fierce placard' were tempted to gaze on the acrobats, danseuses, and grotesques, who
> seemed, in the glamour of limelight, to have leaped from the walls to take part in the show.

A large number of the posters, appropriately for their setting, advertised performance. Many of the 48 by Chéret were theatrical, as well as a dozen by Toulouse-Lautrec, including a version of his Aristide Bruant poster and his poster for the Divan Japonais. The exhibition also featured Frederick Walker's original cartoon for his *Woman in White* poster; Grasset's poster for Bernhardt as Jeanne d'Arc; Aubrey Beardsley's poster advertising *A Comedy of Sighs* at the Avenue Theatre, 1894; a poster by Steinlen of Yvette Guilbert; and the first posters by The Beggarstaffs. Paris had already mounted several poster exhibitions, but for the first time Britons could see

29. Posters on a hoarding by Daly's Theatre, 1899, including Dudley Hardy's poster for the revival of *A Gaiety Girl*, UK, 1899. Photograph by Mills, no. 21.

innovative and influential French posters. They were well received, the critic of *The Sketch* (November 1894) crediting Chéret as 'the originator of the modern school', Grasset as 'the French equivalent of our aesthetic decorators' and Lautrec simply as 'the incomparable' who 'distances all others here'. As the poster artist E. McKnight Kauffer later wrote, the influence of Toulouse-Lautrec 'passed like a comet over the major part of the Western hemisphere'.[11]

Aubrey Beardsley's poster for the Avenue Theatre (plate 30) was commissioned by Florence Farr, the redoubtable actress and manager of the theatre who prided herself on her up-to-date ideas about mounting and advertising plays and who saw Beardsley's artwork as in keeping with her aspirations at the Avenue. Beardsley's design doubled as poster and programme cover for both this and Farr's next production, George Bernard Shaw's *Arms and the Man*. The image caused immediate comment and reaction; the figure of the woman half-hidden by gauze curtains bore no relation to the tone or subject-matter of *A Comedy of Sighs*, a burlesque of romantic comedy, and *Punch* lampooned it, with the pun ''Ave a new poster'. On the other hand, Charles Hiatt in his book *Picture Posters* (1895), wrote that 'nothing so compelling, so irresistible, had ever been posted on the hoardings before'.[12] He noted that some gazed at it with awe, and others jeered at it, but that in its power to provoke attention it had succeeded as an advertisement.

30. Aubrey Beardsley. Avenue Theatre poster, UK, 1894. E. 289-1925

The Beggarstaffs collaborated between 1894 and 1899 producing decorative panels, book illustration and signboards as well as posters. The two met in the late 1880s as students at Hubert Herkomer's art school in Bushey, Hertfordshire. In 1893 Nicholson married James Pryde's sister, Mabel, and through the Pryde family, who knew Henry Irving, Nicholson became a regular visitor at the Lyceum Theatre where Ellen Terry was Irving's leading lady. Nicholson and Pryde became friendly with Ellen Terry's son, the actor Edward Gordon Craig, and in the summer of 1894 Craig commissioned The Beggarstaffs' first theatrical poster for a touring production of *Hamlet* by the Hardy Shakespeare Company, starring Craig as Hamlet.

Both Pryde and Nicholson were well aware of the innovative nature of poster art in France and England. James Pryde later admitted his admiration of Dudley Hardy's theatre posters and of Aubrey Beardsley's Avenue Theatre poster that had appeared in March 1894. Above all, The

Aquarium Exhibition had shown them the work of Toulouse-Lautrec, whom Pryde once called 'one of the few artists who understands what a poster is and should be'. After their *Hamlet* poster of 1894, The Beggarstaffs concentrated on two more theatrical posters that year, both for productions involving Craig, for the Hardy Company's production of *The School for Scandal* and for *Becket* at the Lyceum Theatre. Irving rejected the design for *Becket*, but that did not deter The Beggarstaffs from risking a monumentally large design for another Irving production, *A Chapter from Don Quixote*, mounted at the Lyceum Theatre in May 1895. The full title of the play is not on the poster and it seems probable that The Beggarstaffs learned about a forthcoming production based on *Don Quixote* and did the designs as a speculation. They went to the trouble of making three large designs, the second of which remained in the artists' studio for almost 30 years until 1927, when it was bought from them for £50 by the V&A Museum (plate 31). Each design incorporated lettering integrally, and in its use of the unshaded silhouette for the horse, tone for Don Quixote and a block of black for the windmill, this poster recalls aspects of Toulouse-Lautrec's posters for the Moulin Rouge and Divan Japonais, both of which featured in the 1894 Aquarium Exhibition. The Beggarstaffs were more inspired by the spirit of Cervantes' original story, in which Don Quixote tilts against windmills believing them to be giants, than by Irving's production. Their depiction of Don Quixote looked nothing like Irving, probably one of the reasons why he never used the poster, and when Ellen Terry told him in 1899 that The Beggarstaffs had designed a poster for his production of *Robespierre*, Irving declared definitively 'No more mills!'[13] Although The Beggarstaffs' work was appreciated by critics it did not always meet with approval or comprehension from the public, the advertisers or its intended commissioners. Even the critic Spielmann remarked that their works were 'about as like to Chéret's posy-like *affiches* as a grim and ascetic old Carmelite is like to a lady of the *corps de ballet*'.[14]

Contemporary poster work in France and England varied greatly in quality and artistic aspiration. Titillation drew some audiences as effectively as artistic excellence, and that was the lure of the frilly bloomers and the nudity on posters by Albert Guillaume advertising Lona Barrison's act on horseback at the Folies-Bergère and Carlo Dali's poster advertising the

31. The Beggarstaffs (James Pryde and William Nicholson). 'Don Quixote', UK, 1895. Black and brown paper pasted on white. E.1208-1927

32. Carlo Dali. 'Paris Tout Nu', France, c. 1900. E.519-1939

risqué revue *Paris Tout Nu* at the Ambassadeurs (plate 32). Contemporary English posters advertising burlesque, variety and pantomime often depicted a revealingly costumed female form, but the more overt continental images show how the French earned their reputation of naughtiness in the 1890s. The froth of petticoats and the glimpse of leg in Lautrec's poster for the Troupe de Mlle Eglantine was characteristic of the dance which became the can-can and was made famous at the Moulin Rouge and Tabarin Club.

Effective theatre posters do not necessarily have to concentrate on performers – the audience itself can be a powerful subject. The Belgian artists E.J. Duyck and Adolphe Louis Crespin depicted a fashionable audience at the revue theatre Alcazar Royal in Brussels, 1894 (plate 33), emphasizing the fascination of the audience for the unseen action on stage. This poster also had the practical advantage of advertising for the venue as a whole rather than just for a specific revue. The name and address of the theatre, designed in Art Nouveau style lettering to form an elegant arch above the spectators, are an integral element of the poster, whereas the title of the revue – *Bruxelles Sans-Gène* – added to the blank reserve on the bottom right, could easily be changed for another show. The poster by the English artist Albert Morrow advertising *Edison's Life-Size Animated Pictures*, c. 1901 (plate 34), uses a similar technique. The lettering on the 'screen' would have been adapted to suit any of the picture shows screened by the manager, Waller Jeffs, at Birmingham's Curzon Hall where, by the turn of the century, cinematograph films were the main feature of entertainment.

33. Edouard J. Duyck and Adolphe Louis Crespin. 'Alcazar Royal: Bruxelles Sans-Gène', Belgium, 1894. E.170-1921

34. Albert Morrow. 'Curzon Hall, Birmingham: Edison's Life-Size Animated Pictures', UK, c. 1901. E.3312-1932

A contemporary of Albert Morrow's was the prolific and inventive poster artist John Hassall. He trained as a painter in Antwerp and Paris, but his intention to make his name as a great painter was deflected by his success with a theatre poster for *The French Maid*, prompted by a circular letter from David Allen & Sons asking artists for poster designs. Hassall's work was appealing and commercial; he worked fast, and by 1899 had designed over 600 posters as well as producing illustrations for nursery rhymes and fairy stories. He admired Mucha's work and believed posters should be decorative and witty, as is his poster for a touring production of *The Mummy* (plate 35). Originally produced at the Comedy Theatre in 1896, this was inspired by the contemporary interest in Egyptology. The mummy Rameses' dark face is handled three-dimensionally, as is the bottle and top-hat that he holds, but Hassall treats the white embalming bands unravelling around him decoratively like streamers containing the lettering and fantastic shapes which contrast with the red and blue striped background. The lettering is integral to the design, like the hieroglyphics on the mummy. Hassall disliked lettering dominating posters, as he told *The Poster* (June 1898): 'The less writing the better. Even the principal words should be small; for if the design achieves its object, the public would find the name with a microscope if necessary'.

35. John Hassall. 'The Mummy', UK, c. 1896. E.3307-1932

While Hassall designed posters for a wide variety of commissions, his contemporary artist Charles Buchel devoted himself particularly to the theatre. Buchel worked for most of the leading actor-managers of the day, painting theatrical scenes and portraits for illustrated magazines such as *The Sphere* and *Tatler* – he claimed that he 'probably had as sitters, more actors and actresses than any other living artist'.[15] For over 16 years, Buchel had a special working relationship with the actor-manager Herbert Beerbohm Tree at His Majesty's Theatre, providing illustrations for the lavish souvenir brochures given away at the theatre, murals to decorate Tree's apartment there, oil paintings of Tree in character, as well as posters for at least 35 productions. Tree was careful with his publicity material, and commissioned innovative artwork, as his poster for the Japanese play *The Darling of the Gods*, December 1903 (plate 37), demonstrates. This restrained and surreal design by an anonymous

36. Charles Buchel. 'The Tempest',

UK, 1920. Originally designed in 1904.

E.451-1921

37. Anonymous. 'The Darling of the

Gods', UK, 1903. E.592-1915

artist features a *samurai* sword dripping with blood on which a butterfly has landed. The delicate butterfly contrasts with the harsh sword, while the red blood and the yellow wings stand out dramatically against the neutral background.

Buchel's evocative poster for *The Tempest* (plate 36) was originally designed in 1904 for Tree's spectacular production at His Majesty's Theatre starring Tree as Prospero. For the role of Ariel his daughter, Viola, had to learn the techniques of being flown on wires, and she is depicted on the poster riding serenely on a bat high above the sea. She is framed against the arch of cloud behind her, the gauzy quality of the bat's wings echoed in Ariel's wings, her skirt curling sensuously below her, the glimpse of leg seen through the material recalling posters of Loïe Fuller. The poster for *The Tempest* clearly pleased Viola Tree, since she used it again 16 years later to advertise the production at the Aldwych Theatre, February 1920, which she presented with her own company and in which she appeared as Juno.

The influence of innovative French and English poster work of the 1890s quickly spread internationally at the end of the century, thanks to exhibitions and magazines such as *Les Maîtres de l'Affiche*, Paris, 1896-1900, and *The Poster*, printed in London from 1898 to 1900. Artists in the USA and Europe developed their own interpretation of Art Nouveau, although the most prominent poster artists in the USA at the turn of the century, including Edward Penfield and Maxfield Parrish, were little concerned with the theatre. *The Poster*, March 1899, in an article on American posters, discussed the hideousness of most theatre posters and noted: 'Theatrically the hoardings have not been happy for months past. The best posters have been importations, such as the Hardy and Hassall sheets for *A Brace of Partridges*.

The next important developments in poster design occurred in Germany in the first years of the twentieth century. After the demise of the influential French and English magazines devoted to poster art, it was in Berlin that the poster magazine *Das Plakat* was published from 1910 to 1921. In Berlin too, Lucien Bernhard's mainly commercial posters in the early years of the century created a style that set the tone for subsequent commercial poster design. Bernhard's work inspired other designers, including the Munich poster artist Ludwig Hohlwein; in 1912 *The Studio* magazine declared that Hohlwein was conceivable without Munich, but not Munich without Hohlwein. Trained as an architect, Hohlwein concentrated on poster design from about 1906 and became one of the most prolific and influential German poster artists of the twentieth century, to whose work the entire issue of *Das Plakat* was devoted in May 1913. He also admired the work of The Beggarstaffs and pared his designs to achieve clarity and simplicity, as in his poster advertising a week of Richard Strauss events in Munich, 1910 (plate 38). He used mostly rich, dark colours to great effect, with simple geometric lettering, on posters advertising a wide variety of products and events. In 1912 *The Studio* commented on the Munich style inspired by Hohlwein: 'As far as one can generalise, the poster art of Munich is sane, sober, and concise in effect. It differs from similar work in France, which more often makes appeal to our sentiment, to our emotions rather than to our reason'.

38. Ludwig Hohlwein. 'Richard Strauss-Woche', Germany, 1910. E.348-1921

Hohlwein particularly liked sport, racing and animals, but his range of subject-matter in posters and other ephemera was vast. The power and simplicity of his images made him a leading artist for propaganda posters during the 1914-18 war. The elegant and restrained work of his contemporary, the Austrian artist Julius Klinger, showed the impact of the German poster artists, but the influence worked both ways and one of Hohlwein's posters for the Munich Zoo in 1912 owed more than a passing resemblance to Klinger's earlier sophisticated flamingo advertising the Berlin Zoo (plate 39).

Ballet has also inspired remarkable posters; that of the dancer Nijinsky (plate 40) is a powerful example produced by the artist, Jean Cocteau, who was personally committed to his subject, Diaghilev's Ballets Russes, and especially to its star, Nijinsky. The 19-year-old dancer made his debut in Paris in May 1909 in the rapturously received first season of Diaghilev's Russian Ballet. Cocteau was entranced with Nijinsky from the moment he first saw him dance as the Slave in *Le Pavillion d'Armide*, and as well as dedicating and publishing poems to him, became a devoted follower of the company, executing caricatures of Diaghilev and his entourage which impressed

39. Julius Klinger. 'Zoologischer Garten', Germany, c.1910. E.614-1915

40. Jean Cocteau. 'Ballets Russes': Nijinsky in *Le Spectre de la Rose*, France, 1911. S.562-1980

the scenic artist Leon Bakst. The first season was heralded in Paris by a large poster based on a drawing of Pavlova in *Les Sylphides* by the Russian artist Valentin Serov, in keeping with Diaghilev's aims to introduce Russian art and music to the West. Nevertheless, for posters for the third season of the Russian Ballet in 1911, Bakst recommended that Cocteau be commissioned. Cocteau designed two large posters illustrating respectively Tamara Karsarvina and Vaclav Nijinsky in their roles in *Le Spectre de la Rose*, a ballet to be introduced in 1911. The lettering was not integrated into the design, and was easily changed for subsequent seasons. Cocteau concentrates on the images; Nijinsky, in his rose-coloured costume designed by Bakst, is suspended mid-air in one of his famous 'hovering leaps'. The draughtsmanship of the right arm indicates the work of a young and inexperienced artist, but nevertheless the impact of the poster is powerful. For the same season Cocteau also wrote a publicity text which reflects his portrayal of Nijinsky:

> Young, erect, supple .... his neck long and massive as Donatello, his slender young torso contrasting with overdeveloped thighs, he is like some young Florentine, vigorous beyond anything human, and feline to a disquieting degree.[16]

Cocteau depicted the animal grace of Nijinsky, whereas the poster for the Olympic Games in Stockholm of 1912 (plate 41) by Olle Hjörtzberg displays the male body as a perfect machine, a symbol of supremacy. The original design, of nude athletes, was replaced by a second version in which strategically placed streamers were added – though ironically this had the effect of drawing attention to the nudity. Hjörtzberg depicts the athletes in muscular detail, three-dimensional living statues surrounded (in the modified version) by the billowing folds of international flags and streamers; male and patriotic versions of Loïe Fuller, each with a mission to win. This, the first official Olympic poster, was printed in sixteen languages and three formats, although not distributed in countries where the image was still thought too daring.

The increasing international rivalry that developed within the Olympic Games after their re-establishment in 1894 was reflected in its posters. Classical Realism, for example, appealed to Hitler who chose it as the official style of Nazism, and it was used by Franz Würbel on the posters for the 1936 Olympic Games in Berlin, sponsored by the German Railways (plate 42). Printed in 19 languages and allegedly distributed in 34 countries, this design is dominated by the heroic head crowned with a laurel wreath, towering over the silhouette of sculpture from Berlin's Brandenburg Gate.

41. Olle Hjörtzberg. 'Olympic Games Stockholm 1912', Sweden, 1911.
E.705-1912

42. Franz Würbel, 'Olympic Games', Germany, 1936. E.2905-1980

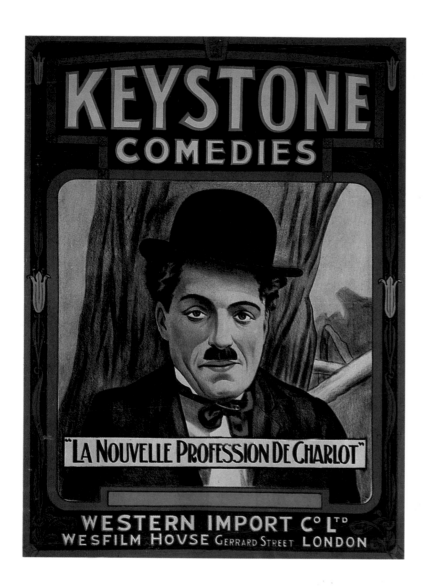

44. Anonymous. 'Something to Sing

About', USA, 1937. E.983-1979

Hollywood led in film production in the early twentieth century, and the American preference for photographic images on theatrical posters was translated into cinema posters. Nevertheless, for the first two decades of its existence in the States, film was such a novelty that little publicity was needed apart from a sign outside the theatre announcing 'Moving Picture Show'. The earliest film posters, c. 1909, resulted from Edison's efforts to establish patent priorities, which sparked fierce competition with other producers. Edison, Selig and Biograph advertised their films like commodities, asserting that their products were the best, and on their earliest posters the producers' trade marks were prominent. In Britain, when film was first introduced at the turn of the century, short programmes were shown in variety theatres as part of an evening's otherwise live entertainment and were billed on the usually typographical posters as if they were another variety act.

When the early silent films were imported to Europe from the States they came complete with photographic posters produced by the studios. Since the actors were largely anonymous at first, these tended to depict dramatic moments from the action, often with a line of dialogue from the film, much like posters for stage melodrama. By 1910 however, with the rise of such film stars as Mary Pickford and Charlie Chaplin (plate 43), posters began to capitalize on their fame. By 1914, stars' names and faces rather than titles dominated film posters, since stars undoubtedly 'sold' films. American films, and posters, after World War I began to cater for the new demand for exoticism and escape from reality. Glamorous stars in costume would be shown in moments of action that promised excitement or sexuality, just as they do on Indian film posters today. By the 1930s it was said that MGM in Hollywood possessed 'more stars than Heaven itself', and their portraits dominated theatre posters, as does James Cagney's as the New York band-leader on the poster for *Something to Sing About* (1937; plate 44). Only posters advertising comedies or horror might depart from this style, and then not if the film included one of the great dramatic or romantic stars. Posters for British films generally placed less emphasis on the images of the stars than on the subject of the films; the Ealing Studios, for example, commissioned a poster for *The Titfield Thunderbolt* (1952) from the illustrator and designer Edward Bawden which featured the much-loved train with the names of the cast on plumes of smoke coming from the engine (plate 45).

The most remarkable and radical approach to film posters in the early twentieth century occurred in the Soviet Union after 1919, when film was declared 'the most important art'. The earliest films seen in Russia were those of the Lumière brothers, imported from France in 1894. Within ten years a home-grown film industry was established, its posters mostly designed in a style

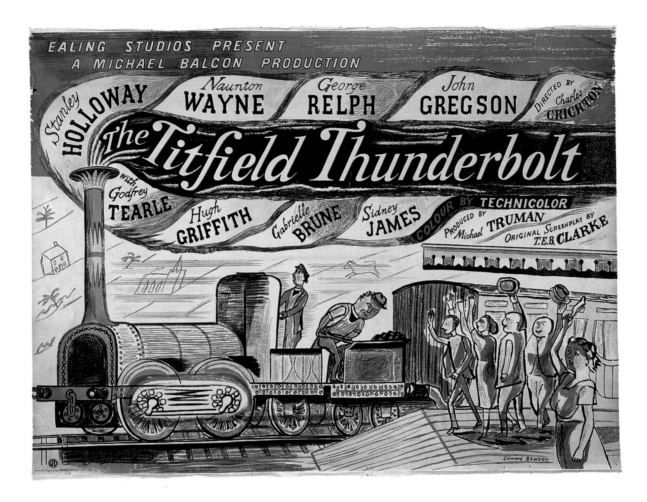

45. Edward Bawden. 'The Titfield

Thunderbolt', UK, 1952. E.181-1980

reminiscent of Russian folk imagery, showing little awareness of the developments of Western poster art. The upheavals of World War I and the 1917 Revolution temporarily halted Soviet film production but, realizing the importance of film as propaganda, Lenin nationalized the ailing industry in 1919, and it went on to produce documentary, education, propaganda and entertainment films. Posters proved immensely valuable in the Soviet Union between 1917 and 1923 for disseminating the new political ideology, and to promote the cinema a brilliant team of Constructivist poster designers was employed by the state-controlled Reklam Film. The most notable artists working for Reklam in the 1920s were the Stenberg brothers, Vladimir and Georgii. Their earliest posters were designed for Tairov's Kamerny Theatre, where they worked as scene designers from 1922/3, and where in 1926 they organized the first Russian exhibition of film posters. Their first film poster was in 1924, and they continued to work together until the death of Georgii in 1933. Their style developed from a narrative depiction of plot, previously used by Russian film poster designers, to one that subtly communicated the atmosphere of a film.

Strikingly powerful and original, their posters combined recognizable images of stars with a strong graphic approach. Faces, usually unsmiling, would draw in the viewer; as Vladimir Stenberg later said: 'We would give most attention to the eyes and the nose .... There would be nothing superfluous'.[17] The rounded, stylized shapes of bodies and inanimate objects, characteristic of the Stenbergs' work, are typical of the Russian Constructivists' experimentation with geometric shapes and the elimination of extraneous detail. The brothers were fascinated with creative precision and

46. Anonymous, possibly by the Stenberg Brothers, Vladimir and Georgi [Georgii] Stenberg. 'The Hero of the Blast Furnace', USSR, 1928. E.1286-1989

technical perfection and though they rarely used photomontage in their posters, they found a way to achieve the sharp photographic quality they wanted. The poster for the film *The Hero of the Blast Furnace* (1928) has stylized features similar to those of the Stenbergs: dramatic faces with Futurist shadowing, superimposed images cut through by abstract shapes, and integral lettering receding to give a three-dimensional effect (plate 46).

Apart from the Soviet Union, the most exciting work in film poster design in the late 1920s was in Germany; this included the influential film posters by Jan Tschichold for the Phoebus Palast theatre in 1927, and Expressionistic posters like Fritz Lang's *Spione*, 1928 (plate 82, chapter 2). German and Russian poster design influenced a brief revival of mainly commercial poster art in Poland in the 1930s, a short period of prosperity before World War II. In post-war Poland however, when private enterprise ceased and commercial advertising was unnecessary, cinema-going became a huge diversion, and film posters had an enormous influence on the development of Polish poster art generally. At first they were very basic and mainly typographic, but in 1947 the state institution that distributed films – Film Polsky – began to commission designers to work on film posters. These brightened up the streets in post-war Poland, and the so-called modern 'Polish School of Poster Design' credits much of its success to film posters, and to the state patronage which also organized

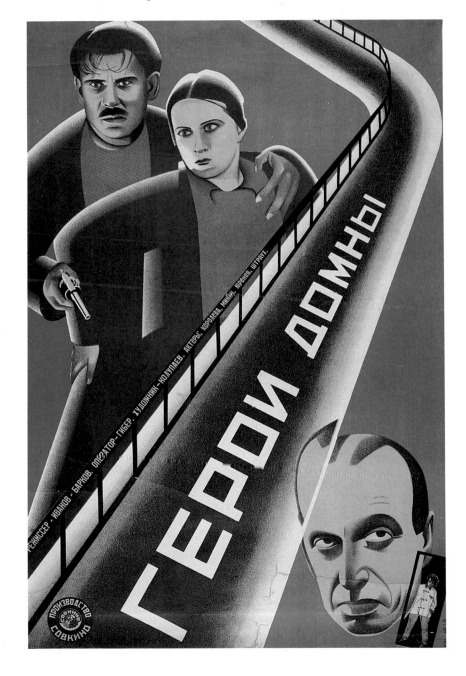

poster design competitions such as the International Poster Biennale in Warsaw. Later, in the 1960s and early 1970s, many Polish artists, including Waldemar Swierzy, Jan Mlodozoniec and Hubert Hilscher, produced witty and strikingly inventive posters for entertainment. On Hilscher's 1970 brightly coloured poster for the circus (plate 47) a performing lion wittily executes a handstand.

The wit and inventiveness of Polish posters advertising entertainment is seen again in Jan Sawka's poster advertising a stage adaptation of Chaucer's *The Canterbury Tales* (plate 48) in Opole in 1976. Sawka, born in Poland in 1946, trained as an architect, a fine artist and graphic designer and was involved in student theatre, first designing sets, posters and record-covers for an avant-garde theatre group at the STU theatre in Crakow. This poster was one of the last he designed in Poland before his expulsion for his political beliefs in 1978. Sawka sees his theatre posters as integral to the whole dramatization, and *The Canterbury Tales* was a controversial production intended to be provocative to Communist authorities, whilst remaining true to Chaucer's original.[18] The pilgrims' journey is interpreted as that of a motley band of contemporary travellers who wend their way over a gigantic and inflated female body, representing the lustful inclinations of the Wife of Bath, as well as symbolizing the degenerate Western values (which were nevertheless the dream of many Polish people under Communism). In the surreal quality of the image, and in the colours and cartoon treatment, Sawka also deliberately referred to the Pop Art posters that had been influential in Poland in the 1960s. There are echoes, for example, of the poster for the film inspired by the Beatles' *Yellow Submarine* (1968).

Just as war was an impetus for powerful propaganda posters, so an outbreak of love, peace and hallucination in the mid-1960s produced an extraordinary wave of poster art. In the USA the roots of the psychedelic poster were established in San Francisco in the early 1960s, when young musicians and artists gathered together, excited by developments in British rock music, especially by the Beatles. In 1965 and 1966 the promoter Bill Graham put on rock concerts at San Francisco's

47. Hubert Hilscher. 'Cyrk', Poland, 1970. E.1084-1976

48. Jan Sawka. 'Opowiesci Kanterberyjskie' (*The Canterbury Tales*), Poland, 1976. S.1104-1996

Fillmore Auditorium and commissioned posters from Wes Wilson (Robert Wesley Wilson), who was then working at a small San Francisco press. Wilson was one of America's earliest psychedelic poster artists, and he did all Bill Graham's artwork in 1966 until May 1967, designing 11 of the first posters advertising the San Francisco group Family Dog. A poster fanatic, Jeff Berger, remembered the excitement of collecting such posters when he was at school in San Francisco:

> Every day, the moment school ended, we'd head up to Telegraph Avenue, and then a whole ritual would begin. We would go into the stores that had posters in their window and ask the proprietor if we could sign the back with, say, 'save for Jeff Berger'. If they had the handbills on the counter, we'd grab a handful. But you've got to realise how intense this all was. The crowd that was into this collecting scene would catapult out from school, go screaming up the hill to be the first to sign the backs.[19]

One promoter recalled the frustration of posting a whole street and returning a few minutes later to find that 90 per cent had been removed, but he admitted that a poster carried home and pasted on a home refrigerator reached the audience he wanted. The hallmarks of the psychedelic posters were their shimmering colours and their impenetrable lettering, which caused friction between Bill Graham and Wes Wilson. These posters went against all the rules – they certainly did not communicate a succinct message but perversely demanded patient study to unravel their message, and because of that they attracted a cult following. Graham understood the desire: 'to bury all the pertinent information underneath all the oozes and ebbs and flows and liquidy movement on the poster',[20] but as a promoter he wanted people to be able to read the information. He told Wilson: 'Just watch people standing there, trying to read your poster! Their bodies actually would be trying to follow the curvature of the words, the lettering'.[21] Lettering fascinated Wilson, who liked the conceit of using the 'negative spaces' of its design and was much influenced by the lettering techniques of the Vienna Secession artists. In his April 1967 poster advertising The Byrds (plate 49), the perspective of the globular lettering of the repeated name of the group gives a three-dimensional effect to the coloured streamer behind the peacock. The sinuous curves are reminiscent of the ornate and highly decorative Art Nouveau forms that Wilson admired, and the black and white, almost Celtic patterning on the peacock is evocative of Aubrey Beardsley's graphic style. Wilson's enjoyment of the contrast of black and white and colour is evident in this poster; he claimed that his colours came from his experiments with LSD. Victor Moscoso, who began designing posters after he saw an early one of Wilson's, related music to his artwork: 'I turned the colour up as loud as I possibly could'.[22]

Promoting pop records, performers or events, entertainment posters of the 1960s became

49. Wes Wilson. 'Byrds, Byrds, Byrds',
USA, 1967. E.396-1968

50. Michael English. 'Love Festival',
UK, 1967. Colour screen-print.
E.38-1968

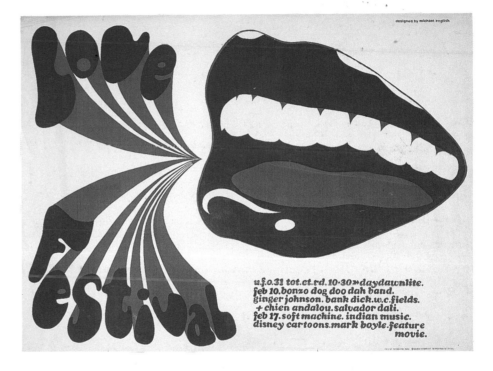

collectable items, and students especially appreciated them as fashionable and cheap works of art to pin on bed-sit walls. In Britain every pop movement produced its own visual style, but the so-called 'underground movement' of the 1960s developed innovative graphics in tandem with the new music, writing and philosophy. In 1967 Nigel Waymouth and Michael English joined forces in London as poster designers under the name Hapshash and the Coloured Coat to advertise events and activities at the underground's London club, the UFO, or 'Unlimited Freak Out'. The club was described in an article in *The Observer Magazine* of 3 December 1967 as '... the first spontaneous and successful attempt to produce a total environment using music, light, and people' which aimed at '... mind-expansion and hallucination at the service of the destruction of the non-hip'. The poster that Michael English designed for the Love Festival at the UFO in February 1967 (plate 50) was his first for the club, combining the image of a Pop Art style glistening plastic mouth

with a flowering text spelling out the words 'Love Festival'. English and Waymouth used the new technology of day-glo colours and metallic inks, which are seen in the studio set-up photograph of Pop posters on a hoarding (plate 51). English recalls that wherever possible many repeats were pasted together to enhance the patterns and effect, and that the *Love Festival* poster made a huge splash on the hoardings surrounding London's Royal Lancaster Hotel when it was being built. The UFO posters were sold at the club, and displayed inside as well as on the street, because of the 'mind-expanding' effect of the ultra-violet light on the colours. Thirty years on, Michael English apologizes for the eclecticism of their work and for stealing the lips in the UFO poster from the work of the American Pop Artist Tom Wesselmann.[23] At the time, however, this fusion of

51. Hoarding of psychedelic posters including the **UFO** 'Love Festival' poster by Michael English, UK, 1967. Photographed by Patrick Ward for *The Observer Magazine*, 3 Dec. 1967.

other styles from Bosch to Beardsley, Mucha to Matisse, was accepted as an essential element of their work, described again by George Melly in *The Observer Magazine* (3 December 1967) as: 'a visionary and hallucinatory bouillabaisse'.

Another artist whose work influenced the Pop Art poster boom in Britain was the Australian Martin Sharp, the artist on the satirical and psychedelic magazine *Oz* started by Richard Neville in Sydney in 1964. Sharp and Neville came to England in 1966 to launch the magazine, and Sharp's artwork so impressed Peter Ledeboer, an *Oz* associate, that he set up Big O Posters to produce, promote and distribute all his work. Sharp's 1967 homage to Bob Dylan, *Mister Tambourine Man* (plate 53), was a hugely popular iconic image.

Styles of graphic design for entertainment posters in the 1960s were nevertheless as diverse as the entertainment they advertised. The acclaimed American designer Saul Bass used strong, simplified elements in the 1962 poster (plate 52) advertising the Otto Preminger

53. Martin Sharp. 'Mister Tambourine Man', UK, 1967. Colour screen-print.

E.7-1900

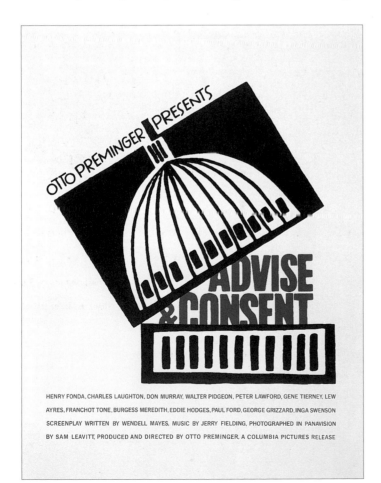

52. Saul Bass. 'Advise & Consent', USA, 1962. Colour screen-print.

E.2926-1980

film about the moral darkness of Washington. An illustrative approach is evident in Joseph Eula's American poster advertising the Supremes' concert at New York's Lincoln Center in 1965 (plate 54).

Colour and rhythmic effects characterize the poster by Robert Rauschenberg for a concert season by the St Louis Symphony Orchestra at the Powell Symphony Hall, St Louis, in 1968 (plate 55). The artist's bravura interweaving of the elements of photomontage and typography become a metaphor for the music itself: classical elements given a contemporary treatment are incorporated and collaged in an apparent disarray, yet are brought together in harmony. The metropolitan ambience is reinforced by the city map as background. Rauschenberg's own life-long love of music (he has worked with John Cage and Merce Cunningham) is apparent.

56. Per Arnoldi.

'Copenhagen Jazz Festival',

Denmark, 1983. E.1420-1983

Similarly, though in a very different style, the poster by Per Arnoldi for a Copenhagen Jazz Festival in 1983 (plate 56) uses colour and form as a direct expression of the spirit of the music: the primary reds and yellows of the saxophone vibrate against the rich blue background, while the letters 'jazz' stretch out along the body of the instrument, as though part of the music-making. In this and earlier posters by Arnoldi for jazz at the Montmartre Club, Copenhagen, including those advertising performances by Oscar Peterson and Dizzy Gillespie, colour is the music and the message.

Other areas of the entertainment business explored the possibilities of photography and photomontage in their poster output. Murray Duitz's celebrated poster of 1970 for the film *Mash* uses photomontage to create an eye-catching and wittily surreal image out of black and white photographs of legs, a hand and an army helmet, perfectly capturing the irreverent spirit of the film. Duitz had worked as a newsreel cameraman during World War II, and later set up his own film studio; by the 1970s his work expressed his particular interest in photography and Surrealism. Surrealism's power to shock and to look at familiar objects in new ways is used powerfully in much of his poster work by the German graphic designer Holger Matthies. Matthies works especially for theatre, rock and pop concerts, and on CD and LP covers. His theatre posters capture the essence of the drama; for the 1975 Kiel Theatre production of *Der Hofmeister* (plate 58), the castration of the schoolmaster was his subject. Matthies creates and takes the photographs himself, and works closely with the printer Bahruth, who has produced his work for 30 years and understands the quality of the images that Matthies demands.[25]

57. Poláčková, 'Nežna'. Poster for showing in Czechoslovakia of the French film *Une Femme Douce*, based on a story by Dostoievski. Czechoslovakia, 1970. E.409-1972

58. Holger Matthies. 'Der Hofmeister', Germany, 1975. E.1580-1979

59. David Hockney. 'Olympische
Spiele München 1972', Germany, 1970.
E.357-1972

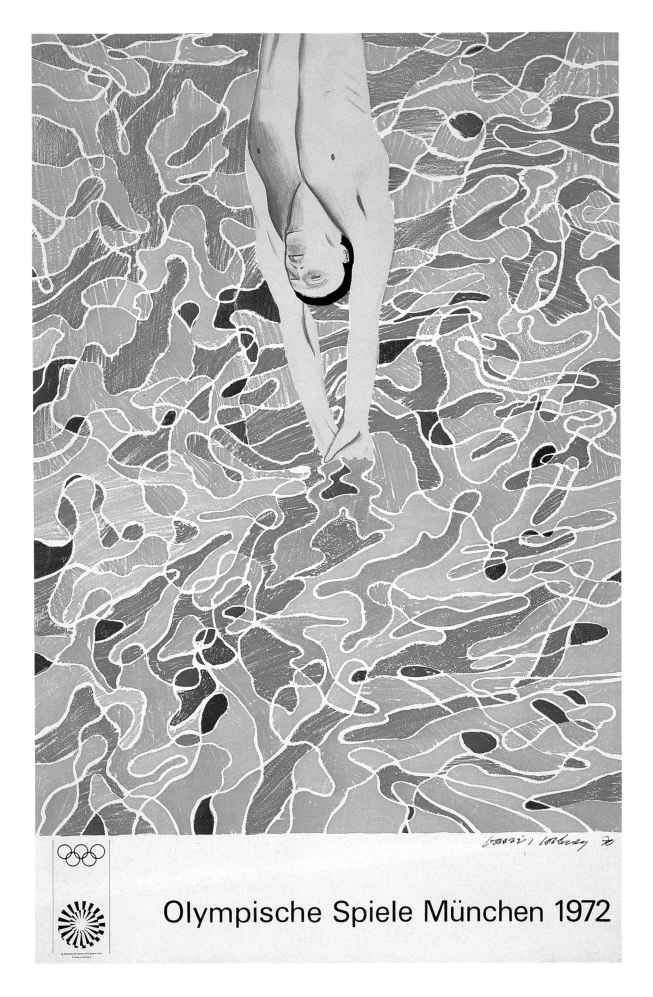

In contrast to the harsh Surrealism of Holger Matthies is the poetic interpretation of David Hockney's poster for the 1972 Munich Olympics (plate 59), one of a series commissioned from well-known artists celebrating the spirit of peaceful competition. Unlike some previous posters for the Olympics, this is an image without any underlying nationalistic message. Hockney concentrates on the perfection of the last moment of the dive, eloquently treating the ripples in the pool like a shimmering mosaic in which the flesh tones of the diver are reflected.

Posters are no longer pre-eminent in London's West End theatrical productions, since leaflets and press advertisements are now seen as the first line of attack. Seventy to eighty per cent of West End theatre posters come from Dewynters PLC, a single agency which designs, prints and manufactures an entire range of advertising and merchandise for productions; it also provides the same service for producers world-wide, including in America, Australia, Denmark and Holland. The poster image can be based on a photographic shot or, for major musicals, a recognizable 'icon' such as cats' eyes (*Cats*) or a mask (*Phantom of the Opera*), which will work on mugs or matchboxes as well as on posters – poster production is part of a 'package'. Designers have to conform to 'contractual billing' whereby the sizes of the typeface for the names of those who appear on the poster has been agreed with producers and agents; this can be a graphic designer's 'typographical nightmare',[26] and a continuation of an age-old problem.

With the exception of some posters issued by the subsidized theatre companies, few contemporary British theatrical posters excite attention, but the medium is taken more seriously elsewhere. The poster by Boris Bućan advertising *The Fire Bird* and *Petrushka* (plate 60) at the Croatian National Theatre in Zagreb in 1983, for example, is a stunningly original creation. In Britain, however, unusual theatre poster campaigns are so rare that there was a huge media reaction when, in 1989, The English

60. Boris Bućan. 'The Fire Bird' and 'Petrushka', Croatia, 1983. Colour screen-print. E.498-1986

National Opera produced their second corporate poster campaign aimed at promoting the accessibility of opera. With vital commercial sponsorship, ENO produced a series of dramatic photographic posters focusing on the back-stage staff. Significantly it was an in-house campaign, the result of brain-storming between the marketing and press departments, with three of the posters, including *High flyer low profile* (plate 62), featuring photographs by a master of dance photography, Anthony Crickmay.

In Britain, the music business is the main branch of entertainment today that most regularly and avidly produces and pastes up posters, especially on illegal poster sites. Marketing departments of record companies contract fly-poster companies to display posters for new albums or singles about a week before their release date, or to publicize concerts by their recording artists. Working in the very early morning to avoid detection, fly-posters, if they have a chance, will post long repeats of identical posters (plate 61). Posters on illegal sites are often short lived but striking; pedestrians and some drivers in traffic jams provide the audience.

61. Fly-posted hoarding, Great West Road, London, 1997.

Photograph by Graham Brandon.

A music business poster temporarily banned for indecency under an 1889 Act was designed by Jamie Reid and John Varnom to advertise the anarchic Sex Pistols' album *Never Mind the Bollocks* (plate 63). Reid and Varnum designed the album cover for its release in 1977, and shortly afterwards produced the poster as a further affront to the authorities who had tried to prosecute a shop owner for indecent advertisements. Reid produced artwork for the Sex Pistols from their first single in 1976, and since the band instantly generated massive media coverage, Reid decided that there wasn't any need to have pictures of them on the graphics:

'What's the point when you're already on the front of *The Daily Mirror* and *The Sun* ... I wanted

the graphics to articulate what the attitude of the song was, what the attitude of the band was ...'[27]

Reid trained at Wimbledon Art College, and his work for the Sex Pistols developed alongside his involvement with the band. Although he designed an immense amount of their promotional material, including posters, album covers, handbills, stickers and flyers, he claimed that the

62. **Sue Coffey**. 'High flyer low
profile', **UK**, 1989.

Photograph by **Anthony Crickmay**.

Poster advertising **The English
National Opera**. S.2806-1995

63. Jamie Reid and John Varnom.

'Never Mind the Bollocks', UK, 1977.

Original artwork advertising the

album by the Sex Pistols. S.761-1990

artwork only took about 1 per cent of his time with them – he was also generally concerned with the running of the band.

In the USA today, Warner Brothers still find posters successful for advertising new artists or established performers with a new image to project. The huge poster advertising Madonna's 1986 album *True Blue* (plate 64) features a seductive close-up of her by Herb Ritts. Madonna, one of Warner's biggest stars, has complete control of all official artwork for her publicity. She and Ritts have worked for several years in a compatible and creative relationship. Since image is of supreme importance to Madonna, the way that image is presented is vital.

Posters advertising entertainment can still be vital in the profile of performance, and the best must be capable of communicating in an instant with a stressed driver or a preoccupied pedestrian. From the poetry of Mucha to the anarchy of Jamie Reid, effective posters work at a glance. Reid was a victim of his own success when he was beaten up wearing a T-shirt printed with the controversial artwork for the Sex Pistols' *God Save the Queen* poster. As Holger Matthies once declared, 'Designing posters is marvellous. Designing posters is agony'.[28]

64. 'True Blue', USA, 1986.

Photograph by Herb Ritts.

Poster advertising a Madonna album.

E.152-1987

2 POSTERS FOR ART'S SAKE

DAWN ADES

There is a fascination with the origins of posters which is closely bound up with the question of their status. Born of the print collectors' cabinets as well as of the street, the poster's hybrid parentage serves as a reminder of a continuous if always re-articulated debate about its artistic status. The fact that the poster is mass produced and that its aims are to seduce, sell, cajole, excite or educate have been regarded as incompatible with pure aesthetic purposes. But, as Susan Sontag points out, to define the poster as being unlike 'fine art forms' because the poster artist works for money and in the interests of a client is not only dubious and simplistic but also unhistorical: 'Only since the early nineteenth century has the artist been generally understood as working to express himself, or for the sake of "art".[1] The label 'applied art' is handy but blurs precisely those tensions, contradictions and ambiguities that have historically animated encounters between artists and poster-making.

The term 'art poster', *Künstlerische plakat*, as opposed to that of 'poster as such' (*plakat als solches*), as the German magazine *Das Plakat* defined it in 1914, was not necessarily a distinction between advertising an aesthetic, as opposed to a commercial product, but concerned rather the status of the designer. When Alfred Barr included posters in *Cubism and Abstract Art* (1936) as an art form in its own right like painting, photography, theatre and film, it was in response to the fact that many artists, such as the Constructivists in Russia, had chosen this mode as a preferred alternative to easel painting.[2]

There has, moreover, been a curious inversion: whereas in its early days the poster aspired to the status of art, in the twentieth century pictorial art has often aspired to the condition of the poster. Barbara Kruger's large-scale mock advertisements, with slogans blazoned across an arresting photographic fragment (*Your body is a battleground*, 1989 – see plate 134 in chapter 3 – or *I shop therefore I am*; 1987), not only visibly parodied the poster but were actually inserted into the commercial arena on street hoardings. A part of Kruger's purpose is to reinvest art with the power to project a specific – in this case feminist – message. When 60 years earlier Berlin Dadaists invented photomontage, they first produced one-off images that played with and against advertising customs; Hannah Höch in particular incorporated magazine advertisements into her montages, which sometimes mimic posters. Their methods were later developed by Heartfield into fully-fledged political propaganda whose primary tool was the uncovering of the meanings of official Nazi propaganda.

Three special conditions attach to the poster regardless of its specific subject: its destination in the public space of walls and hoardings; its means of production as an object of mass production (though the scale can stretch from the fully industrial to the craft-studio); and its function as advocacy. It is in relation to these conditions that I want to look at various instances of the intersection between artists, artistic practices and poster design. The focus will be on the exhibition poster, but first I would like to explore briefly three contrasting attitudes to the artistic status of the poster in its setting.

The images produced in the first great age of the coloured pictorial poster are cherished by museums and collectors, but it was their original impact on walls and hoardings – their intrusion into the landscape – that prompted public debate about their political and aesthetic proprieties. Posters by Chéret, Lautrec or The Beggarstaffs seem as remote from the jumbled typographic mass of advertisements shown in nineteenth-century photographs of London and Paris, or in John Parry's painting of a hoarding near St Paul's in the 1840s, as from the debased mythological nudes, gloomy landscapes and scenes of military exploits of academic Salon painting. They seemed to occupy a new arena, a kind of *terrain vague,* not just between high and popular art, but also because they were in a public space that was not framed for art, as a museum or gallery is, and raised new questions of aesthetics which tangled explicitly with commerce and ethics.

Roger Marx, in his influential prefaces to the five collected volumes of the portfolio *Les Maîtres de l'Affiche* from 1896 to 1900, first published in monthly instalments in sets of four, insisted on both the artistic and social value of the poster, basing his argument on the posters' equivalence to murals, and frequently uses the phrase 'mural chromolithography'. Drawing on both Tolstoy, who had championed an art of and by the people, and on William Morris, he argued both for the value of decorative arts of a high quality, and for the potential educative function of posters. He mentions the use of posters in the classroom in Switzerland and in Britain, where 'To the pupils' watchful eye, the British have proposed huge coloured posters whose subjects are taken from the Bible, legend and country life.'[3] And in France, he mentions the lithographed transcription of 'Puvis de Chavannes' admirable frescoes in the Pantheon', the Poster for the Union for Moral Action, thereby brought to the view of the casual passer-by.

Marx's arguments about the decorative function of the poster are not prescriptive but stem from a conviction of its special role in the modern city: 'The picturesqueness of narrow alleys has been succeeded by the picturesqueness of broad, variegated modern thoroughfares; it is a scene which also has its beauty and of which the poster is the essential element.'[4] But not just any poster: to fulfil its function the poster must fit its setting, and this setting is the public wall.

> It is successful only on condition that it meets the laws of mural decoration. This aspect is hardly taken into consideration by the detractors who are so quick to censure the effects of a technique required to realize the purpose of the poster. For instance, the sharply set off arabesques and lines are an integral part of the poster's design, for, without it, the composition would not be legible from a distance and the first glance could not embrace it in its entirety; likewise, the display outdoors, in order to sparkle in the light of day, demands just as imperiously the use of fairly brilliant colours.[5]

With the mural comparison in mind, it is interesting how diverse responses to its lessons were among the early poster artists. While some tilted the figure towards the passer-by, others emphasized a flat, unmodelled silhouette. Chéret, whose sketches reveal above all his great debt to Watteau (recently rescued from relative obscurity by the Goncourt brothers' study *Eighteenth-Century Painters*), was also an admirer of Tiepolo, and borrows poses from his wall and ceiling paintings of figures turning and suspended in space.

In his first preface Marx compares posters in the street to an open air gallery, recalling the first Salons in the Place Dauphine.

> It is, I know, a museum created by chance, where the work of genius jostles the mediocre, the exquisite adjoins the vulgar, the witty is placed side by side with the absurd – a museum which renews itself with the suddenness of a transformation scene in a fairy play because the poster has the precarious fate of everything that glitters, from the butterfly to the flower, it gleams in the sun, fades in the mist, dangles sadly in shreds ...[6]

Marx's celebration of the enlivening quality of the street poster, and its contribution to the elevation of popular taste, had its conservative counterpart in the strictures of the Right-wing Catholic Talmeyr, who grumbled about the loss of authority in the face of the poster's inviting sensuality, which made it the natural and logical art of an epoch of individualism and extreme egotism.

Isn't that just the modern monument, the paper castle, the cathedral of sensuality, where all our culture and aesthetic sense finds nothing better to do than to work for the exaltation of well-being and the tickling of the instincts?[7]

Both draw the parallel with architecture, though Talmeyr, like Ruskin, deplores the disappearance of the stone monument under the teeming and vibrant ephemerality of the poster. There were mutual accusations of decadence from both sides of the divide; Huysmans famously rubbished Salon painting (Talmeyr's images of authority and aesthetic value): 'their Virgins dressed in pink and blue like Christmas crackers, their grey-bearded God-the-Fathers, their Brutuses made to order, their Venuses made to measure', preferring 'the crudest posters advertising a cabaret or a circus'.[8] It is one of the persistent ironies of the debate that this mass-produced medium was often appealed to as the possessor of true originality and strength. The idea, moreover, that high-quality posters could constitute a 'museum of the street' gains in significance in the context of museum and gallery audiences in nineteenth-century London and Paris, which were far from exclusively elite: visitors to museums included middle- and working-class spectators, who could therefore be seen as being offered an alternative to the Salon or Academy, with the right to judge and choose between these diverse modes of visual pleasure and instruction. Thus the poster could be not just a vulgar alternative to high art, but a flagship in the cause of a demotic modern art.

Wyndham Lewis, not unlike Marx, believed that posters could educate the public in good design, if the walls of London could be 'carpeted with abstractions'.[9] For Fernand Léger it was the overall impact of the new 'murals' rather than any individual poster's status as art that mattered and gave him his source for a new aesthetic: pictorial contrast. 'This yellow or red poster, shouting in a timid landscape, is the best of possible reasons for the new painting; it topples the whole sentimental literary concept and announces the advent of pictorial contrast'.[10] He, Lissitzky and Delaunay all believed that 'the culture of painting' now came from 'the picture gallery of our modern streets...'.[11] Léger was outraged at the attempts to control the spread of billboards (saying that The Society for the Protection of the Landscape was peopled precisely by those who laughed at modern art), and, like Marinetti, hymned the challenge of the street-based, exaggeratedly coloured lithographic poster to nature: 'Multi-coloured billboards on the green of the fields'.[12]

In contrast to this Modernist celebration of the new man and urban industrial landscape, the Surrealists looked with other eyes at the peopling of the streets with new and fantastic creations. In the Surrealist poet Robert Desnos's imagination, the city landscape is transformed into the theatre of an epic encounter between two of the candidates for a modern mythology, both born of the poster: Bébé Cadum, the baby advertising Cadum soap whose gigantic image towered over the Paris streets in the 1920s, and the Michelin tyre man, Bibendum.

65. Roy Lichtenstein. 'Crak! Now, Mes

Petits...Pour La France!', USA, 1963.

E.229-1985

For Desnos, as for Apollinaire and Cendrars, the streets and sky are peopled by a new breed of heroes, witnesses to the strange workings of the human imagination, whose inhuman scale or comic transpositions (of tyres into limbs, for instance) seemed to subvert their advertising function. The Paris billboards with the Bébé Cadum posters, although rising to the height of houses, had additional sections added to the upper edge of the hoardings cut to the outline of the baby's head, so that they do indeed look like giant faces among the chimneys, and it is easy to imagine the city as a huge soapy bathtub with the baby rising like Venus from the foam. The Surrealists were quick to detect the unintentionally irrational aspect of modern product promotion, which in various ways informed their imagery and then in turn was to seep uncontrollably back into the voracious world of advertising. Magritte especially, whose pipe in the *The Treachery of Images* could come straight from a billboard, saw his pictures plundered by the advertising industry.

Exhibition posters have an advantage from the artist-designer's point of view. At one extreme, the one-person exhibition, they are intimately connected with the artist's own project, although this may pose interesting questions about the public face he or she may choose as representative. If the exhibition is of work in other media, rather than an exhibition of posters, there is the problem of translating an image into the poster medium and for another arena. Some artists choose to design specifically for the poster; Roy Lichtenstein's poster (plate 65) for his 1963 gallery exhibition, on the other hand, uses an existing image with comic-book origins which unexpectedly activates a set of associations with partisan propaganda and political posters. Exhibition posters obviously cover a much wider range of activities or product-display than the one-person or group show.

Because of their relatively restricted scope – local and short term – with smaller print runs, posters are not so subject to the need to play for safety that governed advertising for modern manufacturing industry and that Roger Fry so deplored. Fry's argument was that the trade designer had to take care not to offend anyone, because of the huge investment in a large-scale advertising campaign, and thus 'A really creative designer is the last person whom a manufacturer can safely employ'.[13] This is not of course an invariable state of affairs; enlightened clients have sponsored large-scale advertising campaigns of remarkable quality, such as the London Transport posters commissioned by Frank Pick (see page 14). On the other hand compromises were also evident in fine art exhibition posters. The poster for the Fifth Venice Biennale (plate 66) avoided identification with any particular style by resorting to an innocuous, naturalistic, almost tourist-view scene of the city.

66. Augusto Sezanne. 'Fifth
International Art Exhibition, Venice',
Italy, 1903. E.72-1903

67. Austin Cooper. 'Exhibition of
British Industrial Art in the Home:
London', UK, 1933. E.133-1961

Exhibition posters have, though, often functioned as a visual manifesto, and if they are for an industrial or technological exhibition are often positioned on the interface between art and design. But exhibition posters also reflect local tastes and resistances: abstract designs, as Barr pointed out in 1936, were less acceptable to an Anglo-American audience 'accustomed to an over-crowded and banally realistic style'.[14] He reproduced in *Cubism and Abstract Art* (1936) two posters for the Cologne International Exhibition of Printing in 1928, one in a realistic style, with picture and lettering clearly differentiated, the other using flat, dramatic diagonals, which function as a framework for the typography. Austin Cooper's poster for British Industrial Art in the Home (plate 67), however, shows the increasing influence of Bauhaus-inspired design principles. The 'BIA' capital letters are influenced by Moholy-Nagy's emphasis on three-dimensional primary geometrical forms, cone, ball and cube (advocated in his *Von Material zu Architektur,* 1928), whose architectural associations Cooper also hints at.

The posters selected for inclusion in *Les Maîtres de l'Affiche* include many advertising exhibitions; they are highly eclectic in character, regarded as a virtue by Marx. Two posters by Carlos Schwabe (plate 68) and Alfred Roedel (plate 69) were among those reproduced. Unlike the dynamic

68. *far right.* **Carlos Schwabe. 'Salon Rose Croix', France, 1892. E.291-1921**

69. *right.* **Alfred Roedel. 'Exposition publique de Dessins, aquarelles, Pastels, Tableaux, Lithographies, Hôtel des Ventes, Paris, 1895'.**

E.2440-1938

and florid posters by Chéret, where the lettering is usually free floating and often overlaps or is overlapped by the figures, Schwabe carefully frames and isolates the title; the lettering for 'Salon' is Japanese in style, and the whole poster is in a restrained Symbolist manner. Peladan's Rose Croix Salon of 1892 invited works for exhibition 'even if the execution was imperfect', so long as they dealt with Catholicism, allegory and poetry, but rejected 'historical painting, portraits, representations of contemporary life, landscapes, seascapes, still-lifes and anything painted by a woman'.[15] Rejection of the modern world, and even of Impressionism, is evident in the absence of colour and the women's timeless draperies. The woman in black has already broken her earthly chains, while the woman in white, symbolizing faith, reaches to help her ascend 'the steps of mystical flowers that lead to heaven'. Humanity is shown sunk in a murky pool, possibly, as Jane Abdy commented, as punishment for admiring Impressionism.

Roedel's poster by contrast is a down-to-earth description of the bohemian world of the Montmartre artists. Originally designed for the exhibition at the Hôtel des Ventes, another version using the identical image was commissioned by the Moulin de la Galette, the oldest *café-concert* of Montmartre, frequented by the Paris working class. The girl walking down the hill carrying pictures to the sale is probably an artist's model. There is a flexibility in this poster which raises a question common to many of the posters of this period: can one distinguish clearly and at first glance the nature of the product? Almost regardless of what is being advertised during the 1890s – play, book, exhibition, bicycle, absinthe, gas or oil lamps – and whatever the style, the dominant figure is a woman. Willette, like Roedel a Montmartre artist, for instance, portrayed a *grisette* painting a medallion of his head to advertise an exhibition of his own paintings and drawings. Even Schwabe's poster for the Rose Croix Salon could be taken as advertising something else – fashion, say – without the caption. Langorous women abound in all contexts at this period, as did the high-kicking girls of Chéret; the tendency simply to posit the product name in conjunction with the image of a woman could lead the viewer to think at first glance that, for example, 'L'Absinthe' was the name of a novel, or advertisements for electric lamps were for theatres or exhibitions. It is no wonder that during the period of maximum attention to function and efficiency, in the 1920s and 1930s, the pictorial element was minimized or eliminated, and abstract geometrical forms (of pictorial origin) became the designer-typographers' ideal alibi.

Art Nouveau, although a pervasive influence throughout Europe, did not produce a standardized type of design. The curvilinear and arabesque drawn from natural forms was open to variation by the gifted artist-designer. There was little agreement on lettering, which ranged from the relatively simple to patterned wildernesses in which the actual words are lost. In Alfred

Roller's poster (plate 70) for the Sixteenth Secession Exhibition in 1903 the announcement constitutes the whole poster, with only a minimal heraldic design resembling wallpaper filling the background – this is one of the clearest statements of the value of design in its own right, without recourse to the human figure. Roller is here deliberately cutting the lines to the claim to the artistic, made by certain kinds of poster, based upon a pictorial resemblance to the subjects and figurative styles of 'high' or academic art. Van de Velde argued in *Les Formules* against the cultural snobberies that separated crafts, industrial and applied arts from the fine arts. Like William Morris and others he aimed to improve the standards of manufacturing design.

Frank Brangwyn, who influenced Van de Velde, provided a bridge between the simple elegance of the Arts and Crafts Movement and the more dynamic character of Art Nouveau. He worked in William Morris's studio for two years, and then became one of the most prominent of the British designers associated with Siegfried Bing's Paris gallery; Bing, a dealer in Japanese art, made his gallery into the international forum for Art Nouveau for several years from his first Salon in 1895. Brangwyn's unusual poster (plate 71) advertised an exhibition of Art Nouveau organized by Bing for London, which included stained glass designed by Brangwyn and executed by Tiffany.[16] It strikes a sympathetic balance between the stylistic demands of the subject and his sense of social responsibility in the modern world. The subdued decorative linearity in the drawing of the young potter, clearly a modern

70. Alfred Roller. 'Secession. 16 Ausstellung 1903', Austria, 1902.

CIRC 275-1973

working girl, is continued into the scene of chimneys and factory smoke behind, creating a rhythmic merger between arabesques derived from plant forms and the industrial landscape. The carefully hand-held pot positioned in front of the factories is, however, a loaded image, but precisely what it connotes is unclear. It could be an appeal for higher standards in industrial products, or it could represent a contrast between hand-made craft and mass production. Although ambiguous, it points to some of the central debates dominating design in the early part of the twentieth century. The poster itself was part of these debates: while some argued for the 'art poster' which would free artists from the stifling commercial demands of the manufacturers, others used it to promote a closer relationship between artist and industry. Debates about the appropriate relationship between form and function interweave in the first decades of the twentieth century with the development of Modernism in art. The visual simplifications of abstraction heralded new types of formal clarification in the posters of the Russian Constructivists and of the De Stijl group.

The German Werkbund, founded by Hermann Muthesius and others in 1907, had the aim of improving standards of German design and encouraging and facilitating contacts between industry and designers. It established ideas and practices that were to remain influential after the war, in such contexts as the Bauhaus.[17] It established architecture as the model in the field of design, and placed an emphasis on standardization with simplicity, clarity and rationality as primary objectives. Peter Behrens, originally a painter and graphic designer, took on responsibility for all AEG products, and continued to design posters as well as lamps, teapots and sewing machines, after becoming an architect. As he freed himself from the influence of Art Nouveau, he adopted a 'Schinkelesque' classicism; in his poster for the Werkbund Exhibition of 1914 (plate 72), the naked torch-bearing horseman has strong classical overtones. The squaring of the forms seems to have more to do with architectural mass than with any notion of geometrical abstraction. Interesting contrasts can be

71. Frank Brangwyn. 'L'Art Nouveau', UK, 1899. E.450-1965

72. Peter Behrens. 'Deutsche Werkbund-Ausstellung', Germany, 1914. F.279.1982

DEUTSCHE WERKBUND-
AUSSTELLUNG
KUNST IN HANDWERK,
INDUSTRIE UND HANDEL • ARCHITEKTUR
MAI CÖLN 1914 OCT.

A. MOLLING & COMP. K-G. HANNOVER-BERLIN.

73. Adolf Münzer. 'II Kraft-und
Arbeits- Maschinen-Ausstellung,
München 1898', Germany.
E.3314-1932

drawn with an earlier poster by Adolf Münzer (plate 73) for the second Kraft-und Arbeits-Maschinen-Ausstellung in Munich, and with the poster by Leopoldo Metlicovitz for the International Exhibition in Milan marking the opening of the Simplon Tunnel in 1906 (plate 74). Münzer's poster is remarkable in its harmonious formal meld of man and machine in an almost abstract pattern; he uses the strong chiaroscuro of the two thrusting figures not to emphasize naturalistic modelling but to merge with the rhythmic arabesque of the wheel. Münzer, who had been closely associated with Jugendstil, joined the Werkbund in 1912. Metlicovitz's poster is also a surprisingly successful figurative design, foreshadowing the Futurist notion of marriage of man and machine in Marinetti's classical metaphor of the Centaur car/man. It also draws upon mythology, possibly in this case mingling Nordic with classical references. Here the central crouched figure, with a winged helmet, is lit with the red glow from the fire of the engine, and the focus is on the tunnel opening on to the distant vista of Italy, the whole neatly symbolizing the new communications link from North to South.

Muthesius's notion of form was rooted in a rationalist humanism and a timeless stability, and his examples are eclectic: 'Form, that is for us an unique and shining achievement of human art – the Greek temple, the Roman Thermae, the Gothic Cathedral, and the princely salon of the eighteenth century'.[18] One of the founders of Purism, Le Corbusier, attended the Werkbund conference and some of Muthesius's ideas, 'suitably modified', as Reyner Banham says, re-appear in his writings. Purism proposed the selection of manufactured objects based upon pure geometric shapes as subjects for painting.

A different and more generalized notion of simplification of form is evident in the poster for the Second Post-

74. Leopoldo Metlicovitz. 'Simplon
Tunnels Internationale Ausstellung',
Italy, 1906. E.405-1982

Impressionist Exhibition (plate 75) organized by Roger Fry at the Grafton Galleries, London, in 1912; it was 'the result of collaboration among several artists of the English group. It has been drawn by Duncan Grant'.[19] Perhaps the collaboration was responsible for the curiously proto-Art Deco appearance of the poster, with its stepped decorative framing and the strong sweeping lines of the head which may be intended to have a primitive feel. Fry's introduction to the catalogue specifically rejects the Futurist aesthetic. Italian and German artists were excluded, and Clive Bell's essay on 'The English Group', while acknowledging an enormous debt to Cézanne among the English artists, emphasizes 'simplification and plastic design' over any particular style. The muted primitivizing here contrasts with that of Kokoschka's poster (plate 76) for the 1908

Kunstschau in Vienna. Although Kokoschka's lettering is firmly partitioned from the 'cotton-picking girl' in the centre, its deliberately crude, broad and uneven forms are nonetheless echoed in the pictorial design. The simple blockish forms of the figure and the typical three-lobed balls of cotton are in a style recalling the growing interest in children's art and in the expressive possibilities of the woodcut.

The poster designs by David Bomberg and C.R.W. Nevinson offer interesting contrasts in the context of Bell's notion of 'simplification and plastic form'. Bomberg resisted alignment with any avant-garde group, refusing Wyndham Lewis's invitation to have his work reproduced in *Blast* and later the invitation to join De Stijl. Bomberg's pastel design for a poster (plate 77) – which appears not to have been realized – is usually dated c. 1914-18, but bears much more resemblance to paintings and drawings of 1919 and 1920 than to the 'angular form language' of *Mud Bath* (1914) or the mixed Abstract-Realist manner of his war painting *Sappers at Work* (c. 1918-19). Its simple, almost sculptural forms recall rather Gaudier or Epstein, as do two other known sketches for the same composition.[20] Moreover, in 1919 Bomberg did several other commercial commissions, such as the poster for Cameo Corner, London. Unlike his earlier work the figures here are neither flatly geometric nor absorbed into an overall patterning. They form strong blocks which contrast with the black and white areas. Nevinson, like Paul

77. **David Bomberg. 'New Art Salon', UK, c. 1919-20.**

Design for a poster; body-colour and chalk on brown paper.

E.1104-1978

Nash, was an official war artist, but whereas Nash subverted traditional landscape painting to depict the blasted scenery of the Western Front (plate 78), Nevinson used a range of techniques including brilliant adaptations of Futurism. After two exhibitions of War Paintings, his 1919 show at the Leicester Galleries was his 'peace exhibition',[21] and it caused considerable offence, not least for the preface in which he rejected every 'new' or 'advanced' movement; every form of 'ist', 'ism', 'post', 'neo', 'academic' or 'unacademic'.[22] Several of the works exhibited took theatrical or cabaret subjects, like that in the poster (plate 79), that represents a Flanagan and Allen-style pair of male dancers, the spotlights striking out hard angular shadows in a kind of parody of the searchlights Nevinson had depicted in his war paintings. Resistance among the English artists to 'isms' and notions of standardized design is in stark contrast to many of the post-war continental poster designers.

79. **C.R.W. Nevinson. 'Pictures by Nevinson', UK, 1919.** E.3407-1920

ARCHITECTUUR
FRANK LLOYD WRIGHT.
FRANK LLOYD WRIGHT.
FRANK LLOYD WRIGHT.
FRANK LLOYD WRIGHT.
FRANK LLOYD WRIGH.
FRANK LLOYD WRIGH.

TENTOONSTELLING
EERSTE EUROPEESCHE
TENTOONSTELLING
VAN DE WERKEN VAN
FRANK LLOYD WRIGHT
ARCHITECT AMERIKA
IN HET STED: MUSEUM
TE AMSTERDAM VAN
9 MEI TOT 31 MEI 1931

DE TENTOONSTELLINGS
RAAD VOOR BOUWKUNST
EN VERWANTE KUNSTEN

JOH. ENSCHEDÉ EN ZONEN HAARLEM

H. TH. WIJDEVELD AMSTERDAM

80. Hendrikus Wijdeveld. 'Frank Lloyd
Wright Architectur Tentoonstelling',
Netherlands, 1931. E.1436-1991

Although neither of these posters falls into Barr's category of the 'over-crowded and banally realistic style', they are still far from the dynamism and radical abstraction of either the Russian Constructivists or the De Stijl-based design. Hendrikus Wijdeveld's poster for a Frank Lloyd Wright exhibition in Amsterdam in 1931 (plate 80) is an intriguing instance of marriage between typography and abstract form. Although the frontal symmetry is unlike the dynamic balance that Mondrian sought in his compositions of squares, rectangles and lines, the design with the prominent red square is clearly indebted to him.

El Lissitzky, whose ideas fascinated both Moholy-Nagy and van Doesburg, developed his Constructive ideas based upon elementary bodies (cube, cone, sphere) set in 'imaginary space':

> We saw that the surface of the Proun [which Lissitzky described as 'an interchange station between painting and architecture'] ceases to be a picture and turns into a structure round which we must circle .... The result is that the one axis of the picture which stood at right angles to the horizontal was destroyed. Circling round it, we screw ourselves into space ...[23]

Whereas the white space of the horizontal-vertical composition in such examples as Wijdeveld's poster becomes a page, a flat blank space on which the – primarily typographic – message can be inscribed, the destruction of the right-angle axis leads to the construction of indeterminate space, in which objects and letters can float or dynamically interact. Fritz Lang's film poster for *Spione* (plate 82) is a striking example of this; although the pictorial element, the search-lights in the black sky, is controlled by the letters, the spatial drama enacted by the latter is determined by the deep space these beams imply.

In the post-World War II era there has been a marked resistance to standardized design, and, partly as a result of the massive expansion of other forms of media advertising, in film and television, for posters to explore both their own particular pictorial resources and their history. At the same time artists have turned again but in a different spirit from their Dada and Constructivist

81. Richard Hamilton. 'this is tomorrow', UK, 1956. Screen-print. E.176-1994

82. Fritz Lang. 'Spione', Germany,

1928. E.352-1932

predecessors to popular imagery. Richard Hamilton's collage *Just what is it that makes today's homes so different, so appealing?* was made as a contribution to the catalogue for the exhibition *this is tomorrow* at the Whitechapel Gallery in 1956, rather than as a work in its own right. A larger silk-screen printing was used as a poster (plate 81). It was built up of clippings from magazines selected to cover a set of key categories: 'Man Woman Food History Newspapers Cinema Domestic appliances Cars Space Comics TV Telephone Information'.[24] Hamilton's contribution to the exhibition itself was an installation that also used found, ready-made material; like the giant Robbie the robot, '16 feet high and complete with flashing eyes and teeth ... a piece of cinema publicity material borrowed from the front of the London Pavilion in Piccadilly Circus'. These were, Hamilton said, 'produced in a spirit of polemic', and the polemic was against both the formalism of modern art and against a predetermined idea of meaning: 'We reject the notion that 'tomorrow' can be expressed through the presentation of rigid formal concepts .... What is needed is not a definition of meaningful imagery but the development of our perceptive potentialities to accept and utilise the continual enrichment of visual material.'[25] These polemical exhibits and the paintings that were to follow, which emptied, selected and streamlined the imagery of mass commercial culture, were deliberately 'eclectic and catholic'. The attitude was polemical, but the polemics were geared more towards a Modernist art shorn of vital connection with the visual resources of contemporary technology than, for example, towards a critique of the social construction of gender which now seems such a clear component of *Just what is it ...?*

Krzysztof Ducki's 1989 poster *Aurora* (plate 83) is a wittily informal but also nostalgic design. It was made to advertise an exhibition of his own posters, but itself takes on political significance in the context of the unstable conditions in Eastern Bloc countries at the end of the 1980s. Hungary had just abolished the official celebration of the Russian Revolution; *Aurora* was, like *Potemkin*, a battleship associated with the naval rebellion that started the Russian Revolution; it had fired the first shot on the Winter Palace in Leningrad in 1917. The poster therefore could be an expression of nostalgia for the

83. Krzysztof Ducki. 'Aurora', Hungary, 1989. E.157-1991

84. Victor Moscoso.

'Poster Show ... Dallas', USA,

1967. E.724-1970

ideals of the Communist Revolution in its early days, with the sense of the impending end of an era. The rectangles and red squares appropriate to the age of Constructivist design that was so closely bound up with the Revolution are set afloat on crude squiggles of purple paint, like a ship sinking below the waves. Even the lettering resists any consistency, and spreads unevenly across the sheet. This poster is a highly personal response to a political situation.

The psychedelic colours of Victor Moscoso's *Poster Show ... Dallas* (plate 84) absorb rather than bring to the foreground the words. This is a superb example of the 'second look' principle in poster design, in which an arresting image does not at first glance reveal its function. It also looks back to Max Ernst's city/forest paintings of the 1920s, whose structural principles it appears to borrow: that is, an extremely spare abstract design of circle and line which can also be read as cosmic forms. Although this may be a fortuitous connection, it would not be untypical of the sophisticated glancing references to earlier artists and designers. Vjenceslav Richter's poster for the 13th International Biennale of Graphic art at Ljubliana (plate 85), of 1979, is a *tour de force* of monochrome subtleties. The flowing streams of black and white lines recall Art Nouveau plant forms, but as though in sections seen through a microscope. These sweeping lines are occasionally interrupted by a surprisingly sharp angle or fold which enforces ideas of more geometrical patterns or of creases in the human body. The balance between abstraction and figuration plays elegantly with the whole history of poster design. The minimal lettering on the white strip unevenly straddles the drawing, from which it is clearly separated, with the exception of the red '13'. This, like the lettering on a Cubist canvas which hovers between surface and depth, introduces a 'third' surface in the design.

Seymour Chwast, one of the founders in 1954 of the Push Pin Studios, New York, whose work in the field of design has been been among the most creative, is as adept at the use of the visual conceit as in references to demotic imagery: here, the poster for the Brno Biennale (plate 86) is printed in a crude two-colour style reminiscent of childrens' books. The allegorical figure of the United States (Statue of Liberty) riding to the rescue on a motor bike refers to Chwast's opportune last-minute offer to design a poster for Brno (*Issues and Causes* had previously been shown at the AIGA, New York). The conceit rests on the rough elements in the drawing and printing (the uneven black of the bike's tyres for example) which unite a sense of haste with the overall message of urgency. Push Pin's approach was wholly eclectic; while Chwast wanted his own 'graphic personality to be imparted in whatever I do',[26] he did not adopt any one particular style. He believed in the possibility of 'finding a solution from whatever comes to hand, instead of continuously searching for the absolute'.[27]

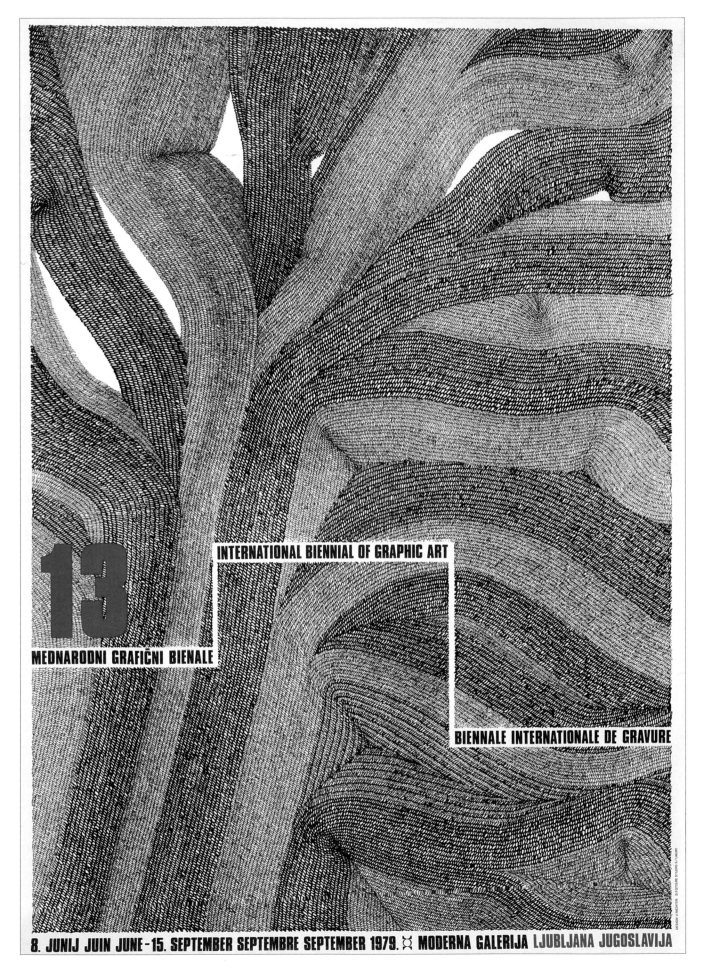

85. Vjenceslav Richter.
'13 International
Biennial of Graphic Art',
Yugoslavia, 1979.

E.481-1981

86. Seymour Chwast. 'Issues and Causes. Brno

Biennale', Czech Republic, 1994. E.189-1997

Exhibition posters have offered here a route across the arena of artists' encounters with poster design and the idea of the 'art poster'. It is no more than a route, because exhibition posters only constitute a 'sub-genre' in strictly functional terms. The selection here represents only a tiny fragment from the V&A's rich holdings, and was intended to explore the widest range of examples; some major areas that belong in this context are missing – most obviously Constructivist designs using photomontage, whose greatest exponent of exhibition posters was probably El Lissitzky.[28] But we have seen how productive and far from one sided the relationship between modern art and the poster has been. It has, for one thing, provided a concentrated model for the interaction of word and image, which has been a recurring interest for the avant-garde. Its

87. Guerrilla Girls. 'Do women have to be naked to get into the Met. Museum?', USA, 1989. E.622-1997

discipline has produced some of the most powerful examples of propaganda art, especially among the Constructivists of Soviet Russia in the 1920s, for whom the style was the polemical underpinning of the message.

The final poster here is salutary for several reasons: as one of the very few examples of work in this publication by women, the campaign to which it belongs is yet again justified, and evidently far from won. In 1985 the Guerrilla Girls – whose operating base was New York and whose identity remains concealed behind the gorilla masks invariably worn in public appearances – began to use public walls and hoardings for posters, stickers and broadsheets attacking sexism and racism in the art world, and targeting museums, galleries and exhibitions. Most of their work presents statistics which effectively reveal the bias that exists in most art institutions against women artists and artists of colour. This poster, *Do women have to be naked to get into the Met. Museum?* of 1989 (plate 87), appeared on rented advertising spaces on buses in Lower Manhattan. It is one of the rare examples of their campaign which seems to proclaim its art context immediately through the image of the Ingres nude. However, it is an ironic contextualization, for art has become a familiar tool to advertise consumer products, and it is through the grotesque montage that this context is denied, just as the museum staple of the female nude is challenged. Moreover, the old issue of 'is it art?' turns out to be still capable of new twists: the Guerrilla Girls were excluded from a show of political posters at the Museum of Modern Art in New York called 'Committed to Print', on the grounds that what they did wasn't art but politics. The curator, according to the Guerrilla Girls, had 'firm criteria: while a poster protesting war could safely be called "art", a poster hanging in a museum protesting museum ethics was clearly "politics"'.[29]

PART II

PROTEST AND PROPAGANDA

3 THE PROPAGANDA POSTER

DAVID CROWLEY

In October 1956 a small crowd gathered in a side street in Budapest to watch a poster being put to the torch (plate 88). One man's gesture, a small part of the courageous uprising of a nation against Soviet rule, would no doubt be forgotten today were it not for the presence of a photo-journalist who captured Stalin's smiling face and benign gesture as the heat from the flames unfurled the poster like a flag and melted the Soviet leader's tunic. The rapt attention of the onlookers testified to the gravity of the moment. This was more than the burning of a sheet of paper coated in ink: it was a public exorcism by fire of a figure who had imposed an illegitimate and loathed political system on Hungary. In fact, the poster – a reproduction of Alexander Gerasimov's 1939 painting *Stalin at the 18th Congress of the Communist Party of the Soviet Union* – was more than just an image; it was understood by Hungarians as an image of injustice. The emotional drama of this iconoclastic act is hard to imagine today: only three years earlier ordinary Hungarian citizens had wept in public at news of Stalin's death, such was the potency of the cult of personality promoted by the Communist Party's ideologues. This brief episode illustrates the power of the poster, as a symbol of authority, sometimes to generate loyalty and, at other times, to provoke hatred.

Just over 30 years later in 1989, the citizens of Hungary and the other states in the Eastern Bloc took to the streets again to do away with an unwanted political system. To rally the enormous crowds that gathered in Heroes Square in Budapest, in Palace Square in Bucharest, in Wenceslas Square in Prague and the other rallying points of the 'year of revolutions', a propaganda poster of a different kind was produced. István Orosz's poster *Comrades It's Over!* (plate 89) – a call for the occupying Red Army to withdraw from Hungary – was made at a moment when the future seemed

88. Burning a poster of Alexander Gerasimov's 1939 painting of *Stalin at the 18th Congress of the Communist Party of the Soviet Union* during the Hungarian uprising in 1956. Illustrated in Reg Gadney, *Cry Hungary*, (Weidenfeld and Nicolson, 1986).

89. István Orosz. 'Tovarishi, Koniets!' ('Comrades, It's Over!'), Hungary, 1990. E.2034-1990

This poster is a later version of a design originally produced during the final phase of Communism in Hungary. Although it was a potent declaration of opposition to the presence of Soviet troops in Eastern Europe, Russian soldiers queued to buy a copy of it as a souvenir when the Red Army left Hungary in June 1991.

far from clear and carried personal risk. The claustrophobic presence of this soldier was more than just an aesthetic effect. On other posters, whether lithographically reproduced or daubed by hand on paper no better than that used to print newspapers, urgent images were pasted on to city walls to spur on the rolling force of revolution. The gulf between the two political traditions, represented by the image of Stalin and Orosz's poster, could not be wider: the former tradition generated celebratory, emollient images, designed by official artists and produced by state printers; the latter produced agitational images sometimes designed by the untrained and printed by any means possible. These two traditions lie at either end of a spectrum which encompasses the history of the propaganda poster in the twentieth century.

MODERN PROPAGANDA AND MASS POLITICS

However, the history of the propaganda poster has deep roots. The tradition of the impertinent political cartoon propped in a bookseller's window or the typographic call to arms posted in town and village on the eve of war are often described as antecedents of the modern propaganda poster. One early image in the V&A's collection is a graphic commemoration of the murdered hero of the French Revolution, the left-wing journalist Jean-Paul Marat (plate 90). The phrase 'L'Ami du Peuple' was both the title of the anti-royalist newspaper which Marat published and, in effect, an epitaph awarded by his fellow leaders of the Revolution. Marat was made into a martyr after his death at the hand of Charlotte Corday in July 1793. The National Convention requested that a number of engravings be made of his image in death for circulation throughout France to record

90. Anonymous. 'Marat. L'Ami du Peuple', France, c. 1793. Etching coloured by hand. E.657-1993

his noble sacrifice. His reputation as a uncompromising *révolutionnaire*, who was responsible for the execution of hundreds during the Prison Massacres of 1792, was replaced by Marat the martyr: plays, poems and hymns were written in his memory and 37 towns in France adopted his name. Marat was reinvented as a kind of secular saint: children were taught in school to make the sign of the cross at his name. In the same way, in this poster, Marat is crowned with a halo of stars. The relatively large size of this hand-coloured etching suggests that this image was produced for public display rather than as a private *memento mori*.

But the propaganda poster as we recognize it today was the product of modern life. Modernity itself was the result of a number of new conditions (of which the French Revolution released an idealistic new conception, that of the 'Third Estate' i.e. 'the people', for the benefit of whom politics were to be conducted).[1] Important determinants included the refinement of chromo-lithographic printing in the 1840s, which allowed colourful posters combining vivid images and exhortatory texts, to be printed in thousands of copies.[2] The potential of the lithographic poster also relied on the increasing concentration of people in urban environments – viewers who could consume the same images and, it was envisaged, might come to hold the same views. In 1888 *Punch*, for example, speculated on the 'effect' of the 'Pandemonium of Posters' found on the walls of 'Horrible London' on the 'legions of dull-witted toilers' (i.e. the working classes).[3]

Above all, the modern propaganda poster was the product of changing political conditions in much of Europe and the United States of America. For centuries, political élites had needed to pay little heed to the opinion of the common man and woman. However, in the last decades of the nineteenth century the transformation of the political constitution of many nations into civic states produced new relations between rulers and the ruled. Extending the suffrage for most males in many states, including the United Kingdom in 1867 and 1884, the USA in 1867 and France in 1875, for example, meant that authority had increasingly to take into account the views of the people and, when it could, shape those opinions to its own requirements to secure loyalty and even obedience. Eric Hobsbawm has identified a connection between the emergence of mass politics and a contemporaneous, self-conscious investigation of the power of irrational and emotive appeals to maintain the social order, a key feature, as we shall see, in the rhetoric of propaganda.[4] In this changing political environment new forces emerged: the 1880s and the 1890s saw, for example, Socialism mature from peripheral political activism conducted by small groups of intellectuals and aired in prolix pamphlets and on the stages of lecture halls, to a popular force which began to capture the imagination of working men and women.

The political iconography of many political parties and the graphic skirmishes which accompanied election campaigns at this time are still with us today. Gerald Spencer Pryse's poster *Workless* (plate 91), commissioned by the Labour Party in 1910, is an early example of a potent and familiar theme in political rhetoric, that of unemployment. Published at the time of a general election, Pryse's social realist image represented the dreadful ennui and impotence of unemployment by depicting the 'workless' as somnambulists slipping into forgotten shadows. In 1978 the Conservative Party returned to this theme in its 'Labour Isn't Working' campaign which included depictions of a long queue snaking outside a job centre; it came out on billboard posters and in a short cinema advert. Reissued in 1979 as *Labour Still Isn't Working* (plate 92) this memorable and latterly notorious image invoked a common fear of modern life, the threat of unemployment, and has often been claimed as a factor in the fall of the Prime Minister Callaghan's Labour administration of the day.

The emergence of mass politics not only explains the flood of political propaganda printed in the last decades of the nineteenth century, but also the forms that many of these posters took. This point can be illustrated by the series of sixteen posters published by Lenepveu in Paris in the aftermath of the Dreyfus Affair which erupted in France in the 1890s. Alfred Dreyfus was a Jewish captain in the French army who was falsely accused of spying for Germany in 1894. Although no substantial evidence was brought against him (and that which did appear was shown to be forged),

91. Gerald Spencer Pryse. 'Workless', UK, 1910. Published by the Labour Party. E.3141-1913

This is one part of a three-panel poster. The titles of the other two images are 'Landless' and 'Forward! The Day Is Breaking'. Pryse's poster was reissued in 1929 as the threat of mass unemployment revived.

92. Saatchi and Saatchi Advertising (Andrew Rutherford and Martin Walsh; photographed by Bob Cramp). 'Labour Still Isn't Working', UK, 1979. Published by the Conservative Party. E.141-1986

"WORKLESS"

PUBLISHED BY THE LABOUR PARTY, 28 VICTORIA STREET, LONDON. S.W. & PRINTED BY DAVID ALLEN & SONS Lᴅ. HARROW. ETC.

a coalition of aristocratic, nationalist officers kept Dreyfus imprisoned in the notorious penal colony, Devil's Island. The venom poured on Dreyfus was motivated by anti-semitism in influential quarters of French society and fuelled by waves of xenophobic hysteria. The Dreyfus Affair was a prism which threw tensions in French society into sharp perspective. Voices in support of Dreyfus were few: a tidal wave of anti-semitism swept the country calling for boycotts on Jewish shops and raising petitions to expel the Jews from France.

This series of posters must be seen as part of this intense, 'popular' strain of nationalism. In one (plate 93), Dreyfus is caricatured as a Hydra, a monster with many heads, which when cut off are succeeded by others, run through with a sword bearing the accusation 'le Traître!' (No other caption was required, such was the familiarity of Dreyfus's face in the French press.) The symbolism of a serpent thwarted by the cruciform sword, a chivalric weapon associated with myths of saints and dragons, was an easily understood metaphor for 'Christian good' slaying 'Jewish evil'.[5] And the capacity of the Hydra to restore itself when under attack suggested a kind of Jewish conspiracy in which another 'traitor' would take Dreyfus's place when called. Such images were hard to misunderstand, and the use of such common symbols and popular imagery, often reworked in a limited but widely understood repertoire, has been a notable feature of graphic propaganda. The representation of one's enemy as a serpent has appeared with regularity throughout the twentieth century. Moreover, in circumstances contorted by common fears and popular prejudices, producers of graphic propaganda have tended not to overestimate the intellectual capacity of their audiences. In fact, one might claim that the singular intelligibility of the propaganda poster has been one of its distinctive features. The layers of meaning which make the study of a work of fine art so rich and rewarding are not normally a feature of effective propaganda.

93. V. Le Nepveu. 'Musée des Horreurs. le Traître!', France, c. 1899-1900. E.835-1985

This caricature of Alfred Dreyfus was produced as the sixth image in a series of posters entitled 'Musée des Horreurs'.

Not all nationalisms in the late nineteenth and early twentieth centuries were fuelled by the kind of mean xenophobia driving the Dreyfus Affair. A growing awareness of the power of popular political will underpinned campaigns of independence mounted by nations living under imperial rule. Nationalists representing 'small peoples' such as the Poles, the Irish or the Finns sought to strengthen conviction in national claims on sovereignty. The poster became an influential medium to press these claims and to consolidate a lexicon of national symbols and historical figures. Irish nationalists, for example, sensing a relaxation of British interest in Ireland, distributed depictions – both as posters and prints for the home – of 'Ireland's Latest Martyrs' (i.e. Fenians prosecuted by the British), and images of desolate Erin accompanied a stringless harp before a sunrise to presage the future ascension of a free Ireland. British voices of authority, as well as Unionists in Ireland, responded with counter-propaganda. For example, in 1910, a year of two general elections, the National Union of Conservative Associations satirized nationalist desire for Home Rule in Ireland. G.R. Halkett depicted John Redmond, the leader of the Irish Nationalist Party, carrying a green banner for Irish independence and leading politicians Asquith, Lloyd George and Churchill by the nose 'to disruption' (plate 94). The results of the first election in January left the Liberals and Conservatives with almost equal representation in the House of Commons with the Irish Parliamentary Party holding the balance of power, and brought the Home Rule question to the forefront of political debate. *Their Irish Master* suggested that the 'proper' relations of powerful Britain over subaltern Ireland were reversed by Redmond's wily political opportunism.

94. G.R. Halkett. 'Their Irish Master',
UK, 1910. Published by the National
Union of Conservative and
Constitutional Associations. E.185-1968

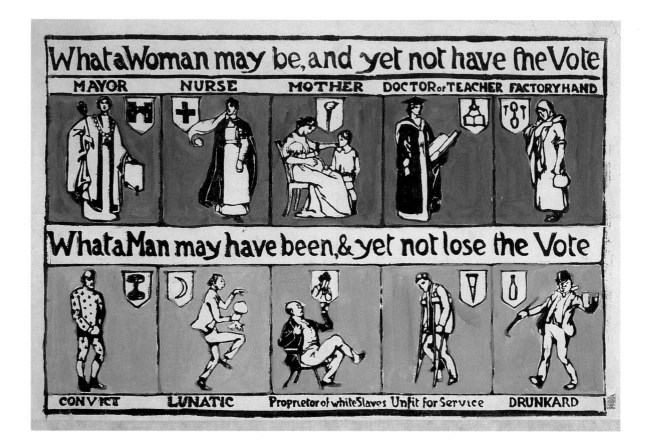

95. Suffrage Atelier. 'What a Woman may be, and yet not have the Vote', UK, 1913. Woodcut, coloured by hand. E.646-1972

In nineteenth-century Britain, as elsewhere, attempts to shape public opinion tended to be framed by the limited form of democracy which had been adopted. Moreover, in most countries women were excluded from the franchise. This was part of the wholesale removal of women from many aspects of public life. The ideology of the 'separate spheres', which confined middle-class women to domestic responsibilities as keepers of the home and as mothers, was vigorously contested by the Suffragette movement which swelled from the 1860s and climaxed in the years of militancy before World War I. The prevailing, conservative and idealized image of femininity enjoyed endless reproduction and, as Lisa Tickner has shown, permeated the legal, social and political organization of British society.[6] Consequently, Edwardian Suffragettes produced counter-representations to contest these repressive images of femininity. George Bernard Shaw reflected on the domestic containment of Edwardian women in *The Quintessence of Ibsenism*, writing 'if we have come to think that the nursery and the kitchen are the natural sphere of a woman, we have done so exactly as English children have come to think that a cage is a natural sphere of a parrot: because they have never seen one anywhere else'.[7] Shaw was prompted to write these words after seeing a poster produced by the Suffrage Atelier (plate 95), a society formed in 1909 to 'encourage artists to forward the Woman's Movement, and particularly the enfranchisement of women, by means of pictorial publications'. *What a Woman may be, and yet not have the Vote* was printed as a block print in 1913 by members of the Atelier; this relatively unsophisticated technique was a consequence, in part, of limited funds. But it also allowed 'fresh cartoons [to be] got out at very short notice'. The poster not only pressed the case for female suffrage but also reflected the view held by many early twentieth-century feminists that the moral and ethical standards of British society needed improvement. Just as women were expected to live by a clear moral code so, it was argued, should men. The Atelier's poster includes amongst its gallery of rogues, a 'proprietor of white slaves', i.e. a man who coerced women into prostitution, and a drunk – men who had abrogated their social responsibility, yet were still fit to vote.

WORLD WAR I

Before 1914 the resources invested in the propaganda poster had been relatively slight. Those often modest political lobbies like the Suffrage Atelier produced graphic propaganda which matched the scale of their organizations. World War I, however, saw the resources of states being invested in poster production on a scale which was hitherto unknown. This conflict is often claimed as the first truly modern war because of the industrialized methods and chemical weapons used in battle, as well as the ways in which the war broached the confines of the battlefield. Moreover, it was fought in a changed world where popular support for the war was, more than in any other previous conflict, a necessary condition for success. Populations were sometimes coerced and, at other times, compelled to enlist as soldiers; cajoled to lend money to the state in the form of war bonds; and persuaded to work harder in their domestic occupations or in munitions factories. In an age before television and radio broadcasts and when the cinema was still in its infancy, the lithographic poster was a mature and established form of graphic communication supported by a range of professions – specialist printers, designers and advertising agents responsible for securing space on hoardings.

Britain did not introduce conscription until January 1916 when the authorities were encountering difficulties attracting volunteers. With a far smaller standing army than those of her enemies, the War Office established the Parliamentary Recruiting Committee (PRC) in August 1914. One of the ways in which the PRC sought to encourage recruitment was through posters issued by its Publications Sub-Department. In 1920 M. Hardie and A.K. Sabin, in their review of the posters produced by all sides, estimated that the PRC had commissioned 100 designs published in editions of up to 40,000 copies before conscription was introduced.[8] Many of the British posters found in the V&A's collection were designed in printers' 'art departments', i.e. by untrained designers whose careers had been spent producing the sentimental and painterly images used in commercial advertising. It comes as no surprise therefore that many wartime posters resembled such advertising in format and syrupy imagery. Typically these designs were 'volunteered' by eager printers who submitted their designs to the PRC for official approval. Although the earliest posters were typographical appeals usually invoking 'King and Country', the most famous posters published by the PRC involved more sophisticated appeals to instinct, combining image with text. Savile Lumley's poster, captioned with the notorious question 'Daddy, what did YOU do in the Great War?', is one of the best known and most reproduced British recruiting posters (plate 96). It was conceived by a printer, Arthur Gunn, who is reported to have imagined himself as the father in question. In fact, after having a sketch of this scene made up by Lumley in 1915, Gunn joined the Westminster Volunteers. It typifies what, in many ways, became one of the most controversial and denounced forms of hortatory poster after the war, that of an emotional or moral reproach. It shows, in a rather conventional style, a moment after the war when the daughter, studying a history of the conflict, asks the question which captions the image. The father, in the clichéd pose of the pensive man, stares steadily out at the viewer. In this exchange of gazes, the male viewer is encouraged to imagine himself as the subject of the poster at a time when the social pressure to volunteer was remarkably strong. The young boy playing with toy soldiers reinforces the message: he seems to be about to place a soldier on the floor to join his comrades in arms. The primary audience for this poster is clearly intended to be those men who have yet to enlist, but a second audience is also addressed, i.e. families, whose responsibility, as defined by this appeal, was to act as a persuader, or an agent for the state.

The explicit message of Lumley's poster is, as propaganda, hard to misunderstand. Yet the way in which this image constructs and mobilizes meaning is not solely the product of the efforts of PRC propagandists. It relies on a combination of graphic codes and particular ideologies current in Edwardian and wartime Britain outside the direct control of Lumley and the PRC. The poster, for example, represents recruitment through an image of the domestic realm. Ideologies of masculinity and femininity had in the Victorian period effectively gendered the home as a feminine space.[9] The concept of the 'separate spheres', whilst under threat from the women's Suffrage movement and changes in employment and legislation over property rights, underwent a rehabilitation in wartime Britain. Some suffragettes, for example, agreed to suspend their

Daddy, what did YOU do in the Great War?

96. Savile Lumley. 'Daddy, what did <u>YOU</u> do in the Great War?', UK, 1915. Issued by the Parliamentary Recruiting Committee. CIRC 466-1969

97. Howard Chandler Christy. 'Gee! I wish I were a man. I'd join the Navy', USA, 1917. Colour half-tone letterpress. E.118-1918

campaign for the vote 'for the duration'. Consequently, to encourage the male viewer of this poster graphically to identify himself with the father inside the home was to issue a challenge to his masculinity, a challenge that would only be met if he traversed into the public 'setting' of the forces. Any male viewer who had not volunteered was uncomfortably feminized by such images (see also plate 97).

The effectiveness of this poster was predicated on its 'matter-of-factness'. Posters that effortlessly confirmed, for example, popular conceptions of masculinity and prejudices about the enemy, or virtuously affirmed the British 'way of life', were likely to be most successful with the public. War came to seem just and 'natural'. In the instance of Lumley's design, the decision to volunteer is represented as a decision to ensure the future of one's children, although the nature of the threat that they faced was not made clear. In this sense, some propaganda, particularly that produced by hegemonic institutions such as the state, can be seen to function as an untroubling confirmation of the 'way things are'. Moreover, such images rely 'parasitically' on other representations – both literary and visual – in order to achieve this 'naturalization'. Most World War I posters drew upon and extended a reservoir of themes which had an increased valency in the charged atmosphere of war reporting. Knowledge drawn from other images or texts gave the viewer of these posters 'information' with which he or she could confirm the meaning of these usually drawn, historically unspecific, visual tropes.

This point is illustrated by the American poster, *Hun or Home?* designed by Henry Raleigh (plate 98). It depicts the hulking figure of a German soldier, identified by his spiked helmet, emerging from the shadows towards a young woman clasping a baby in her arms. This image was printed after April 1917 when the USA declared war on Germany, and was designed to secure support for her war effort in the form of Liberty Bonds. Like many British images, Raleigh's poster drew upon a vein of notorious 'atrocity propaganda'. American citizens had been a considerable audience for such material as the British mounted a campaign to draw in America as a military ally. The press, for example, was encouraged to report in lurid detail 'war crimes' committed by German troops in occupied territory. Ghastly stories appeared (apparently confirmed by material published by Wellington House, the Secret War Propaganda Bureau) which offered accounts of rape and child murder, and tales of the mutilation and the abuse of British corpses in 'cadaver factories'.[10] After the war the majority of these tales proved to be fictitious or highly distorted. Raleigh's poster depicts one such event. In graphic form, it employs a much-mythologized stereotype which had particular wartime currency. As Steve Baker has shown, this stereotype of the 'Hun' was a

**98. Henry Raleigh. 'HUN or HOME?',
USA, c. 1917. E.156-1919**

particular construction of 'Germanness' which drew upon the latent currency of misunderstood Darwinian thinking ('survival of the fittest' and 'that man descends from animals like apes') and the 'principles' of physiognomy.[11] In particular, certain graphic codes were almost invariably used to signify 'innate' German traits: weak-jawed, corpulent, pig-eyed characters prevailed. On occasion, as Raleigh's poster suggests, the caricature of the 'Hun' was exaggerated into an ape-like character to suggest the regression of the German 'race' along the evolutionary path. Such caricatural representations of the German officer served to reinforce public perceptions of the inhumanity of their foe.

After 1918 some commentators were highly critical of British and American wartime posters of the kinds described above. In their 1920 survey, Hardie and Sabin made a somewhat odd, though not unusual, assessment of the British designs. Schooled in the aesthetic 'standards' of poster-artists such as Henri de Toulouse-Lautrec and The Beggarstaffs, these high-minded critics found them 'vulgar' and 'insipid' when compared to those produced by continental designers, including the Germans and Austrians who displayed a keen understanding of 'modern' principles of design such as the poster announcing the 'Eighth War Loan' by Julius Klinger (plate 99). Another image of good triumphing over evil symbolized as a serpent, Klinger's poster achieved dramatic graphic impact by reducing the design to simple elements. The number '8', for example, functions as both a textual and a graphic device. In contrast, British design appeared as conservative and emotionally charged as pre-war advertising. But propaganda, as many of its critics and advocates in the inter-war period were keen to emphasize, required assessment not by aesthetic standards but by effects. Much of the literature on the British posters of World War I claims that they scored a great victory in, for

99. Julius Klinger. '8 Kriegsanleihe' ('8th War Loan'), Austria, c. 1914-18. E.2602-1920

example, securing the recruitment of 24 per cent of available men in the first 18 months of the conflict. Yet many factors, such as poverty and the relatively good pay offered by the army, may have been instrumental in encouraging recruitment.[12] Consequently, it would be difficult to retrieve the meanings attached to these posters by contemporaries on the basis of the images alone. In fact, diaries and letters occasionally throw up evidence to suggest that some viewed with disdain the mawkish sentiment of these posters and their attempts to provoke feelings of guilt. Lady Cynthia Asquith, writing as the first clouds of poison gas spilled across the battlefield at Ypres, for example, recorded on 8 May 1915 in her diary:

> London, I think, looks distinctly more abnormal now – more soldiers, more bandages and limps
>
> and more nurses – quite a sensational sense of strain. Raw recruits led by band still make one
>
> cry and everywhere the rather undignified, bullying posters – very, very dark at night.[13]

Nevertheless, such expressions of dissent remained largely in the private realm. It was only in the post-war period that public debate about the effects of the propaganda of World War I took place.

AFTER THE TRENCHES

It would be no exaggeration to say that World War I was the critical moment in the history of the propaganda poster. In the British context, where poster artists had been unstinting in the bellicose approaches that they used to promote the allied cause, the poster was seen as an important factor in victory. Even Hitler in *Mein Kampf* (1926) described British propaganda as being as 'ruthless as it was brilliant', and he acknowledged that many of the characteristic strategies of Nazi propaganda, such as the use of emotional blackmail, originated in British practices. However, in Britain many commentators felt aggrieved at the gulf between the image of war in propaganda and their own experiences, as proof emerged to show that 'Hun atrocities' had been grossly exaggerated. In the mood of post-war recrimination and reflection, the British poster also came under attack. George Orwell, writing about the ways in which covert pacifism amongst schoolboys during World War I developed into a contempt for militarism in adulthood in the 1920s, famously recalled:

> 1914-1918 was written off as meaningless slaughter, and even the men who had been
>
> slaughtered were held in some way to blame. I have often laughed to think of that recruiting
>
> poster, 'What did you do in the Great War, Daddy?' ... and of all the men who must have been
>
> lured into the army by just that poster and afterwards despised by their children for not being
>
> Conscientious Objectors.[14]

All critics, whether pragmatic apologists recognizing the state's need to influence public opinion or strident critics of 'pernicious' strategies of deception, shared the view, however, that the propaganda of World War I had been successful.

One major effect of the inquisition into the conduct of the campaigns to influence public opinion was that most post-war British governments were reluctant to be seen to engage in propaganda, coming to view it as 'un-English' and only made necessary in circumstances of war. One commentator argued that it broke with British '*laissez-faire* tradition'.[15] And in 1932 a civil servant working for the Foreign Office admitted that in his job as a publicist he avoided using the word 'propaganda', because it was in 'particularly bad odour for some time after the war'.[16] British governments did, however, engage in the production of 'publicity', and some voices associated with the state argued strongly for its continued usage in peacetime. Using the anodyne and carefully inoffensive euphemism, 'national projection', Stephen Tallents, a civil servant and the author of *The Projection of England* (1932), suggested that the national characteristics of 'reticence and modesty' would act as guarantors of dignity in the production of official propaganda. He proposed that agencies working on behalf of the nation should produce material to promote trade within and outside the Empire; to encourage tourism; and to sustain national prestige overseas. This kind of propaganda proposed by Tallents was intended to be an affirmation of English 'virtues'.

Various state-sponsored propaganda programmes of the period reflected Tallents' concerns with 'dignified national projection' (plate 100). The Empire Marketing Board (EMB, 1926-33), for example, was a major patron of graphic designers and film-makers through its schemes to promote the products of Empire, largely foodstuffs, in the United Kingdom.[17] But the design and content of the posters were self-consciously 'superior' to those of advertisements. The EMB commissioned 'by invitation' many well-known artists including Edward McKnight Kauffer and Gerald Spencer Pryse. Often the terms of the 'brief' were firmly pre-determined by the EMB and artists would be asked to re-submit work that failed to display sufficient technical accuracy or lapsed into fantasy. The tone of the captions used to accompany these painterly images was characteristically sober and restrained, unlike the hyperbole of modern advertising. In fact many of the posters were printed on stiff card and distributed to schools or reproduced in educational textbooks. The aim of these designs was to make the public aware of the products of Empire, whether South African fruit, dairy produce from Australia or Rhodesian tobacco, but in a more general sense these posters were effective propaganda for imperialism *per se*. The temperate and informative tone of EMB posters was a careful strategy to avoid the accusations of deception and

MOTOR MANUFACTURING

mendacity which the propaganda of the Great War had attracted. Nevertheless, there was still public concern about propaganda. In particular, perceptions about the science of psychology, the force of advertising and the uses of propaganda by the totalitarian states in Europe accentuated the sense of fear attached to this concept.

In Europe, the Right and the Left – whether governments in Germany and the Soviet Union, or those contesting the Spanish Civil War (plate 101) – made significant and systematic investments in propaganda in the inter-war years. One can detect a strong stress on the importance of propaganda in the early writings of the architects of the Communist and Fascist systems: Hitler in *Mein Kampf* (1926); and Lenin in *What Is To Be Done?* (1902). From its earliest

100. Clive Gardiner. 'Motor Manufacturing', UK, 1928. Issued by the Empire Marketing Board.

E.443-1932

Gardiner's design was one of a six-part poster entitled 'Empire Buying Makes Busy Factories'.

101. Amado Oliver. 'La Garra Del Invasor Italiano Pretende Esclavizarnos' ('The claw of the Italian invader grasps to enslave us'). Issued by the Council for the Defence of Madrid, Spain, 1937. E.1182-1937

Oliver was associated with the Union General de Trajabadores, a Socialist trades union. His poster was published to rally opposition to 50,000 troops who had arrived from Italy in March 1937 to support Franco's aim of capturing Madrid.

days, Soviet Russia initiated programmes of propaganda which were designed to elicit support for the Revolution in a massive country populated by a largely illiterate, peasant people. For example, Glavpolitprosvet (Chief Committee for Political Education) was established in November 1920, and it exercised influence through the system of Party offices spread across the country. The main challenge facing this body was the elimination of illiteracy amongst the peasantry. However, this pedagogic task cannot be divorced from its propagandistic function. In 'reading huts', peasants were taught to read with political posters. Whilst the new regime held the modern technical inventions of the twentieth century in high esteem – Lenin had, after all, famously proclaimed that 'Communism is Soviet power plus the electrification of the whole country' – the backward condition of the post-war USSR demanded pragmatism. Resourceful strategies were developed by artists and designers associated with the avant-garde to promote the Bolshevik cause. Good examples of these were the 'Rosta windows' issued from October 1919 by the Russian Telegraph Agency (plate 102). These striking wall newspapers comprising four to twelve sequential images on a single sheet were reproduced from stencils. Their lucid forms and bold colours reflected not only the limitations of the technique but also the taste of their avant-garde designers, schooled in Futurism and Expressionism and enthusiasts for the traditional Russian *lubok* (vernacular woodcut). Rosta windows, based on a familiar range of stereotypes, were easy to understand, even by an illiterate peasant who had never encountered the Russian aristocrats, bourgeois industrialists and French generals that they featured.

The poster was a means by which artists could commit themselves to the Revolution. Figures associated with the Constructivist avant-garde, such as Alexander Rodchenko and El Lissitzky, became increasingly involved in the production of photographic propaganda as the optimism and utopianism that had shaped their abstract, quasi-architectural compositions of the early 1920s dissipated. The photograph was favoured because its mechanical character suggested modernity, and its reproducibility suggested democracy. In particular, the practice of photomontage was claimed by Rodchenko as a way of fixing the inherently open and fluid meaning of the single photograph.[18] Despite this step towards popular comprehension, the hardening of political and aesthetic culture that occurred under Stalin unleashed serious criticism of the avant-garde. Gustav Klutsis's photomontage poster, *Under the Banner of Lenin for Socialist Construction*, published by the State Publishing House in 1930 (plate 103), is an interesting work produced before the Stalinist aesthetics froze. An ally of the avant-garde as a member of the October Group, Klutsis too was damned as a formalist, yet his celebration of the industrialization that had occurred under the first Five Year Plan contained themes inextricably associated with Stalinist aesthetics. Despite, for

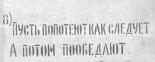

102. Mikhail Cheremnykh. 'In the Luxury Wagon ...'. 12-panel ROSTA window issued by Glavpolitprosvet, Soviet Russia, 1921. Colour stencil. E.1241-1933

This series depicts the progress of a delegation, instituted by the allied powers and led by Joseph Noulens, investigating famine in Russia. The texts, probably by the poet Vladimir Mayakovsky, read:

1. In the luxury carriage, in the salon wagon, three Frenchmen travel and talk amongst themselves.

2. Noulens says, shaking with laughter, 'What fun we'll have.

3. When we reach the famine areas we'll issue a manifesto.

4. If you want to eat to your heart's content, then down with Soviet power.

5. Here is your Tsar and your Tsarina, and here is rye and wheat.'

6. Says Gireau[?], winking slyly,

7. 'That's nothing — we'll get them up against the wall first.

8. Let them sweat a bit, as they should, and then they can eat.'

9. Says General Bravy[?], 'We know you will feed the whole crowd,

10. we'll reduce their numbers a bit, and leave the quiet ones.

11. Anyone who looks like a trouble maker — we'll give them trouble.'

12. Friends, go away at once. Russia is not your homeland.

example, Lenin's widely recorded distrust of his future successor, Klutsis suggested that Lenin and Stalin shared the same vision (in the most literal sense by sharing the same eye). In fact, Lenin had warned against mythologizing his leadership after his own death (in January 1924). Nevertheless, this image reinforces the dual cult of personality (of Lenin's and of Stalin's) prevalent in Stalin's Russia.

The Soviet investment in propaganda was matched by that of Nazi Germany. In fact, during its formative years – mythologized as the *Kampfzeit* ('years of struggle') before 1933 – the NSDAP (Nationalsozialistische Deutsche Arbeiterpartei/Nazi Party) borrowed many political symbols from their political opponents on the Left. In the Saxon elections of October 1926, for example, a Nazi poster represented a muscular proletarian, bathed in red light and stripped to the waist, destroying a parliamentary building captioned 'international high-finance' (plate 105). This poster was designed to illustrate the Nazi promise to deliver dramatic solutions to pressing social problems, which the democratic system had been unable to solve. Anti-parliamentarianism was a distinctive feature of both Left- and Right-wing activism and, in fact, the figure of the proletarian towering over a parliamentary chamber was a typical theme of Kommunistische Partei

103. Gustav Klutsis. 'Under the Banner of Lenin for Socialist Construction'. Published by the State Publishing House, USSR, 1930. E.404-1988

Deutschlands (German Communist Party) posters. The treatment of this figure, of the subject as well as the colour scheme, was almost indistinguishable from the political imagery employed by Communist designers in Germany. Only the swastikas on the iconoclast's belt-buckle and his tool (and perhaps the black letter instruction to vote National Socialist) identify the Nazi Party as the poster's subject. However, after securing power in 1933, Nazi propaganda became increasingly and powerfully concentrated within a limited repertoire of themes: the image of the Führer as a singular genius; the racial stereotype of the Aryan and the mythical German community of the *volk*; and the threat posed by the 'Jewish-Bolshevik conspiracy'.

Propaganda became a major feature of state activity after March 1933 when Joseph Goebbels formed the Reichsministerium für Volksaufklärung und Propaganda (Ministry for People's Enlightenment and Propaganda).[19] Its chief agency, the Reichskulturkammer (National Chamber of Culture), established in September 1933, extended total state control over the public media, nationalizing radio broadcasting and the press and making unequivocal use of the poster and the cinema. A number of highly skilled and renowned designers quickly offered their skills to the Nazi cause. Ludwig Hohlwein, for example, had been a leading poster designer in Wilhelmine and Weimar Germany. His sophisticated if inflated treatment of the body in *Give, in*

104. Gustav Klutsis. 'Politbureau ZKVKP(B)' (Central Committee of the All Russian Communist Party [Bolshevik]), USSR, 1935. E.1267-1989

Klutsis's design uses graphic scale to indicate political significance, hence Stalin's prominence. One figure has been inked out by hand, illustrating the rapid turn of political events in the 1930s when once prominent Bolsheviks fell from grace.

А. И. Микоян   М. И. Калинин   В. М. Молотов   Л. М. Каганович   К. Е. Ворошилов   Г. К. Орджоникидзе
С. В. Косиор   В. Я. Чубарь   А. А. Андреев   И. В. СТАЛИН   Кандидаты ▬▬▬ П. Постышев Г. И. Петровский А. А. Жданов Р. И. Эйхе
Секретарь ЦК ВКП(Б) И. И. Ежов

ПОЛИТБЮРО ЦК ВКП(Б)

the Struggle against Hunger and Cold of 1933 (plate 106), contrasts with that represented in the Saxon election poster of seven years earlier. Hohlwein's, sharing many of the same elements, including the reliance on black, white and red as well as the male figure, was produced to procure charitable aid during the regime's first winter (when Germany was in the pit of economic depression). Nevertheless, the Nazi body is now Aryan, a mythical, racial 'ideal'. This German's musculature is not a sign of labour but of breeding. Even in a poster calling for charity one can detect a reference to the Nazi's spurious and vicious claim of German racial supremacy.

105. Anonymous. 'Wählt nationalsozialistisch!', Germany, 1926. E.1365-1931

106. Ludwig Hohlwein. 'Opfert zum Kampf Gegen Hunger und Kälte. Winterhilfswerk Des Deutschen Volkes 1933-34' ('Give, in the Struggle against Hunger and Cold. Winter relief work of the German nation 1933-34'), Germany, 1933. E.386-1934

PROPAGANDA ON THE HOME FRONT

In 1939, at the outbreak of World War II, the Ministry of Information (MOI) was re-established in the United Kingdom to inform and, to some degree, shape public opinion at home. The MOI utilized modern media, including radio broadcasts and cinema newsreels, as well as established print formats, including posters. Through its Campaigns and Exhibitions Divisions, the MOI managed the production of graphic propaganda. It employed over 60 designers, typographers, cartoonists and printers. In this war, however, there was no great drive to recruit men, as conscription had been introduced in anticipation of the war in April 1939. Nevertheless the MOI was responsible for campaigns to secure the recruitment of other sections of society such as women into industry, as well as to encourage thrift, self-sufficiency and public safety.

During the so-called 'phoney war' of 1939-40 the MOI was criticized as a scaremonger. One early poster provoked controversy: a widely displayed typographic design, in which the words '*YOUR* COURAGE, '*YOUR* CHEERFULNESS, '*YOUR* RESOLUTION WILL BRING US VICTORY' were capped with a crown, prompted a writer in *The Times* to remark:

> the insipid and patronising invocations to which the passer-by is now being treated have a power of exasperation which is all of their own. There may be no intrinsic harm in their faint, academic piety but the implication that the public morale needs this kind of support ... is calculated to provoke a response which is neither academic nor pious [20]

Tom Harrisson of Mass-Observation, in a report of October 1939 commissioned by the MOI, anxious to gauge public responses to their efforts, found that Britons were remarkably unaware of this poster despite a large print run of 836,000 copies. Harrisson judged that the poster, in adopting a literary format and employing elevated language, was inflected with class. It seemed to invoke the rhetoric of World War I posters which, in retrospect, had encouraged working-class sacrifice for the benefit of the Establishment. Other early MOI campaigns also backfired. After the evacuation of the British forces from Dunkirk at the end of May 1940 and British defeats in Norway, an invasion seemed increasingly likely. The MOI sought to raise public awareness of the risk of Nazi spies by spreading rumours of a 'Silent Column' at work in Britain. This campaign, coinciding with prosecutions of British citizens for spreading defeatist rumours, had a divisive effect in British society.

Those wartime posters which have now entered into the popular, nostalgic memory of the conflict were produced after this inauspicious start. They were remarkably different from the Great War images. In general, the MOI's domestic propaganda campaigns placed an emphasis on information over persuasion, on promises rather than threats, and on rational appeals over fear. And unlike Nazi Germany or Soviet Russia, the leaders of Britain and her allies were rarely depicted as heroic models to be imitated, nor were the enemy represented as evil embodied. The chief subject of these posters was the British people. As Churchill noted, 'The fronts are everywhere. The trenches are dug in the towns and streets. Every village is fortified'; and, largely as a consequence of the bombing, more British civilians died than soldiers during the first three years of the conflict.[21] The inescapable fact that this was a 'People's War' was reinforced in MOI propaganda. Donald Zec's poster *Women of Britain Come into the Factories* (plate 107), for example, followed the 'call up' of women into war work in December 1941 (bar those exempt because of their domestic responsibilities). Commentators have detected an echo of the archetypal image of the Soviet proletarian woman in Zec's treatment – a graphic trace of the mood of egalitarianism in wartime Britain, as well as a reference to the popular alliance made with the Soviet Union in July.

107. Donald Zec. 'Women of Britain Come into the Factories'. Issued by the Ministry of Information, UK, probably 1941. E.135-1973

GIVE 'EM

BOTH BARRELS

JEAN CARLU

DIVISION OF INFORMATION
OFFICE FOR EMERGENCY MANAGEMENT
WASHINGTON, D.C.

Appeals to the noble, 'higher' motives of patriotism and duty rarely featured in MOI posters. War was 'naturalized' in the claim that it was being fought with the democratic consensus of an informed people. The British authorities gained much legitimacy by emphasizing the truthfulness and accuracy of the information which they made available for public consumption. But, as Arthur Marwick has noted, in conditions of total war social groups that were traditionally lacking in political influence and power were able to exert an indirect influence on social policy.[22] The state made a *de facto* contract with the British people – not least in poster propaganda – in order to bolster the 'war effort', whether by growing food or by joining the Auxiliary Territorial Service. These graphic pledges often literally offered a vision of a new Britain in the peace to

108. Jean Georges Leon Carlu. 'Give 'Em Both Barrels', USA, 1941. Issued by the US Division of Information Office for Emergency Management. E. 2916-1980

Carlu's poster, like many produced in Britain, drew a graphic connection between the war effort at home and that made on the battle front.

come. In a 1942 poster designed by Abram Games for the Army Bureau of Current Affairs, for example, a decaying terrace of brick housing – an index of the poverty of the Depression – crumbles to reveal a gleaming, modernist social housing scheme captioned with the words 'Your Britain'. Such images, in effect, were part of the expectant re-evaluation of British society which led to what has been described as 'Welfare Capitalism' after the war (i.e. in which the state took responsibility for improving employment, health, diet and housing of the people whilst encouraging business to pursue profit). Traces of this vision of the extended role of the state can even be found in other less optimistic images. Reginald Mount's 1943-44 poster entitled *VD. Hello boy friend. Coming my way?* sought to influence the sexual habits of the serviceman (plate 109). In what today seems a macabre triangulation of death (symbolized by the skull), exotic sexual encounter (in the fleshy, sexual orchid) and feminine attraction (the pink veil), the soldier was reminded of the risk of sexually transmitted diseases. Nevertheless, this poster was part of a health programme which demonstrated the state's awareness of its own responsibility for increasing public knowledge of a preventative approach to disease.

Although the egalitarian aims of the Labour government, which won a landslide victory in the first post-war election, were slowly relinquished in the face of the dire economic circumstances in which Britain found itself in the 1940s, all British governments accepted an extended range of social responsibilities until the late 1970s. Moreover, Welfare Capitalism was predicated on the view that political activism should be conducted within the frame of party politics. This did not necessarily mean the wholesale abandonment of propaganda posters. The state, through the agency of the Central Office of Information (the official publicity service which emerged from the MOI in 1946), as well as officially supported bodies and charities

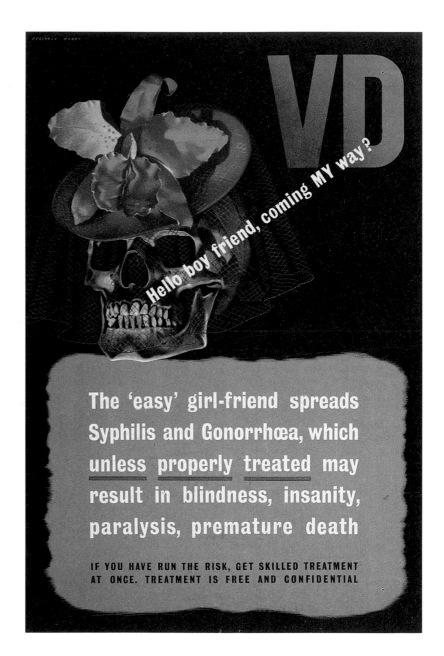

109. Reginald Mount. 'VD'. Produced by the Ministry of Information for the Ministry of Health and the Central Council of Health Education, UK, c. 1943-44. E. 2914-1995

such as Royal Society for the Prevention of Accidents, continued to commission propaganda posters in their least controversial form. In a spirit of paternalism, designs were printed which maintained a role – consolidated during the war – of protecting and informing the people. Posters reminding Britons to 'Keep Britain Tidy', to 'Buy British' and to give up smoking, and in recent years to promote other health matters such as AIDS awareness, maintained the consensus which endorsed the state's social responsibilities. Generally such campaigns have not been controversial: they seem unquestionably to be in the 'public interest'.

111. Anonymous. 'Smoking is Very Glamorous', USA, 1972. Produced by the American Cancer Society. E.70-1974

One in a series of posters which stressed the consequences of smoking, this deliberately ambiguous image debunks the long-established associations of cigarettes with glamour and sexuality particularly found in Hollywood movies.

110. Dorothy Braddell. 'Which Kind Of Alphabet Do You Like?'. Issued by the Health and Cleanliness Council, UK, 1920s. E.720-1978

Charities had often produced posters on welfare issues before World War II. This one draws a connection between cleanliness and happiness.

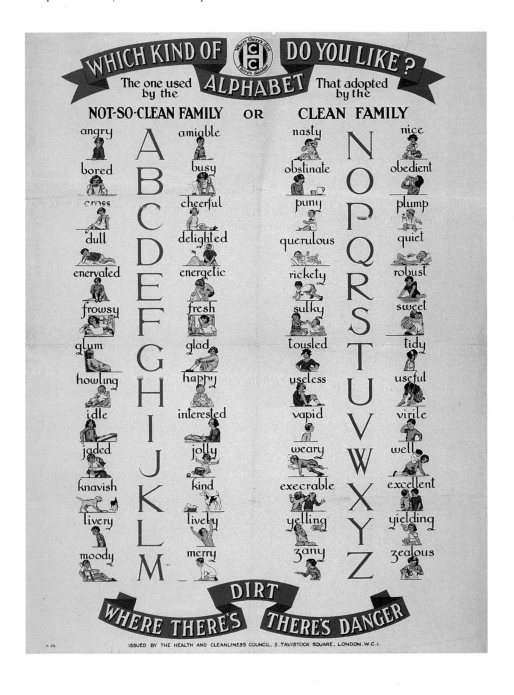

THE COLD WAR

After Germany's attack on Russia in June 1941, the MOI sought to influence public opinion about Britain's new Soviet ally. As Michael Balfour has shown in *Propaganda in War 1939-45* (1979), support for the Soviet Union was remarkably high and the MOI aimed to keep this enthusiasm in 'safe hands and bounds' by organizing a network of Anglo-Soviet committees and events. A number of exhibitions of Russian propaganda posters were held to show the common conditions and deprivations faced by both peoples. Kukriniksi, three cartoonists working under a pseudonym, represented the Anglo-Soviet alliance in a poster entitled *Meeting Over Berlin* (plate 112) which depicted two pilots shaking hands as they discharged their load of bombs over the city. Kukriniksi's design was a sequential '*TASS* Window', reproduced quickly with a stencil like the Rosta windows in the 1920s. It posed as graphic reportage, pasted up as a wall newspaper to report events in the war.[23] However, the friendship of 'brother-nations' that Kukriniksi depicted was short-lived, as the lukewarm and distrustful alliance froze into the Cold War. After 1945 America and her allies actively mounted a campaign to promote the extension of democracy in Europe. This propaganda took various forms. As Ralph Willet notes of American attempts to 're-educate' Germany after the war, 'Baseball took its place beside films and lectures as a corrective to Nazism and a guarantee against a resurgence of German nationalism'.[24] Similarly, the Marshall Plan, announced in 1947 and launched one year later, was not just a programme of American aid for the devastated countries of Europe: it was also

112. Kukriniksi. 'Meeting Over Berlin',
USSR, c. 1942-44. **E.2175 1946**

The Kukriniksi co-operative worked
from the 1920s. This particular version
of the poster in the V&A's collection
was probably printed for display in
MOI exhibitions in Britain during
World War II.

113. Gaston van den Eynde. 'Par Le Plan Marshall Coopération Intereuropéenne Pour Un Niveau De Vie Plus Elevé' ('European Co-operation for a Higher Standard of Living with the Marshall Plan'), Netherlands, 1950. E.1900-1952

114. Reginald Mount and Eileen Evans. 'Little scraps of information can add up to a whale of a lot ... and the net is wide!' Central Office of Information, UK, 1960. E.450-1995

a means of promoting Capitalism and Democracy and, above all, of inhibiting the spread of Communism across the continent. Gaston van den Eynde drew on a simple metaphor to express the purpose of the Marshall Plan in his 1950 poster (plate 113) by representing it as a solid wooden stake supporting a young blossoming tree. The caption accompanying this rather open symbol made the more concrete promise that co-operation between European states would guarantee a higher standard of living.

It would seem that during the Cold War Western democratic states largely withdrew from the production of explicit graphic propaganda. An espousal of free speech and the right of all peoples to self-determination did not sit comfortably with overt campaigns to mould public opinion. There were, of course, notorious exceptions to this, such as the anti-Communist witch-hunts held in the USA in the late 1940s and 1950s. Nevertheless, a small number of Cold War posters produced in the West can be found. Reginald Mount and Eileen Evans, for example, designed a poster captioned with the warning 'Little scraps of information can add up to a whale of a lot ... and the net is wide!' This 1960 image (plate 114) depicted small pieces of printed paper shaped as fish, being trapped in a dark net by an unseen hand. The words on each piece appear on first inspection to be a kind of miscellany, selected by chance. On closer inspection, particular words stand out: Eastern

Europe, NATO, British economy and nuclear power. This poster, for display in British government and military offices dealing with 'sensitive' material, reminded employees of the interest that Britain's Cold War enemies might have in this information. Despite the slow thawing of East-West relations under Khrushchev, the 1950s – opening with the defection of the British diplomats Guy Burgess and Donald MacLean and concluding with Soviet triumphs in the space race – were framed by constant anxiety about the 'Soviet threat'. Whilst not self-consciously ideological, Mount and Evans's poster drew upon the fear of infiltration and espionage which fuelled Cold War paranoia and East-West enmity.

In the Soviet Union, China and other Communist states the poster continued to have an important place in the promotion of the political ideals of the regimes (plates 115 and 116). After World War II, Communist ideologues in Moscow's newly acquired European satellite states used

116. Anonymous. 'Chairman Mao goes to An-yuan'. Based on an oil painting by Liu Chunhua, China, 1966-67. Private collection.

This poster was widely exhibited and reproduced during the Cultural Revolution. It is estimated that about 900 million were printed in different formats. The image typified the cult of personality which operated during the Cultural Revolution and placed Mao as the central figure in all aspects of life in China. In Liu Chunhau's image the young Mao is depicted as a unique man of vision, his eyes seeing a better future.

115. Anonymous. 'Tiananmen Square', China, 1950. Colour half-tone letterpress. FE.20-1994

A small poster that celebrates the founding of the People's Republic of China, it depicts crowds hailing portraits of Communist leaders.

毛主席去安源

posters to promote a largely unwanted and disliked political system. Although Soviet domination over this part of Europe sometimes took the form of brutal repression, as events in Hungary in 1956 cruelly showed, for much of the period national Communist parties sought to win over the people through propaganda. In fact, during the early years of these regimes most forms of culture – carefully shaped and censored by the state – had the character of propaganda. Nevertheless, the poster continued to play an important role because of the relatively poor economic and technical condition of these states. Ownership of television, for example, was not widespread in some Eastern European states until the 1970s. And so an imported calendar of national holidays, such as May Day and the anniversary of the October Revolution, was fortified by countless thousands of posters pasted up on streets or in public offices which depicted the 'father of the Revolution', Lenin, or the beaming faces of the young dressed in the characteristic uniform of the party activist and carrying the red flags of Socialism and banners calling for World Peace (plate 117).

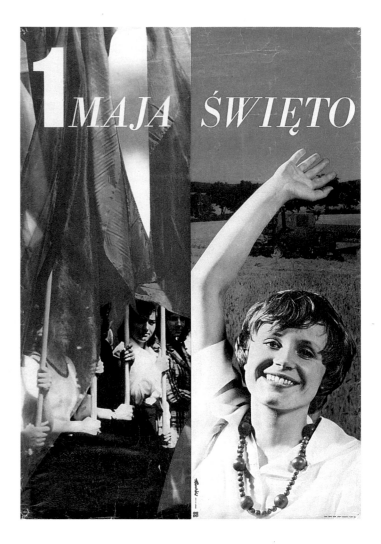

117. Anonymous. '1 Maja Święto' (May Day Holiday), Poland, mid-1970s. Photographs by K. Lipski. E.135-1994

An archetypal poster from Moscow's satellite state, Poland, drawing on a familiar repertoire of clichés: smiling, young party activists; billowing waves of red flags; and a rural setting suggesting plenty.

118. Anonymous. 'Pax Sovietica', Poland, c. 1982. Printed on an underground Solidarity press during a period of martial law. E.1398-1993

Under pressure from the USSR to regain control after the Solidarity-led strikes of 1981, General Jaruzelski resorted to military force on 13 December 1981, crushing Solidarity and imposing martial law. This witty protest, fusing the symbols of war and peace, satirizes the 'Soviet-style' method of restoring order.

During the years of political reform in Russia after 1986 associated with *Perestroika* (Restructuring) and *Glasnost* (Openness), and the revolutions of Eastern Europe in 1989-90, the poster enjoyed a revival. Critics of the Communist system (whether 'within' the party like supporters of Gorbachev or 'without' like Solidarity in Poland) used this medium more than any other to press for the development of civic culture. In Poland, for example, opponents of the regime in its final years had limited means to promote their views. Moreover, television and radio had been discredited by the lies that had been broadcast on behalf of the regime. The poster was used to activate and represent widely held but largely unspoken aspirations. One of the most memorable images of the June 1989 elections which marked the beginnings of the democratic revolution in Eastern Europe was Tomasz Sarnecki's poster *High Noon* (plate 119). It represented the forthcoming election as the moment in which the Party and its illegitimate regime would be brought to justice. The pistol that Gary Cooper had once carried in the 1952 Hollywood film was

**120. Iu. Leonova. 'Stalinism!',
USSR, 1989.** E.966-1990

A prize-winning entry in a poster competition, 'Perestroika and Us', dedicated to the 70th anniversary of the VLKSM (All-Union Leninist Communist Youth League). Stalin, despite his blank eyes and mouth, is immediately recognizable. Gorbachev, when promoting *Glasnost* in political life, had called for the blank spots in the historical record of Stalin's rule to be investigated and corrected.

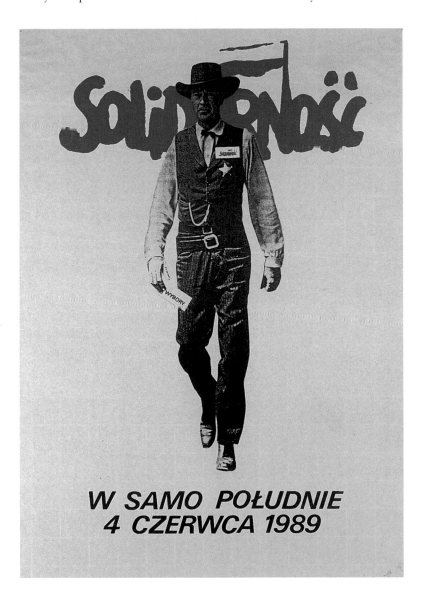

**119. Tomasz Sarnecki. 'High Noon
4 June 1989'. Election poster for
Solidarity, Poland, 1989.** E.3125-1990

replaced by the ballot paper, metaphorically identifying an impending change from rule by force to rule by ballot box. Above all, this image from a Western movie summed up the desire of many Poles to escape from Moscow's influence and join the West. This was unmistakably a political poster: yet it made no direct reference to ideology or party programmes. It was not an image of an actual cowboy but of a film star. It would seem as if Sarnecki's design hinted at the form of political culture which had become dominant in the West, that of staged spectacle and razzmatazz.

COUNTER-CULTURE

With a few exceptions, in the West the state's interest in the propaganda poster began to decline in the 1950s. Some commentators viewed the reinforcement of stable parliamentary democracy in Western Europe and North America, coupled with a 'consumer boom', as the beginning of a new phase in history. American commentator Daniel Boorstin in his studies *The Genius of American Politics* (1953) and *The Americans: The Colonial Experience* (1958), stressed that the American experience had rendered utopian dreams irrelevant. It seemed that advanced, Western societies were about to enter an age in which scarcity was becoming a thing of the past. Technological innovation and sound economic management by a technocratic middle class seemed to augur a virtuous circle of economic good fortune. The prosperity offered by economic boom was bolstered – at least in the British context – by the security provided by the Welfare State and the extension of the education system. The old fear of poverty seemed anachronistic. The fact that demands for food and housing were still behind public riots in places like Poland, where ideology reigned supreme, added force to such views. It seemed in the West that the prospect of the kinds of political agitation experienced between the wars was increasingly remote. Yet these certainties were shaken by a new wave of strong-willed activism.

The late 1950s saw the emergence of new kinds of politics concerned with moral and ethical issues, and the extension of civil rights. After the Soviet invasion of Hungary in 1956 as well as

121. F.H.K. Henrion. 'Stop Nuclear Suicide'. Issued by the Campaign for Nuclear Disarmament, UK, 1963.

E.3910-1983

Henrion's design has entered the notorious category of banned posters, as London Transport deemed that it contravened its *Conditions Covering the Acceptance of Advertising*. These terms prohibited images which were likely to cause political controversy.

Khrushchev's revelations about the brutality and criminality of Stalin's rule emerging from Moscow, the authority of orthodox Marxism collapsed amongst Left-wing intellectuals. New issues became the focus of Left-wing dissent: civil rights for ethnic minorities and women; atomic weapons; and, from the mid-1960s, the war in Vietnam. Direct action, 'sit-ins' and demonstrations shifted responsibility away from autocratic and centrally structured political organizations of the 'Old Left' to the individual. Many in Britain were galvanized by the marches from London to the Atomic Weapons Research Centre at Aldermaston organized by the Campaign for Nuclear Disarmament (CND) which was founded in February 1958. CND attracted the support of some prominent intellectuals and public figures as well as the talents of some skilled graphic designers including Ken Garland and F.H.K. Henrion. Henrion's 1963 design *Stop Nuclear Suicide* (plate 121) was a simple photomontage in which an image of a skull was laid over that of a 'mushroom cloud', and a peace symbol was added in the lower left-hand corner. Protest against the Bomb took a variety of forms, from the display of such posters to demonstrations where protesters lay down in the street outside the Ministry of Defence. Such direct approaches to political activism were

122. Paul Peter Piech. 'They Killed the Dreamer, But Not His Dream', UK, 1979. Linocut on green paper. E.769-1986

Piech, an American living and working in Britain, produced this linocut to commemorate the life and ideas of Martin Luther King, the civil rights leader murdered in 1968.

extolled in the late 1960s by sections of the counter-culture who sought to politicize all aspects of everyday life: 'The personal,' it was pronounced, 'is the political'.

Protest against nuclear weapons was an important catalyst for the radicalization of young Britons. In America this role was played by the movement for civil rights, which campaigned to end the legalized segregation of the races that existed throughout many parts of the USA. In some southern states black Americans were barred from sharing facilities such as buses and drinking fountains with whites. Such public forms of apartheid were part of a pervasive system of exclusion which prohibited inter-racial marriages and excluded blacks from juries. Whilst attacks were made on segregation in the 1930s and 1940s, a swelling wave of black consciousness and Supreme Court judgements against segregation in schools bolstered a committed civil rights movement in the 1950s. Martin Luther King, a Baptist minister who advocated a philosophy of peaceful direct action, became a prominent spokesman for the movement (see plate 122). By 1960 segregation was a urgent social issue which politicized black Americans as well as many young whites. The Student Nonviolent Coordinating Committee (SNCC) published a series of posters illustrated with photographs by Danny Lyon, a young photographer who documented the movement between 1962 and 1964. In one powerful design (plate 123), Lyon's photograph of two young black men taking part in a SNCC demonstration was simply captioned with the word 'Now'. Civil rights had been raised so high on the political agenda in America that a single word could stand as a powerful demand.

In America the experience and influence of civil rights activism had a powerful effect in shaping the counter-culture which developed through the

123. *above* 'Now', USA, c. 1962.

Student Nonviolent Coordinating Committee.

Photograph by Danny Lyon. E.2740-1995

124. Ben Shahn. 'McCarthy Peace', USA, 1967.

E.377-1973

Eugene McCarthy stood on a peace ticket in the presidential election against Lyndon Johnson. Ben Shahn was a renowned Left-wing artist.

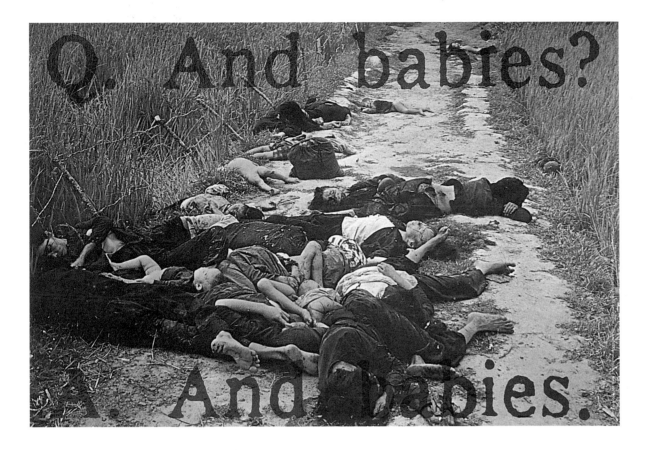

125. Art Workers' Coalition. 'Q. And babies? A. And babies.', USA, 1970. Photograph by Ron Haeberle.

E.233-1985

course of the 1960s. Non-violent campaigning methods led to numerous sit-ins and happenings, from protest against American foreign policy or the annual Miss America Pageant to opposition to the escalation of the war in Vietnam after the Tet Offensive in 1968, which provoked some of the most inventive designs. Most of the images which appeared before this watershed tended to reflect rather more on the USA (plate 124) than on Vietnam, whether in the form of commentaries on patriotism, conscription or on the views of American politicians. But perhaps the most striking anti-Vietnam poster produced to move public opinion against American conduct of the war was *Q. And babies? A. And babies.* designed by the Art Workers' Coalition in 1970 (plate 125). An army photographer, Ron Haeberle, had been present at the massacre by American soldiers of hundreds of Vietnamese, including children, at My Lai in March 1968 and taken colour photographs of the terrible scene he witnessed. Although early reports of the event caused little public concern, the slow pressure of newspaper articles and an army investigation encouraged Haeberle to release his images to the press in 1969. These photographs were shown on national news broadcasts – the camera passing slowly from image to image in silence, as if words could not explain this dreadful act. The impact of these terrifying images was remarkable: doubts that ordinary American servicemen had been responsible for this vile massacre began to dissolve. My Lai exploded into a national controversy. One soldier present at My Lai told a television interviewer that his lieutenant had ordered all the villagers to be killed. 'Men, women and children?' asked the interviewer. 'Men, women and children', the ex-serviceman replied. 'And babies?' he asked again. 'And babies,' came the reply. Haeberle's image and the CBS interview became international news. To keep pressure on the American administration, in 1970 the Art Workers' Coalition, a New York alliance of artists working with the support of the Museum of Modern Art, captioned Haeberle's photograph with the soldier's words as they had appeared in newspaper reports. Although the Museum trustees later tried to withdraw their support for the project, over 50,000 copies of the poster were printed by the Lithographers Union. This easily understood image of summary (in)justice was a remarkable indictment of American claims to be fighting for freedom and democracy in Indo-China. Somewhat inadvertently, this poster also testified to the dominance of broadcast media over the paper-bound format of the poster. The currency of this image drew from the power of television to enter into the lives of all in a way that posters no longer could. Moreover, this poster was rarely encountered *as a poster* – it was paraded in front of another famous anti-war image, Picasso's painting *Guernica* (1937), or carried as a banner for the benefit of newspaper photographers, and it featured on the cover of Yoko Ono's record 'Now or Never'. In other words, this image entered into a conditional relationship with other mass media.

The year 1968 was also a watershed year in Europe. In Paris students took to the streets in a prolonged period of strikes and civil disorder. Fuelled with optimism, these young revolutionaries believed that in alliance with the workers a new society could be fashioned which was not based on capitalism or consumerism. Such utopianism stimulated the founding of an Atelier Populaire at the École Nationale Supérieure des Beaux-Arts during the occupation of Paris's Quartier Latin in May. This anarchistic though well-organized studio produced posters, wall newspapers and happenings for the city streets (plate 127). The Atelier's posters functioned as counter-propaganda to contest hostile reports in the media and President de Gaulle's attempts to discredit the students. One underground pamphlet published in London reported:

> Mural propaganda is an integral part of the revolutionary Paris of May 1968. It has become a
> mass activity, part and parcel of the Revolution's method of self-expression. The walls of the
> Latin-Quarter are the depository of a new rationality ... much of it Situationist in inspiration ...
> 'long live communication, down with telecommunication', ... 'under the Paving Stones, the
> beach' ... 'When examined, we will answer with questions.' ... 'Never Work' ... 'Humanity will only
> be happy when the last capitalist has been strung up with the guts of the last bureaucrat ...'

126. Grapus. Untitled, France, c. 1975-76. Colour screen-print. E.1585-1979

Grapus, a Left-wing alliance of poster designers, was established in France in 1970. The group's three founders met at the Atelier Populaire (see plate 127) in 1968. They were opposed to the 'sweet poison of advertising' and, until 1977, chose to work for Left-wing clients such as the Confédération General du Travail. This simple poster combines a Vietcong flag with the smiling face of a Vietnamese girl and was probably produced to celebrate the end of the war in Indo-China in 1975.

127. Atelier Populaire. 'SS', France, 1968. E.225-1985

Printed on 18 May 1968, this poster shows a policeman wielding a truncheon and carrying a riot shield bearing the letters 'SS', so a comparison is drawn between members of the French CRS (Compagnies Républicaines de Securité) and the Nazi SS (Schutz-Staffel).

These posters were simple, single-colour screen-prints, stencils and lithographs. A low-tech means of reproduction like screen-printing was both cheap and easily learned. The ostensibly crude style of the Paris posters was a self-conscious challenge to the spectacle of the professional media. And unlike much propaganda which operates by confirming received opinion or at least by exploiting popular prejudices, these posters, appearing overnight on the streets of the French capital, were unsettling and questioning. An Expressionist image of a girl hurling a brick, captioned 'La Beauté est dans la rue', could not be interpreted as a political statement by any traditional view of politics.

French posters had a contingency and immediacy because they were produced in response to events rapidly unfolding in Paris. In fact, the Atelier Populaire published a book of their posters in 1969 to encourage other activists to follow their example and produce posters in response to local circumstances.[25] The counter-culture's commitment to direct action and a conception of personal political responsibility led to the establishment of various poster workshops such as the Red Dragon Print Collective in London which operated in the 1970s (see plate 128). In a philosophy loosely encapsulated in the contemporary slogan 'dig where you stand' (which, in other words, advocated individual responsibility and actions, not least at a local level), a number of different workshops produced posters dealing with libertarian causes. The idea of designing, printing and distributing one's own posters was not only claimed as a means of allowing marginalized voices to be heard, but also as a social process in which the passivity which characterizes most people's relationship to the mass media could be turned into action (a kind of 'resistance work' as it was dubbed at the time). Pen Dalton's poster, *Parity Begins at Home*, produced in 1974, is a good example of this localization of political activism in both its message and the way it was produced (plate 129). A witty design making reference to the austere proverb 'charity begins at home' as well as to the famous image of a cook in the Edwardian poster for Edwards' Desiccated Soup, Dalton's design reminded Socialists that their egalitarian views should be practised at home as well as in the workplace. Moreover, in an echo of the Suffrage Atelier over 60 years earlier, she screen-printed the poster *at home* and sold it directly to Left-wing bookshops and at conferences.

The ambitious and optimistic libertarianism which motivated political activists in the 1960s was on the wane by the mid-1970s, enervated by failure and constricted by economic recession. Nevertheless many of the issues that continue to attract the support of committed campaigners, such as man's treatment of the environment, anti-sexism and anti-racism, were often shaped by the counter-culture. The early and general concerns about man's abuse of the environment raised by

IF IT'S EMPTY TAKE IT

128. Red Dragon Print Collective. 'If It's Empty Take It', UK, 1974. Colour screen-print. E.527-1975

129. Pen Dalton. 'Parity Begins at Home', UK, 1974. Colour screen-print. E.1577-1991

130. Robert Rauschenberg. 'Earth Day 22
April 1970'. Issued by the American
Environment Foundation, USA, 1970.
E.3035-1991

131. Yellowhammer Advertising Company
Ltd. 'It takes up to 40 dumb animals to
make a fur coat ...'. Photograph by David
Bailey; copy line by Bryn Jones. Issued
by Lynx, UK, c. 1986-87. E.3041-1991

Robert Rauschenberg's poster, *Earth Day*, issued in 1970 (plate 130) – a photographic catalogue of environmental abuse overlaid with the supreme symbol of America, the eagle – have in the last three decades continued to spawn a range of dedicated groups. In 1985, for example, Lynx was established as a splinter group from Greenpeace to protest against the fur trade (plate 131). Although relatively small in size, it raised public awareness of this issue extremely successfully. Drawing upon professional designers, photographers and film directors who shared the charity's objections to the fur trade, Lynx produced some of the most hard-hitting poster imagery of the 1980s (to such an extent that the fur industry retaliated through the courts).

Committed lobbying groups such as Greenpeace have tended to focus their campaigns on public opinion and, even when the state has had no objection to a particular issue, have often been more effective propagandists than governments. The promotion of AIDS awareness is a good example of this. The British government in the 1980s was relatively quick to recognize the threat posed by the HIV virus, and in 1986 the Ministry of Health mounted a poster and leaflet campaign under the slogan *AIDS How big does it have to get before you take notice?* Although largely typographic, the poster suggested a tombstone carved with this slogan (plate 132). This and other morbid imagery was strongly condemned by those who felt that the state was covertly attacking civil liberties when it should have been offering clear and detailed advice about sex and drug use. It is perhaps not surprising that an administration which had emphasized 'family values' found this issue so difficult to deal with. Fearful of offending potential voters, most governments have avoided being seen to condone lifestyles and sexual practices outside convention. Whereas, in contrast, single issue groups established to promote AIDS awareness (such as the Terrence Higgins Trust formed in London in 1983) – though still subject to laws on obscenity and the codes of practice within the advertising industry – are able to grapple with the task with frankness and imagination.

132. Malcolm Gaskin and David O'Connor Thompson. 'AIDS. How big does it have to get before you take notice?' Ministry of Health and Social Security, UK, 1987.

E.177-1987

DECLINE AND FALL?

The continued use that different lobbies make of the poster today testifies to its continued purpose. AIDS awareness campaigners, for example, can speak to those at greatest risk of contracting the HIV virus using direct language – even sexual slang – and graphic symbols that are easily understood, and in places – clubs and cafés – which the sweeping reach of broadcasting media passes over (plate 133). Similarly, in the atmosphere of reaction which has now taken over Poland under the sway of Right-wing governments and the Catholic Church, feminists pasted up Barbara Kruger's poster, *Your body is a battleground*, to remind the people of Warsaw that women's rights are under threat by moves to ban abortion (plate 134). Nevertheless, over recent years there have been a number of predictions about the imminent decline and disappearance of what increasingly seems an anachronistic medium. As early as 1971 Maurice Rickards wrote a book, influenced by Marshal McLuhan's vision of the global village in the electronic age, entitled *The Rise and Fall of the Poster*. And more recently, István Orosz, the designer of *Comrades It's Over!* has claimed that the political revolution in Eastern Europe at the end of the 1980s marked 'the swan-song of the poster'.[26] This format, he claimed, enjoyed a brief Indian summer at the service of the underground movement. The arrival of democracy put the poster back into retirement. But reports of the 'death' of poster, like the famous and apocryphal notice of Mark Twain's demise, have, it seems, been 'greatly exaggerated'. Whilst it is true that the traditional role of the propaganda poster has been largely usurped by electronic media, the poster has not expired. It has entered into new relationships with the now ubiquitous broadcasting media. It is noteworthy that British politicians during the gencral elections of 1992 and 1997, far from abandoning the campaigning poster, deployed it as a means of generating valuable 'photo-opportunities'. A speech is one way of delivering a political message through the television screen, but a speech delivered in front of a graphic symbol and slogan is more likely to register in the mind of the inattentive viewer. The unveiling of a poster depicting 'Vatman' or 'Labour's Double Whammy' can make what might otherwise be an announcement of a dull policy *an event*. The election poster may now be news but, as one journalist noted in 1992, the man in the street would be hard pressed actually to find one.[27] Our encounters with political posters are mediated (like the conditional relationship with the media enjoyed by the Art Workers' Coalition poster, *Q. And Babies?* almost 30 years ago) but it seems as if the task of influencing public opinion through the combination of pithy slogan and graphic image – the basic elements of the propaganda poster – endures.

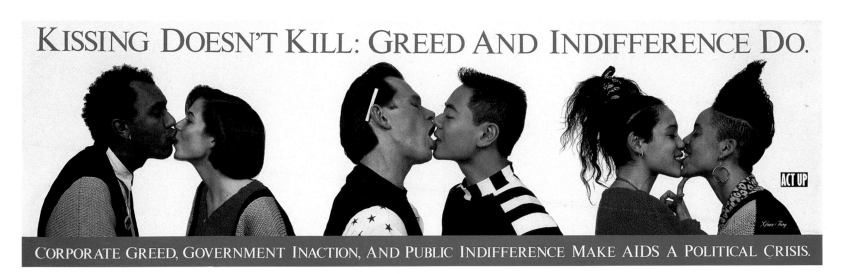

KISSING DOESN'T KILL: GREED AND INDIFFERENCE DO.

ACT UP

CORPORATE GREED, GOVERNMENT INACTION, AND PUBLIC INDIFFERENCE MAKE AIDS A POLITICAL CRISIS.

133. Gran Fury. 'Kissing Doesn't Kill: Greed And Indifference Do.' Sponsored by AmFAR (American Foundation for AIDS Research), USA, 1989. E.472-1993

Gran Fury, a collective of artists and designers within **ACT UP (AIDS Coalition To Unleash Power)** dedicated to promoting **AIDS** awareness, has produced many inventive and thought-provoking posters. **AIDS** activists had used the strategy of the 'kiss-in' — large public demonstrations of affection by gays and straights — drawing fire from conservative commentators. This advertisement, designed to run on public transport in New York and San Fransisco in 1989, ridicules small-mindedness and reminds the authorities of their responsibilities in combating **AIDS**.

134. Barbara Kruger. 'Twoje Ciało To Pole Walki' ('Your body is a battleground'). E.2217-1997

First designed to promote a **Pro-Choice** march in Washington in 1989, it has been reproduced in various languages: this edition was issued in Polish in 1991.

▣ FOUR IN FOCUS

RUTH WALTON

'EMOTION is the motive power of man's will.'   *Frank Brangwyn, RA*

Propaganda posters (other than those specifically for information) sell attitudes, ideas and ethics, and their primary function is to provoke the viewer to action. The issues and causes they promote – whether political, social, ethical or ecological – condition the world in which we live and can therefore be profoundly affecting. Our responses depend on the degree to which we, as individuals, identify with the propositions.

These four posters, selected from the disturbing situations of four significant twentieth-century conflicts, express both official and opposition viewpoints. They all function essentially through appeals to emotion, but use very different means of persuasion and motivation to get their messages across.

'PUT STRENGTH IN THE FINAL BLOW. BUY WAR BONDS'

Auto-lithograph by Sir Frank Brangwyn

Issued by the National War Savings Committee, 1918

Frank Brangwyn deliberately presented the reality of war in all its horror. His personal identification with the fate of Belgium, his birthplace, and its people was expressed through the emotional intensity of his images, which sought through their realism to arouse sympathy and motivate the viewer to action. However, such explicit imagery was not appreciated by the government, whose Parliamentary Recruiting Committee (PRC), responsible for issuing official recruiting posters, refused the gift of Brangwyn's first recruiting poster design,[1] drawn at the request of Frank Pick, commercial manager of the Underground Electric Railways Company of London Ltd (plate 136).

135. Frank Brangwyn. 'Put Strength In The Final Blow. Buy War Bonds', UK. Lettered: Auto-lithograph by Frank Brangwyn, A.R.A. Issued by the National War Savings Committee.

E.2319-1918

In spite of his dislike of war, Brangwyn considered it his patriotic duty to use his art on behalf of the war effort. But it was not until 1918 that he was officially commissioned, by the National War Savings Committee, to prepare a poster for their autumn War Bonds campaign. However, the American government commissioned from him a recruiting poster for the US Navy as soon as the United States joined the fighting. Most of his war posters, therefore, were for fundraising charities helping the victims of war and their dependants, and supporting the troops.

136. Frank Brangwyn. 'Britain's Call to Arms', UK, 1914. E.2681-1914

Brangwyn's first war poster, published by the UERCL, was displayed with adjacent text in stations throughout the network.

THE ONLY ROAD FOR AN ENGLISHMAN

Through Darkness to Light

Through Fighting to Triumph

137. Gerald Spencer Pryse. 'The Only Road For An Englishman', UK, 1914. Auto-lithograph. E.4257-1915

Pick, who refused to hang the PRC's posters in his Underground stations because of their poor design, began in 1914 a policy of commissioning and publishing war posters by accomplished artists, starting with Brangwyn and followed by Gerald Spencer Pryse. Although *Britain's Call to Arms* was criticized for depicting death and destruction, it provoked men to enlist in such huge numbers that the War Office, after asking Pick to remove Brangwyn's posters from all the stations because 'they showed too much of the horrors of war', relented.[2] Pryse's delicate draughtsmanship seen in his recruiting poster, *The Only Road for an Englishman* (plate 137) , was more acceptable. Here, the violence is expressed through the shattered buildings, and the emotive appeal is to comradeship and communal responsibility. Pryse travelled around the Belgian Front with lithographic stones in his car and drew the scenes he witnessed straight on to the stone, even under fire,[3] which lent spontaneity and urgency to his images. The emotional involvement of both these artists with the fate of Belgium invested their drawings with a conviction remarked upon by contemporary writers.

The power of these images was fully conveyed through the sensitivity of lithography, which was Brangwyn's favourite print medium. A consummate draughtsman, he maximized its expressive power by drawing straight on to the stone. 'Lithography is a medium in which you can let yourself go ... express yourself exactly as you feel ... the *only* medium in which an artist can have his drawing reproduced without any deterioration in his work. It's the finest of all the graphic arts – gives back truly all that the artist puts on stone.'[4]

The impact of his poster for the National War Savings Committee, *Put Strength in the Final Blow. Buy War Bonds*, published in 1918, was such that, on seeing it, the Kaiser is reputed to have put a price on his head.[5] Whether or not this was true, Brangwyn believed it and relayed it to his assistants, and it is recorded in a small notebook at The Jointure, Brangwyn's house in Ditchling, Sussex, where the poster is described as 'Bayonet. Price on FB's head (also Will Dyson)'.[6] The scene in the poster is imaginary, as Brangwyn did not see combat, but he knew that accuracy of detail was essential for it to be convincing and insisted on borrowing for his models British and German uniforms from the Imperial War Museum.[7]

Put Strength in the Final Blow. Buy War Bonds is a brutal image, depicting a British soldier in the act of killing a German. According to Reginald Praill of The Avenue Press, who supervised the printing of almost all Brangwyn's war posters, it 'gave the War Bond Committee somewhat of a shock' but the chairman agreed with Brangwyn that 'nothing could be too drastic to fight the Germans with [sic]'.[8] It has been described as 'certainly one of the most vicious posters that the war produced'[9] and an incitement 'to actual violence'. This scene, showing a bayonet piercing the enemy's chest, boldly flouts the convention of the day that preferred a symbolic representation of death. 'Killing people, when you got down to pictures of it – even if it was the enemy, even if only on posters – was somehow wrong.'[10] Even the slogan, although using current phraseology, carries an overtly belligerent message, re-enforced by the dead body lying on the ground.

The lines of the design are crucial to its impact. Brangwyn immediately draws the viewer into the action by directing the eye down the barrel of the rifle, straight to the pain and terror of the German's face. Strongly lit to emphasize his expression, it is framed by his arm and both guns, and placed at the centre of the arc tipped by a helmet at each end.

The composition is structured on strong diagonal axes, to convey movement, as well as a complex series of triangles and parallel lines. However, although logic suggests that the thrust of the bayonet has lifted the German off his feet, neither the British soldier's stance nor his position in relation to his adversary is convincing for such a manoeuvre. Perhaps Brangwyn sacrificed these realistic elements in the overriding interests of the design: the Tommy's back foot is in line with his hand, forming the base of the equilateral triangle headed by the falling helmet; and the solid weight of his body is needed to counter that of the overbalanced German.

The infinitely more difficult attitude of the figure in mid-air has been rendered much more effectively, but its similarity to the almost identical posture, in reverse, of a rugby player by S.T. Dadd reproduced on the front cover of *The Graphic* (plate 138) some years earlier, is too striking to ignore. Brangwyn's illustrations for *The Graphic* had provided his main financial support during the 1890s; therefore, given his tendency to keep interesting images to use in his own work,[11] it is quite possible that he had seen it and kept it.

In any case, the German figure, the main part of the strongest diagonal, carries the action. Having lost his balance on the sloping ground, he topples backwards from the force of the blow, momentarily suspended in mid-air while his body rotates. The line of the body rises, its dark tones and square mass conveying weight and, therefore, its inevitable fall. But it is his plummeting helmet that actually expresses the downward momentum. Placed at the apex of the triangle formed by hands and feet, the helmet anchors the composition.

138. Stephen T. Dadd. 'A Rugby Football Match at Blackheath: "Handed Off"'. Half-tone letterpress. Cover illustration, *The Graphic*, Saturday 9 January, 1897.

The German carries no identification. He is largely in shadow and his upturned helmet is not the distinctive German *stahlhelm*, which is strange, considering Brangwyn was so concerned for accuracy. He appears to have obscured any tell-tale features, focusing on the German's humanity rather than his nationality. Bareheaded, he is simply a man on the point of death.

Brangwyn's integration of the words with the image – the only example among his British war posters – enforces its meaning: the slogan visibly supports the design and, sinking into the foreground, unites those at home buying War Bonds with the fighting forces in a graphic expression of how the money could empower the army. Brangwyn retained tight control of every stage of the poster, marking up and colouring the proofs himself. One proof (plate 139) shows his attempt to integrate fully the lettering with the image by means of a coloured background.

Two very similar versions of the War Bonds poster were published. Reginald Praill suggested that both were issued simultaneously,[12] but bearing in mind the costs involved this is unlikely. Since the autumn War Bonds campaign was announced on 30 September 1918, only six weeks before the cessation of hostilities, the most logical explanation seems to be that Brangwyn was asked to prepare another, milder, version, *Back Him Up. Buy War Bonds* (plate 142) when the original caused offence or, possibly, as hostilities drew to a close. The identical production codes lettered on each poster imply that the second version simply replaced the first in the print/publication schedule; two separate designs published simultaneously would almost invariably have had individual codes.

A small watercolour (plate 140) shows the artist's first thoughts for *Back Him Up. Buy War Bonds*. This brief sketch, entitled *He Needs Your Help Now. Buy War Bonds*, expands the

139. Frank Brangwyn

'Put Strength In The Final Blow.

Buy War Bonds', UK, 1918.

Proof coloured in hand by the artist.

E.3511-1931

basic composition and places the figures on level ground in a much wider landscape, focusing less on the action. It also shows the intended colour composition of the poster (plate 141), although the final version was printed in different colours. Both image and slogan are less aggressive: in the printed poster the bayonet has not yet caused injury, although the intent is clearly symbolized, once again, by the dead body, while the message has been reduced from an exhortation to a plea.

Another soldier has been added in the foreground, whose face completes the curve of hands, helmets and heads in an attempt to introduce some movement into the design.

The slogan drawn by Brangwyn on an unlettered proof (see plate 141), 'He Needs Your Help Now. Buy War Bonds', was never published. The published version, *Back Him Up. Buy War Bonds*, alters the emphasis and, focusing on the British soldier, conveys both the moral and military support endowed by the War Bonds' money.

Brangwyn felt strongly about the human cost of war. He was deeply

140. Frank Brangwyn. 'He Needs Your Help Now. Buy War Bonds'. Watercolour over pencil, UK, 1918. Private collection.

This tiny sketch of only 10 x 15 cm (4 x 6 ins) was realized as a poster measuring approximately 101 x 151 cm (3 ft 2 ins x 4 ft 10 ins).

affected by the fact that his own nephew (in America) had responded to his recruiting poster for the US Navy and had been killed in action six weeks later. Philip Macer-Wright, Brangwyn's biographer who knew him well, comments, 'On a mind as sensitive as Brangwyn's the folly and cruelty of it worked like poison'.[13]

Considering his sense of guilt then, the brutality of Brangwyn's more aggressive War Bonds poster is not surprising: war means killing. It fulfilled its propaganda purpose by appearing to show a British soldier in victorious combat with the enemy. But it also offered Brangwyn a chance to use his art in the service of humanity:

> Art ... must be the expression of the emotions derived from a serious sympathy with one's fellow
> men .... a chief means of raising man to a higher plane of intention... EMOTION is the motive
> power of man's will .... But unless it is used for this purpose it can be of no real use to mankind. [14]

Brangwyn perhaps took this opportunity to make his own, very personal, anti-war protest.

141. Frank Brangwyn. 'He
Needs Your Help Now. Buy War
Bonds', UK, 1918. Monochrome
proof, coloured in hand by the
artist. E.3513-1931

142. Frank Brangwyn. 'Back
Him Up. Buy War Bonds', UK,
1918. Lettered: *Auto-lithograph
by Frank Brangwyn, A.R.A.*
E.2318-1918

'CARELESS TALK COSTS LIVES'

A Series of Eight Posters issued by the Ministry of Information in February 1940

Fougasse (Cyril Kenneth Bird)

Fougasse's gossiping cartoon characters (plates 143 to 150) injected some welcome humour into British government propaganda posters in February 1940, and their popularity set a new tone for official mass communication. Despite an extended and illustrious career as a cartoonist, illustrator and commercial poster designer, it is probably for his 'Careless Talk Costs Lives' posters that Fougasse is best remembered today.

The first government posters of the war had been a failure: their text-only format, pompous language and the enormous cost of the campaign had alienated many and given rise to much criticism. The Ministry of Information commissioned Mass-Observation[15] to discover the reasons for the public's dissatisfaction. This detailed study, which measured individual responses to each particular poster, revealed that most people did not identify with them and, therefore, did not feel the messages were aimed at them personally.[16] It also revealed that the posters against careless talk had hardly registered at all. Language such as, 'Warning. Do not discuss anything which might be of national importance. The consequences of any such indiscretion may be the loss of many lives', was far removed from the personal significance of, for example, whether a loved-one was sailing tonight or tomorrow.

The Ministry of Information prepared the trial design of a small poster for Mass-Observation to test in pubs and bars. This time the text was in rhyme, with the refrain, 'Keep It Dark', and fitted to the catchy rhythm of 'She'll be coming round the mountain, when she comes'. Here at last was a poster in a popular idiom, and in principle it received overwhelming approval.[17] From there it was only a short step to cartoons.

Many of Mass-Observation's interviewees had requested images: 'The ordinary man in the street needs something more than words to help him',[18] and several people even cited Leete's Lord Kitchener poster (see plate 157) from the previous war. But humour, and cartoons in particular, were what most people wanted: '... need ... cartoons. Cheer us up a bit, there's no community spirit without that.' One of the observers went so far as to comment that people seemed to 'yearn for humour'.[19]

Fougasse, who was art editor of *Punch* when war broke out, offered his services to the government free of charge[20] and produced propaganda material for almost every ministry. He believed that the unifying quality of humour (in which the common understanding of the joke

CARELESS TALK
COSTS LIVES

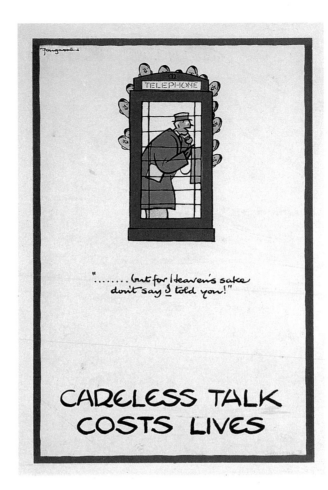

CARELESS TALK
COSTS LIVES

CARELESS TALK
COSTS LIVES

CARELESS TALK
COSTS LIVES

143. 'Don't forget that walls have ears!' E.2167-1946

144. '... but for Heaven's sake don't say I told you!' E.2168-1946

145. 'Of course there's no harm in your knowing!' E.2169-1946

146. 'Strictly between you & me ....' E.2170-1946

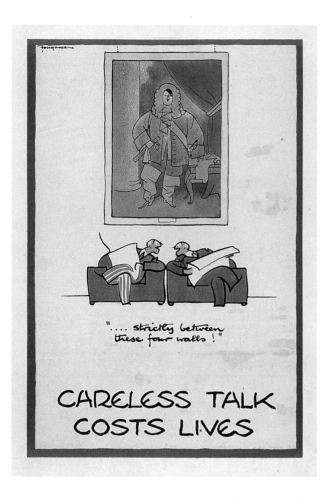

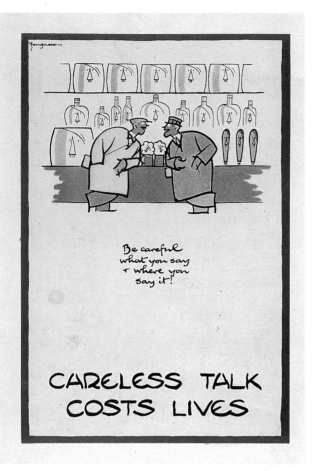

147. '... strictly between
these four walls!'
E.2171-1946

148. 'Be careful what you
say & where you say it!'
E.2172-1946

149. '... but of course it
musn't go any further!'
E.2173-1946

150. 'You never know who's
listening!' E.2174-1946

creates a bond) rendered it ideal for persuasion without causing resentment. He was right. His 'Careless Talk' cartoons were so popular that they were even reproduced on handkerchiefs and dress fabrics (examples are held in the V&A's Department of Textiles and Dress).

In his analysis of humour, *The Good-Tempered Pencil*, Fougasse explained how kindly humour can make the individual 'aware of his ridiculousnesses either through the inner glow of his own sense of humour or the exterior illumination of that of others'.[21] In the 'Careless Talk' posters he made the chattering men and women look foolish because of their irresponsible behaviour. But the real point was more subtle – losing control of the information. Fougasse tried to convey through his captions the compounding nature of gossip, and in his BBC talk on 12 February 1940, 'Strictly Between These Four Walls ...', described it in simple but effective terms: '... in passing on a bit of news you cannot possibly say with truth "Strictly between you and me ...". All you *can* say is "Strictly between *you* and *me* and everyone *you* are going to tell and everyone *I* am going to tell and everyone *they* are going to tell and not only *them*, but everyone else who happens to overhear in the process".' He had already designed a stick-on label (plate 151) for telephone cradles so that lifting the handset would reveal a caricature of Hitler listening, while the slogan, 'Careless Talk Costs Lives', faced the speaker.

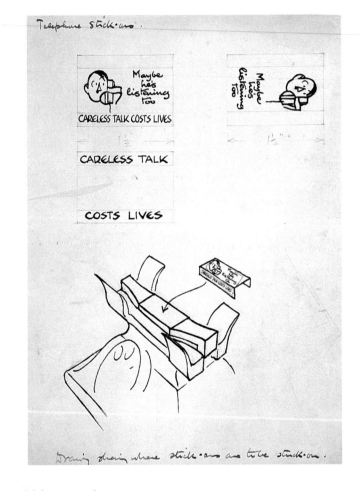

151. 'Careless Talk Costs Lives. Maybe he's listening too.' Pencil and indian ink on board. E.172-1976

Preliminary sketches for a telephone stick-on label, c. 1940.

The posters posed a greater challenge. People had to be persuaded to read them, to be convinced that the message applied to them personally, and then motivated to act on it. Fougasse had already created a basic design for maximum impact in his commercial posters, and presented his government posters in a similar idiom. The red border and white space surrounding each image isolated it from the 'fruit salad of advertisements covering the walls of our stations'.[22] Fougasse then engaged the viewer fully by deliberate intrigue.[23]

Each cartoon, drawn in Fougasse's characteristic and well-known style, presented an everyday situation with which a passer-by could identify. Its simple shapes and bright colours, and the main slogan in capital letters, could be seen from a distance, but in order to enjoy the joke, the viewer was forced to come near enough to read the small caption and then to participate intellectually by drawing his own conclusions. This personal contribution was, Fougasse believed, the key to remembering the message and carrying it out. Since the posters were to be voluntarily displayed, following the public outcry against the cost of the first poster campaign, and in indoor locations (except at railway stations), the posters had to be desirable. The humour made them attractive for display in shops, pubs, restaurants, factories, etc., while the variety of images ensured that the public would not become bored with the message.

The 'Careless Talk Costs Lives' campaign was launched in February 1940 and constantly reinforced throughout the war,[24] both for the public and for the forces. It included a variety of poster designs and graphic techniques by different artists and encompassed every form of publicity, including film and broadcasting. The Ministry of Information had responded to criticism, and the new tone of official mass communication used everyday imagery, colloquial language and catchy slogans. In embracing popular idioms, especially humour (plate 152), the government bound the nation together and boosted morale. John Gloag, writer and design historian, called humour during the war 'Britain's Secret Weapon'.[25]

In his BBC talk, broadcast a few days after the publication of his posters, Fougasse justified his use of humour for such a deadly serious subject. By placing it within a British cultural context he explained its emotional function of enabling people to deal with the difficult truths they do not wish to confront. It is precisely their lack of realism that enables cartoons to communicate powerful ideas in a non-threatening manner.

Fougasse's rendering of Hitler and Goering successfully conveyed the serious consequences of indiscretion, while his skill in showing people how *not* to behave enabled them to see themselves and learn the lesson without humiliation. The then Princess Elizabeth once remarked, 'How carelessly we should have talked during the war but for Fougasse'.[26]

153. Abram Games. 'Your Talk May Kill Your Comrades'. Issued by the War Office, UK, 1942. CIRC 297-1971

Unusually for a propaganda poster, this shows the death of an Allied soldier. Whilst dramatic, it also makes an appeal to reason by illustrating the consequences of thoughtless gossip. Games invented a very literal and powerful graphic device to represent how sensitive information might circulate.

152. Henry Mayo Bateman. 'The Wife Who Squandered The Electricity', UK, 1943. E.158-1973

Bateman was well known for his cartoons illustrating anti-social behaviour. This poster is one of a series including 'The Husband Who ...' and 'The Brother Who ...' issued by the Ministry of Fuel and Power.

'I WANT OUT'

An anti-Vietman War Poster published anonymously by The Committee to
Unsell the War, USA, 1971

Protest against the Vietnam War, which had subsided in the late 1960s, surged with renewed vigour on university and college campuses when President Nixon announced in 1970 the spread of US military involvement to Cambodia, bringing the war in Indo-China once again to the forefront of American politics. *I Want OUT* (plate 154) was published in 1971 as part of a nationwide, multi-media donated campaign to accelerate the withdrawal of US troops from combat.

The concept of a publicity campaign to 'Unsell the War' had been generated by Ira Nerken, a political science student at Yale University, after a nationally broadcast CBS documentary, 'Selling the Pentagon'. This programme had exposed not only the range and extent of the US Defense Department's propaganda activities but also its manipulation of the press and even of the news itself.[27] Nerken concluded that as it was possible to 'sell' the war to the nation, then surely it must also be possible to 'unsell' it.[28] His introduction to David McCall, the president of LaRoche, McCaffrey & McCall, a large New York advertising agency, turned this idea into action. McCall and McCaffrey mobilized the support of the advertising community and formed a committee to organize a major campaign. The brief was for 'advertising in all forms that will help unsell the war .... we are not interested in cheap, superficial, anti-American work. We are interested in thoughtful and honest advertising, created by people who love their country.'[29]

Designs were submitted for approval, and after evaluation by a panel that included the president of Yale, a retired marine general and a former US ambassador to Japan, they were published at a press conference. Media space and time were donated, and *I Want OUT*, the only poster in the campaign, addressed Americans from billboard sites all over the country.[30] An unexpected avalanche of requests for reproductions indicated the extent of popular support. Without the manpower or financial resources to cope, the committee licensed a New York publishing house to reissue the poster[31] and handed the campaign over to Clergy And Laymen Concerned, a religious anti-war organization with an established nationwide structure.

In this poster the voice of the people is expressed through the iconic figure of Uncle Sam. The original Uncle Sam was a real person, a well-liked and respected provisions merchant of Troy, New York, called Samuel Wilson, who supplied the US Army during the War of 1812. He was formally acknowledged by the Senate on 15 September 1961 as 'the progenitor of America's

154. Daniel and Charles Agency:
originator and copywriter: **Larry
Dunst**; art director: **Murray Smith**;
photographer: **Steve Horn**.
'I Want OUT'. US poster, first
published anonymously by **The
Committee to Unsell the War,** 1971;
poster reissued and distributed by
Darien House Inc. E.365-1973

I WANT OUT

national symbol of 'Uncle Sam'.[32] Legend has it that a joker suggested that the letters 'US' (to denote United States), which were stamped on the barrels of meat for the army, stood for 'Uncle Sam', and so it began to be applied by the soldiers to everything in 'Uncle Sam's army'. Use of this term by the troops is documented in a Troy newspaper in 1813, and soon federal government employees in Washington claimed to be working for Uncle Sam. By association with Samuel Wilson, who seemed to 'epitomize the plain American – honest, self-reliant, and devoted to his country',[33] Uncle Sam gradually became established in American folklore as the personification of the United States.

155. Anonymous. 'A Family Quarrel'.
Caricature in *Punch, or The London Charivari*, 28 September 1861, p.127.

In this British view of the American Civil War, the figure symbolizing the northern Union States already manifests some features later adopted to characterize Uncle Sam.

His pictorial representation, however, originated in cartoons. He evolved from the fusion of Brother Jonathan, a British caricature of the typical American (as a counterpart to John Bull or Britannia) with the symbolic northern American Yankee Doodle. Recognizable as a tall, thin character with clothes featuring the stars and stripes, the Uncle Sam we know today acquired his characteristic beard and became more or less standardized through the cartoons of Thomas Nast in *Harper's Weekly* during the 1870s.[34] However, it was James Montgomery Flagg's Uncle Sam on his recruiting poster of 1917 (plate 156) that imprinted itself on the minds of the nation and became a cultural icon. The subsequent satirizing and parodying of this image rendered it a

156. James Montgomery Flagg.

'I Want YOU for U.S. Army',

USA, 1917. Photolithograph.

Imperial War Museum

cat. no. 2747.

powerful vehicle for expressing national dissent. Flagg's Uncle Sam, a self-portrait, wore the costume the artist had made for the purpose,[35] and presented Uncle Sam as a real person, a strong authority figure with whom the viewer could identify, just as in Britain Alfred Leete's famous 1914 recruiting poster had presented Lord Kitchener (plate 157). The emotional appeal of this poster, addressed personally to each viewer, gave an immediacy and urgency to the message and made it highly effective. Although Flagg did not acknowledge Leete's influence, it is almost inconceivable that he had not seen the poster, at least in reproduction. Susan Meyer, a respected Flagg biographer, comments, 'For an artist who freely dispensed ideas, he did not hesitate to borrow either. How well the idea was handled was far more interesting to him than its origin.'[36]

Exposure in both world wars made Flagg's Uncle Sam the best-known American poster of all time, symbolizing the pride, vigour and optimism of America. *I Want OUT* reverses Flagg's recruiting poster, both conceptually and visually, and its power lies in its automatic evocation of the original, which invites a direct comparison. Here, even the model photographed as Uncle Sam bears an uncanny resemblance to Flagg himself; still addressing the viewer, he is now, however, a white-haired old man, wounded and weary from years of fighting, who has lost his former vigour. The beseeching attitude of his hand, enlarged as if reaching out from the picture plane, inverts the original pointing gesture, and his urgent call for enlistment has now, ironically, become a plea to be released. His hat, once worn with pride, is crushed under his arm and his uniform is in tatters.

This image of enfeeblement was, at the time, iconoclastic and shocking. The poster presented uncomfortable truths: American military power was not supreme, and the injured Uncle Sam was a bold reminder of the high cost of American lives, one of the issues most likely to motivate anti-war popular support.[37] He was also a metaphor for the nation's wounded pride.

It is difficult to assess the impact of 'Unsell the War' on the acceleration of America's withdrawal from Vietnam. It came at a time when support for the anti-war protest movement was growing. Revelation of the My Lai massacre (see plate 125, chapter 3) had shamed and shocked the nation; April 1971 saw a weekend of protest by Vietnam war veterans, who threw their medals on to the steps of the Capitol, followed by the largest civilian anti-war demonstration on record since 1969.[38]

Uncle Sam was mercilessly pilloried in popular culture for the sacrifice of American lives (plate 158) . He became 'the enemy of a people no longer heeding his call to arms or willing to die in a senseless massacre far from home, and fed up with the abusive authority and barbaric atrocities he came to represent.'[39] The ferocity with which he was attacked reflected the strength

157. Alfred Leete. 'BRITONS [Lord
Kitchener] Wants YOU', UK, 1914.
Photolithograph and letterpress.
Imperial War Museum cat. no. 2734.

158. Anonymous. 'I Want YOU For
U.S. Army', USA, c. 1972.
Imperial War Museum cat. no. 2524.

This bitter parody of Flagg's World
War I recruiting poster was published
by Personality Posters, Inc.

of popular feelings and was born, paradoxically, out of love of
country; such posters adorned walls in homes throughout the
land, reflecting society's increasing will and power to shape the
world in which we live. As the cheapest and most accessible
form of art, the poster is often at the vanguard of change. And
because of its intimate relationship with our everyday lives it is
also an important and powerful political weapon.

'56.10.23 [23 OCTOBER 1956]

Péter Pócs

Published independently by the artist in Hungary, 1989

Péter Pócs's poster (plate 159), commemorating in its title the 1956 popular Hungarian uprising crushed by Soviet forces, portrays in no uncertain terms the end of Communism. The red star, symbol of the Red Army, is held powerless in a reversal (expressed through the date written backwards) of the events of 1956. The smaller size of the '1989' indicates that, although the revolution has finally succeeded, the year is arbitrary – it was bound to happen sooner or later. This feeling of inevitability reflects the artist's awareness of the new political situation and his desire to make an active contribution to the change away from Communism.[40]

The poster was published on the occasion of the memorial ceremony for the reburial of Imre Nagy, the Hungarian statesman who led the revolutionary government of 1956, and the other executed revolutionary leaders. The public staging of this event in Heroes Square on 16 June 1989, its attendance by Prime Minister Miklós Németh, although not by Hungarian Socialist Workers' Party (the Communist party) officials, and its nationwide television broadcast amounted to an official acknowledgement of the political rehabilitation of the dead men. The impact of this event on the nation cannot be overestimated, since it symbolized the ultimate success of the revolution begun in 1956. Although the poster had originally been commissioned by one of the new political parties, the Alliance of Free Democrats, when they saw the design they were afraid to publish it. The artist therefore went ahead on his own, challenging the censorship regulations which forbade publication by individuals.

Communism in Hungary was not overthrown in 1989 by a popular revolution. Rather, the transition to democracy was the inevitable outcome of a gradual lightening in the political atmosphere, which had gathered momentum when the Hungarian Socialist Workers Party reformed itself in 1988 and paved the way for increasing liberalization. The most significant changes had been early in 1989, when the Party had not only agreed in principle to a multi-party political system but also officially re-evaluated the events of 1956 as a 'popular uprising' rather than as a 'counter-revolution' and admitted that the leaders had been wrongly executed. This crucial decision turned into a political trap in which the Communist regime found itself mortally wounded.

159. Péter Pócs. ''56.10.23' [23 October 1956] Hungary, 1989

Photographed by László Haris. E.153-1991

160. Péter Pócs. '1er Expo en France de

Péter Pócs' ('Péter Pócs's First Exhibition in

France'), Hungary, 1988. Photographed by

László Haris. E.149-1991

Pócs's imaging of the destruction of the red star to express the erosion of Communist power had begun with the poster advertising his first exhibition in France, in August 1988 (plate 160). Rusty old farm implements, symbolizing a bygone era, lie against a crumbling wall, on which hangs a red star that is beginning to rot. But it was his poster *Hasonlat* ('Simile'; plate 161) that catapulted him to fame and demonstrated the political power of a poster. Ostensibly an advertisement for an exhibition by Péter Stefanovits, it communicates its main message in the crucified red star, already in the throes of death. Strict regulations governed the publication of work, 'but,' said the artist, 'there were always ways of cheating the system if you wanted to communicate with the people'. The poster was printed without official approval and pasted up in streets all over the country in what the artist called, 'a little revolution by the art world'.[41]

The authorities tried to remove the offending image but, since their grip on the media had weakened, they were unable to suppress the reporting of their activities on national television news. Ironically, this coverage gave the image maximum exposure for several days and had a powerful impact on the political atmosphere. In making concrete an intangible truth the artist had rendered it the reality. It was a sequel to the earlier public act of iconoclasm, the burning of Stalin's image, described in the previous chapter (plate 88). Pócs's articulation of a longed-for dream made it seem attainable, and its message struck deep into the soul of the nation. The fact that this image was freely shown on television revealed the changing political situation and encouraged other artists. Among them was Krzysztof Ducki, whose exhibition poster a few

161. Péter Pócs. 'Hasonlat' ('Simile'),

Hungary, 1988. Photographed by

László Haris.

Published by the Novotoys Publishing

House. E.146-1991

months later (plate 83, chapter 2) portrayed the sinking battleship *Aurora*, once a proud symbol of the 1917 October Revolution but now signifying the loss of power.

'56.10.23 expressed a political truth. But it was also Pócs's own philosophical statement on the inherently flawed nature of Marxism and Leninism, which he saw only as theories, unable to work in long-term practice.[42] Having conceived the poster as a social document, Pócs therefore constructed an image made from real objects. The background floorboards are typical of a domestic loft or cellar – the kind of place where a mousetrap is kept, rusting away, until needed.

The red star in the poster is raw meat: the artist wanted to render Communism as a live force, in order to convey its active oppression as well as its demise. He therefore persevered with the difficulty of cutting from frozen meat a star good enough to use, since each tended to lose its shape when defrosted! The raw flesh caught in the trap is disturbing. Glistening in the strong light, it seems to writhe in agony as the metal bites. The force with which the red star is held, therefore, seems to express the artist's – and the nation's – passionate feelings of relief and, even, revenge after the years of oppression.

Pócs deliberately challenges the flat paper form by creating an illusion, which he describes as 'optical cheating', when a 'live, 3-dimensional object becomes a 2-dimensional reality.'[43] His working methods aim to lend plasticity, and therefore life and immediacy, to his printed images, which maximizes their impact. First he makes the models to be depicted and paints them. They are then strongly lit to enhance the colours and emphasize the form, and photographed from three different angles, chosen by him, to vary the lighting and mood. The selected image is printed and then over-painted, adding the extra depth and vitality to the printed poster image. A perfectionist, Pócs controls every aspect of production, even to the point of making adjustments to the colours at the printing stage. Such commitment reflects his emotional involvement in his work, and it is this dimension which lends conviction and therefore power to his posters. Katalin Bakos, a Hungarian art historian, says, 'Pócs throws his whole soul into the posters. His works are aggressive. They shout, roar, mock insomuch that we cannot pass them indifferently.'[44]

162. Anonymous. 'The Red Ploughman', Soviet Russia, 1920. E.2444-1921

This Bolshevik poster expounds the new Communist ideology through the destruction of Tzarist symbols. Aimed at the mainly rural population, it adopts the style of a traditional *lubok* (folk woodcut) to convey its message. The lettering in Cyrillic reads: 'On the wild field amid the ruins of evil Lordship and Capital we shall drive our plough and gather the good harvest of happiness for the whole working people!'.

At the time, in 1989, *'56.10.23* could be seen only in exhibitions. Although the artist would infinitely have preferred it to be seen on the streets, because 'I really do believe that posters are the art of the streets,'[45] he was confident that the vast exhibition attendances and the television arts coverage resulted in its being seen by a significant proportion of the population. By defying the censor and publishing the poster, Pócs was conscious of helping to change history. His visual imagery aimed to undermine the power of the regime, and give strength to those who demanded democracy by encouraging them to believe it could and would happen.

István Orosz, a Hungarian poster designer (see plate 89, chapter 3) and film animation director, said, 'It is common knowledge that revolutions are not made by professional politicians, especially not in these parts .... It is the writers, the poets, the artists who are likely to be at the forefront.'[46] There is no doubt that in Hungary the power of the poster contributed to the crumbling of the Communist regime. It is ironic to think that posters, which became a political instrument in the service of Communism, should ultimately have accelerated its downfall.

163. **Valentina Kulagina. '1905. The Road to October', USSR, 1929.**

Published by State Publication, Moscow, Leningrad. E.1274-1989

Valentina Kulagina, like her husband, **Gustav Klutsis, was an exponent of photomontage. This Soviet propaganda poster commemorates the suppressed Revolution of 1905, an important staging post to the triumphal Revolution in October 1917. The overthrow of the Tzarist regime is expressed through the trampling of its symbols by the Constructivist figures.**

PART III

COMMERCE AND COMMUNICATION

5 COMMERCIAL ADVERTISING AND THE POSTER FROM THE 1880s TO THE PRESENT

JULIA BIGHAM

The pictorial commercial poster burgeoned in the 1880s, following significant innovations in chromo-lithography and the expansion of advertising.[1] Of particular significance was the advent of the 'artistic poster', which dominated advertising in France by the late 1880s and 1890s and had a dramatic influence on the rest of Europe and America. Furthermore, this revolutionary breakthrough was widely acknowledged by all contemporary sources to be due to the work of one man, Jules Chéret.[2] It was Chéret who redeemed colour lithography from a mere reproductive process to an artist's medium – and having seen his work, a number of artists, including such avant-garde masters as Bonnard and Toulouse-Lautrec, decided to experiment with both posters and colour prints.

The conferral of high art status on the poster in France in the 1890s came after a much wider debate beginning in the 1860s which questioned the hierarchy of the arts previously established by the academies, where fine arts were elevated over applied and popular arts. The debate was led by two groups – the Indépendants and critics who sought to apply Republican democratic ideals, and the promoters of the decorative arts, in particular the Union Centrale des Beaux-Arts appliqué à l'Industrie, who wished to become accepted within the academies' conservative value system. The poster benefited from both arguments, although the latter group eventually elevated it to high art status as a result of the work of Chéret.

In 1889 Chéret was made Chevalier of the Légion d'Honneur for 'creating a branch of art, by applying art to commercial and industrial printing'. By the 1890s some art dealers were specializing in posters, and periodicals such as *L'Estampe et l'Affiche* reviewed posters as well as commissioning them for collectors (plate 164). The decision of Paris, the art capital of the Western world, to accept posters as an art form was conclusive. Now poster artists elsewhere in Europe and America 'did not have to concern themselves with their artistic legitimacy'.[3]

Equally important for the profession of poster artists and the role of posters in advertising for the next 50 years was the fact that Chéret 'altered the concept of advertising from illustration and description of a product to sales through sensual appeal of colour and design'.[4] Chéret was always keen to communicate to his biographers[5] that his first consideration was for his numerous

164. Pierre Bonnard. 'L'Estampe et L'Affiche', France, 1897. E.151-1921

clients, ranging from bookshops, publishers, department stores and shops (such as the Magasin des Buttes Chaumont), pharmaceutical and cosmetic manufacturers, makers of lamp oil (Saxoléine; plate 165), sewing machines and other appliances, to railway companies and resorts, and also to billstickers and printers' distributors. Although

165. Jules Chéret. 'Saxoléine. Pétrole de Sûreté', France, 1891. E.123-1921

repetition was a common advertising strategy in the nineteenth century, Chéret's clients admired his work so much that they would commission different designs from him rather than repeat the same poster.

Alphonse Mucha was another among many poster artists who helped to establish the high reputation of French 'artistic' posters. Czech born, he came to Paris in 1887 and was initially involved in illustration and poster design for financial reasons, but despite thinking of himself primarily as a painter, he was later glad 'to be involved in an art for the people'. According to his son, his main reason for giving up posters was exploitation by his printer, Champenois. Printers were dominant in poster design; they had commercial businesses to run, and Champenois insisted on a contract obliging Mucha to work exclusively for him, and execute all his commissions, in return for the generous sum of over 30,000 Frs a year. Champenois was hoping to upgrade his business to include higher quality work for larger firms, and Mucha was therefore asked to design for such prestigious clients as Bières de la Meuse (see plate 11 in Introduction), the cigarette paper manufacturer Job (plate 166) and the biscuit manufacturer Lefèvre-Utile. Champenois also re-sold Mucha's designs to different commercial clients, making slight modifications, and therefore ensuring maximum financial returns. The pressure of work on Mucha was immense and was intensified by his design methods, which were those of a painter: he made preliminary life studies, worked up full-scale designs, traced them on to the stone and meticulously hand coloured the first proofs.

166. Alphonse Mucha. 'Job', France, 1897. E.583-1953

Poster advertising cigarette papers.

Competition between printers led to a number of them issuing their own advertising posters, including Charles Verneau, an enthusiast of the 'artistic' poster and *affiche murale*. He commissioned Théophile Steinlen to execute one of the artist's favourite subjects, an enormous street scene, called *La Rue* (plate 167), and advertised his business simply by the sheer quality of the press-work: the glowing colours, the enormous size (2.38 x 3.4 metres; 7 ft 10 ins x 11 ft 2 ins) and the perfect registration of the six sheets.

An early poster historian, Ernest Maindron, whose *Affiches Illustrées 1886-1895* was published in 1896, collected over 10,000 posters. In his writing he emphasized the role of the artist rather than of the client, but set out the factors governing the costs of commissioning a poster: the

artist's fee (according to reputation), the size of the print run, the tax stamp (according to size) and the billsticker's fee (according to location and duration). Maindron stressed the importance of choosing the right billstickers and of placing the poster in the correct area for the target audience. Commerce and art too were linked by the English collector Joseph Thacher Clarke in 1894: 'Undoubtedly the commercial poster still exists in France, but the most astute advertising agent, looking at the matter from the commercial point of view, finds that the really artistic work pays better in cash results'.[6]

The earliest Belgian posters, influenced by French work, were by avant-garde artists; commercial posters evolved from the mid-1890s. Many advertised coffee and cocoa, products of

167. Théophile Steinlen.

'La Rue', France, 1900 C.601 1037

Poster for the printer Charles Verneau.

Belgium's flourishing trade with its empire. An outstanding example is the famous poster for Rajah Coffee (1897; plate 168) by the illustrator and print-maker, Henri Meunier, showing how quickly the printers had learnt the new skills of commercial lithography. Like their French counterparts, many Belgian artists such as Privat-Livemont and Victor Mignot drew directly on the stone. This practice and the high-quality printing contributed to the inclusion of Belgian posters in the 'artistic' poster movement. Henri van der Velde, later a founder of the Deutsche Werkbund (1907), took poster design further: he designed a poster and packaging for the food manufacturer Tropon and moved from realism to more abstract forms; shapes and colours evoked the egg white and yolk, as well as the three sparrows' trademark of the manufacturer (plate 169).

The 'artistic' poster was adopted in Italy only at the end of the 1890s. The music publisher Ricordi commissioned nearly all the leading poster artists, such as Adolfo Hohenstein, Giovanni Mataloni, Leopoldo Metlicovitz (plate 170) and Franz Laskoff, as well as printing high-quality commercial posters. Hohenstein and Metlicovitz emphasized the heroic subject. For example in Metlicovitz's poster celebrating the opening of the Simplon Tunnel of 1906, a winged mythological

168. Henri Georges Meunier. 'Rajah',

Belgium, 1897. E.440-1939

Poster advertising coffee.

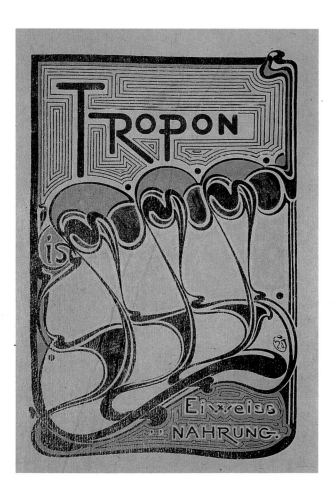

169. Henri van der Velde. 'Tropon',

Germany, 1897. CIRC 992-1967

Poster for processed egg whites.

170. Leopoldo Metlicovitz. 'Olio
D'Oliva', Italy, c. 1905-10. Printed by
G. Ricordi & Co., Milan. E.406-1982

figure sits on the front of the train as it emerges from the tunnel
(plate 74, chapter 2). Other commercial advertisers commissioned
artists who worked in a more decorative, linear style, with solid
blocks of colour, such as Franz Laskoff (plate 171).

Advertising in Britain expanded considerably during the nineteenth century, largely due to
the growth of manufacturing and developments in press advertising. Posters became recognized
by leading manufacturers as commercially essential, and humble advertising agents were
transformed from selling advertising space for the newspapers to large group agencies offering
specialist services, including design. The repeal of heavy newspaper and advertisement taxes in
the 1850s led to an enormous expansion of publicity, particularly with the advent of national
campaigns in the new daily papers. Packaging and branding of goods were introduced, and

171. Franz Laskoff. 'Caffaro', Italy,
c. 1898. E.1414-1963

Poster for a periodical.

competitive brands used advertising extensively in order to differentiate their products from those of their rivals (plates 172 and 173).

Some very large advertisers ran their own publicity directly, using agencies only for placing press advertising. The most obvious examples were the two soap barons, T.J. Barratt of Pears Soap and Lord Leverhulme of Sunlight, who heralded 'artistic' advertising in Britain. Besides using the work of fine artists, 'artistic' advertising was characterized by a dominant image, with copy kept to a minimum. The most famous example is that of J.E. Millais' *Bubbles* (plate 174), which Barratt bought for £2,200 from the editor of *The Illustrated London News* in 1886. With the addition of a bar of soap and the name of the company, Barratt created a high-quality chromo-lithograph advertisement. The print, which used over 25 lithographic stones to attain its subtle colouring, was then presented to Millais for his approval. Many contemporaries praised its fine reproduction.[7] His son, however, claimed that Millais was horrified that his work was being used as an advertisement,[8] and a number of commentaries in journals like *The Magazine of Art*[9] focused on this issue of the degradation of art. Thus in the 1880s many artists were discouraged from contributing to advertising, but others felt that it brought art on to the streets. Barratt himself stated: 'I maintain that we personally can do more good for the spread of art and culture than your Royal Academy or your endless galleries'.[10] For Pears, 'artistic' posters were effective advertising,

172, *left* **Nathaniel Lloyd & Co. (Printers). 'Lazenby's "Chef" Sauce and other delicacies On Every Table', UK, 1910. E.67-1973**

173. Leonetto Cappiello. 'Cirio', Italy, 1923 E.86-1973

These posters depict numerous examples of contemporary packaging.

appealing to its targeted middle-income customers, but they were not the only technique employed by Barratt to establish Pears as a household name: he used catch phrases ('matchless for the complexion' and 'Good Morning! Have you used Pears Soap Today?') and testimonials, such as from the actress Adeline Patti, and he also staged elaborate stunts. His main aim was to equate soap with the product Pears.

During the same period Lord Leverhulme, who spent over £2 million on his soap publicity, was a collector of English paintings. He used some of these in advertising, for example John Baron's *The Wedding Morning* (1892) and William Powell Frith's *New Frock* (1889), mainly with slight adaptions or changes in title. Biscuit manufacturers also used art. Peek Frean adapted a painting by T.B. Kennington, originally called *The Toy Shop* (1891), to depict a group of children gazing at the biscuit packets in the shop window (plate 175).

'Artistic' advertisements, however, were greatly outnumbered by the mass of undistinguished posters on the hoardings. For this reason the poster exhibition at The Royal Aquarium in 1894-95 received wide press coverage. It showed over 200 posters by French artists, such as Chéret, Lautrec and Bonnard, and a small

171. Sir John Everett Millais. 'Bubbles', UK, 1886. Chromolithograph of the painting before conversion into the Pears' advertisement.   E.1660-1931

175. Anonymous. 'Peek, Frean & Co.'s Biscuits London', UK, c. 1891. Poster after the painting *The Toy Shop* (1891) by Thomas Benjamin Kennington. E.2256-1983

Biscuit manufacturers made early use of eye-catching labels for tins and packaging.

selection of British work. The organizer, Edward Bella, was aiming at an audience of collectors and, more significantly, advertisers. He printed commercial posters and also acted as an agent finding suitable designs for advertisers. Thus he exhibited some speculative designs, including the work of The Beggarstaffs (James Pryde and his brother-in-law, William Nicholson).

For The Beggarstaffs, poster designing in the 1890s was an artistic challenge, and they devised an innovative technique using collage and stencils to produce simple, bold compositions with no extraneous detail. Some of their work was 12-13 ft high, and they worked slung from ladders rather than using easels. Although they preferred painting, they thought posters would provide an income. They began by imitating the practice of printers and took designs to advertisers. It was not until they began to use the Artistic Supply Company as their agent, however, that they were successful. This company advised them to design a speculative poster for Rowntree's new advertising for Elect Cocoa. The company described it as 'striking' and 'original' and used it in two sizes nation-wide, having paid The Beggarstaffs £30 (plate 176). The Beggarstaffs would never compromise on the integrity and simplicity of the total composition, so their commercial posters contained no 'reason-why' copy, additional information or illustration of product packaging. Rowntree's got round this potential marketing problem by presenting the poster as a puzzle, and the accompanying press advertising challenged people to guess the subject.

Some found The Beggarstaffs' work too stark and 'gloomy' and preferred colourful, lively posters by Dudley Hardy. His first poster for Jerome K. Jerome's *To-Day* magazine in 1893 depicted a woman in a yellow dress, subsequently nicknamed 'The Yellow Girl'. Hardy's biographer, A.E. Johnson, wrote:

> The effect was startling and no advertisement ever achieved its purpose more simply or more completely. The Yellow Girl refused to be ignored. There was something almost immodest in the way she danced, with mincing steps along the decorous streets of London.[11]

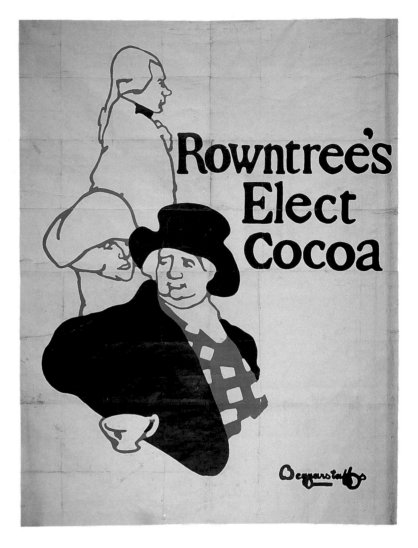

176. The Beggarstaffs (James Pryde and William Nicholson). 'Rowntree's Elect Cocoa', UK, 1896. E.1209-1927

178. John Hassall. 'Skegness Is SO Bracing', UK. First published in 1908 by Great Northern Railway; reissued by LNER, c. 1925. E.1326-1931

The Poster magazine frequently referred to Hardy as the English pioneer of 'artistic' advertising. He was the link between the French 'artistic' poster pioneered by Chéret, whose women had inspired Hardy, and a new, characteristically English approach: the use of little, if any, background, few details, bold colours, clear outlines and integrated lettering (plate 177).

Like Hardy, who influenced him, John Hassall was also a painter, an illustrator in black and white and a poster artist designing for the printers David Allen & Sons for seven years. In *Pearsons Magazine* (16 March 1905), Hassall listed the essentials for a successful poster, emphasizing the need for simplicity and bold colours in England's misty climate. It 'should catch the eye, or, to put it more strongly, should hit the passer-by right in the eyeball. This is best attained by a huge splash

177. Dudley Hardy painting his design for *To-Day* magazine, 1893.

of one colour ...'. He did not, however, discuss the humour of his characters, which made his posters so memorable (plate 178).

Hassall, Hardy and The Beggarstaffs strove to create posters that were both artistically edifying and commercially successful. Most criticism voiced by artists in *The Poster* was aimed at advertisers: they rarely had a clear initial idea, but later wanted to make radical changes which ruined the artist's composition and concept; and they were deeply suspicious of new ideas. W.S. Rogers in 1899 wrote of advertisers who 'would rather I made a base imitation of a hackneyed design, than produce an original idea of my own'.[12] Finally they often wanted to add lettering, to the detriment of the design.

By the 1880s, agencies were designing and laying out press advertisements. By the turn of the century, a number of the larger agencies in Britain, including Mather & Crowther and S.H. Benson's, also offered elaborate 'outdoor advertising' facilities. Samuel Herbert Benson set up in 1893 to introduce a new concept of total campaign management, including efficient distribution of stock and registration of trade marks. Immediately successful, he soon became a chief spokesman for advertising.

Benson's publications between 1901 and 1915 show how far advertising strategy had progressed.[13] In his *Facts for Advertisers* (1905), he estimated that for a 'commanding' display of posters in greater London, 32,800 double crown sheets would be required and 8,000 advertising stations. In about 1912, he published a detailed analysis of the structure and functions of the agency. The Outdoor Advertising Department would be involved in every campaign from the outset, deciding the numbers of posters in appropriate towns, selecting suitable hoardings and negotiating with the contractors. The Studio would then work on the designs. Once the posters were printed, the warehouse would sort, send out or store them, and a nation-wide network of inspectors would periodically examine the hoardings for the duration of the contract, feeding back local information to the London office. By 1912 Benson had created the first market research department in an agency, the Trade Development Office.

Benson stated that poster designs must be suited to the 'policy' or campaign. Early on the Studio was called in either to design the posters or to contribute by 'criticizing' and improving designs submitted by printers or outside artists. In the large top-lit studio five 16-sheet posters could be designed at the same time, and there would be extensive discussions between the Studio, the directors and the clients. The Literary Department would work with the designer on the copy. 'Thus the evolution of a poster ... takes place in an atmosphere of constant suggestion, criticism and improvement. No trouble is too great to take, provided it will make the finished poster a more efficient instrument for the purpose for which it is intended.'[14] Benson believed all this must take place under one roof.

The founding account for Benson was Bovril, whose owner first suggested that Benson should open the agency; as a result the new product was successfully launched and established as a household name. The campaign involved spectacular stunts and competitions as well as press and outdoor advertising. Its most famous early posters, including W.H. Caffyn's '*Alas! My poor brother*' (plate 179), and '*Wherever did I put that Bovril?*', were, as was customary in the early days, all bought in from printers. The same images would be used for the posters, colour throwaways, black and white advertisements and plaster models for shop window display. Benson however also believed in collaboration: 'The poster-artist should work in close co-operation with the thinking advertising man, should understand the object he is after and work to it'. His favourite example was the Louis Weierter poster for Edwards' Desiccated Soup of 1901, whose appealing homely character became so identified with the product that she was later also used on the packaging. By 1900, at Benson's and elsewhere, commercial posters were part of a larger campaign, and were being designed by specialist poster artists.

As in Britain, the early history of the American advertising agency was closely related to press advertising. By the 1890s the modern agency offered services including planning, advice on media, copy, illustration, design and print production. Among the pioneers were Lord & Thomas, N.W. Ayer & Son and J. Walter Thompson, but research and art departments in the agencies were the norm only at the beginning of the twentieth century. By 1906, *Printers Ink* could describe Madison Square as 'the new hub of the advertising universe'.[15]

Historically, imagery for posters came from printers, and American advertising drew on a tradition of high-quality chromo-lithography among German immigrants, skilled, technically qualified craftsmen and draughtsmen trained in formal composition and near-photographic realism. This tradition persisted through the 1890s, by which time 700 printing firms had sprung up, employing 8,000 people with a

179. Anonymous. '"Alas! my poor Brother"', UK, c. 1905. Based on the orginal design of 1896 by W.H. Caffyn. Printed by the Avenue Press. E.147-1973

180. Anonymous. 'Willimantic Spool

Cotton', USA, 1887. E.2887-1980

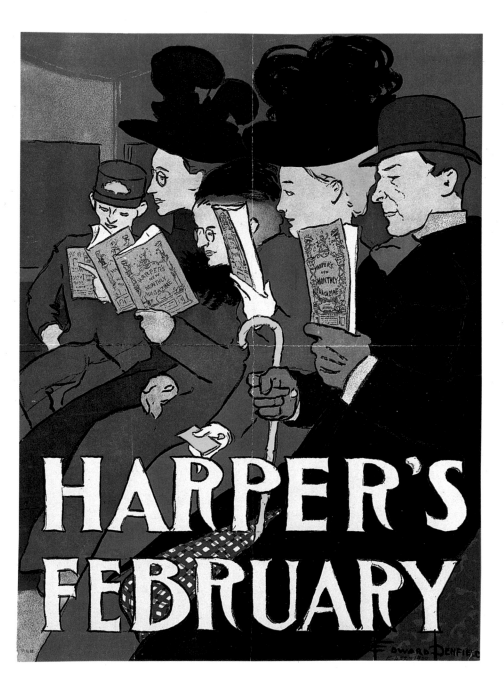

181. Edward Penfield. 'Harper's February',

USA, 1897. E.452-1939

yearly production worth $20 million. Part of their work was for ever-increasing advertising, in particular for soap and patent medicine manufacturers, and part was the mass reproduction of oil paintings. In some advertisements they were able to combine the two, adding the advertiser's name to a high-quality chromo-lithograph of a painting (plate 180). However an innate conservatism meant that, according to a contemporary, 'year after year the same old pictorial horrors were scattered [across] city and country'.[16]

A change in American poster advertising in the 1890s was led by book and magazine publishers, who knew the value of good illustration. They were aware of the French 'artistic' poster (Grasset was commissioned by *Harper's Magazine* in 1889) and recognized the need for distinctive images to distinguish, for the leisured, educated and wealthy classes, their productions from the rapidly expanding mass of publications. In April 1893 *Harper's Weekly* began issuing monthly posters for display on newsstands and in bookstores, all drawn by their art director, Edward Penfield, who designed, laid out and supervised production for all Harper's and Brothers' publications (plate 181). Penfield's designs were a complete contrast to the printers' realistic detailed imagery with stippled shading and were distinguished by sensitive pen outlines, blocks of a limited number of colours and simple compositions, often of a single figure reading. These posters inspired other publishers such as Scribner's, The Century and Lippincott's to follow suit. The posters were all small, on average 19 x 14 ins; they were printed on the publishers' own presses and signed by the artists. Both the large publishers and the small literary ones commissioned a wide range of artists, including unknown young artists and a number of women: Ethel Reed was 19 when she designed her first poster. Competitions also attracted new talent: in 1896 The Century Company's competition for a poster for its Midsummer Fiction Number was won by Joseph Leydendecker, and the second prize by Maxfield Parrish (plate 182), whose poster was used the following year.

182. Maxfield Parrish. 'The Century
Midsummer Holiday Number. August',
USA, 1897. E.85-1925

Bicycle manufacturers too were conspicuous in American advertising. The widely publicized introduction of the safety bicycle in the late 1880s created a bicycling craze. By 1898, bicycle promotion constituted 10 per cent of all national advertising, and leading artists such as Edward Penfield (who worked for Stearns, Orient and Northampton cycles), Maxfield Parrish (Sterling) and Will Bradley (who produced at least four posters for Overman Wheel Company's Victor bicycle; plate 183) were commissioned. The status of the poster artist, however, remained ambivalent. Even Will Bradley, who had trained in the printing trade, wrote that he would not call Edward Penfield a 'poster artist' as 'such a title leaves an

183. Will. H. Bradley. 'Victor Bicycles', USA, 1896. E.414-1921

184. Edward Penfield. 'Hart Schaffner & Marx Clothes for men', USA, c. 1910. E.130-1925

unpleasant impression on the mind and one prefers to speak of him simply as Edward Penfield Artist' (plate 184).[17] A number of artists continued to believe that advertising products, particularly on billboards, tarnished their reputations.

The majority of products in the 1890s were advertised on billboards about 10 ft high or on enormous painted or electric signs. Billboard posters were generally produced by printers' studios, whose antipathy to 'artistic' advertising was emphasized in the trade journal *Billboard Advertising* which described the work of Bradley and Penfield as 'weird and hideous'.[18] It was a rapidly expanding business. There were hoardings in the cities and on suburban and country roads, and from the 1880s on transport, particularly on street cars. To promote national advertising, a regulatory and co-ordinating body, the Association of Billposters, was founded in 1891, and by the 1920s it had graded hoardings, standardized rates and had established a directory of members and voluntary controls.

185. Anonymous. '"Force" The Wheat-Malt Cereal', **USA**, c. 1903. E.56-1973

These hoardings promoted soaps, cereals and other highly competitive, mass-produced goods. Many posters featured brand characters. Perhaps the two best known cereal characters were the Quaker Oats' 'Quaker', and 'Sunny Jim' for Force, the latter created by the advertising agent Earnest Elmo Calkins for the manufacturer Edward Ellsworth. The Sunny Jim campaign included press advertisements, story books and posters, and had immediate short-term success: the first trial month, costing $25,000, doubled sales, and Sunny Jim became as well known a character as Robinson Crusoe (plate 185).[19]

By 1905 most US advertising agents had art departments run by an art manager where specialist artists familiar with the relevant technologies and aesthetics focused primarily on communicating the message graphically. The use of free-lance artists, like Maxfield Parrish, gradually became exceptional, the agency artists thereby becoming part of the emerging modern advertising profession with its specialized jargon and techniques. By 1918 the American Association of Advertising Agents could describe the functions of the agency as: studying the product, analysing the market, distribution and sales, buying space, seeing through production (including writing and designing advertisements), checking display and auditing accounts.[20]

In addition, in the 1920s many of the outdoor advertising companies also had art departments, for example the General Outdoor Advertising Company, which covered the eastern USA. Work from both the agencies and the outdoor advertising companies tended to focus, however, on conservative, realistic illustrative techniques and ignored European Modernism. The outdoor advertising expert at J. Walter Thompson stated: 'our public does not take to the German type of flat colour poster, preferring more realistic pictures such as those used by Camel or Palmolive'.[21] Thus, when European artists Lucian Bernhard and A.M. Cassandre went to America at the height of their reputations in the 1920s and 1930s, their work was not well received, while that of Ludwig Hohlwein was instantly successful (see plates 187, 189 and 191). Furthermore, agencies put most of their energy into press advertising.

In France, Leonetto Cappiello bridged the gap between the 'artistic' poster of the 1890s and the modern poster. In a career of over 40 years he produced 3,000 posters and influenced the next generation. Initially his posters reflected his work as a caricaturist but after 1903, with his poster for Chocolat Klaus, he began using bold compositions, with bright contrasting colours. He also began to associate the product with an often fantastical figure or animal which would become a type of brand character. For Chocolat Klaus he invented a women in a green dress on a red horse. Café Martin was represented by a Turk jumping out of a cup (plate 186). The designs, some of which were being repeated for over 20 years, stood out through their use of these dynamic figures on a plain background, leaping or dancing towards the spectator. The majority of his clients were drink manufacturers, but he received all his commissions through his printers, Devambez.

The work of the next generation of designers began to appear in the mid-1920s. A.M. Cassandre (real name A. Mouron) thought he was taking on his 'pen name' for only a short interlude in his painting career while he experimented with posters. He made a sharp distinction between the individual lyricism of painting and the poster, which he described as:

> a utilitarian art. It strives to do away with the artist's personal characteristics, his idiosyncrasies and traces of his personal manner. It is meant to be a mass-produced object existing in 1000s of copies – like a fountain pen or automobile. Like them, it is designed to answer certainly strictly material needs. It must have a commercial function.[22]

His style reflected the impact of Cubism – 'Some people have called my posters cubistic. They are right in the sense that my method is essentially geometric and monumental ...' – but he saw architecture as his influence. He always emphasized that the lettering was central to the design, but his best known precept was:

> The poster is only a means, a means of communication between the seller and the public – somewhat like a telegraph. The poster artist is like a telegrapher: he does not DRAFT messages, he DESPATCHES them .... all he is asked to do is to communicate clearly, powerfully and precisely.[23]

186. Leonetto Cappiello. 'Café Martin', France, 1924. E.15-1926

187. A.M. Cassandre.

'Etoile du Nord',

France, 1927. E.224-1935

Cassandre's first railway posters were commissioned in 1927 by Maurice Moyrand, whose father was a director of the Chemin de Fer du Nord, and who was the agent for the printer L. Danel of Lille (plate 187). During the 1920s and 1930s, Cassandre received many poster commissions from manufacturers, shipping lines, railways, shops and newspapers, and in all cases he adopted a more Modernist approach and departed from realism.

German artists created their own particular style at the turn of the century. Manufacturers commissioned posters from printers as there were no advertising agencies in Germany until the 1920s, when Dorland's and Crawford's arrived. The leading printing firm in Berlin was Hollerbaum & Schmidt, which created a very distinctive style of poster. Its own publicity posters emphasized the new importance of its artists; their signatures were given equal prominence with the printers' name. It formed a studio of high-calibre artists, such as Lucian Bernhard, Julius Klinger (plate 188), Edmund Edel, Julius Gipkens and Hans R. Erdt. In 1902 Bernhard devised a new style of poster in which the product was portrayed in splendid isolation, accompanied only by its name (plate 189); he drew both elements directly on to the stone as one integrated composition. Many artists associated with the printers followed his example, the effectiveness of their work much depending on high-quality printing and richness of colours. This style remained popular until the outbreak of World War I. Ludwig Hohlwein's approach was very different (plate 191); he started in 1906 and for the next 40 years in Munich and the USA continued in a realistic style, depicting carefully composed isolated groups of figures or animals. He worked on his own but had an enormous and popular output. By 1924 he had produced over 3,000 posters for a wide range of clients.

188. Julius Klinger. 'Lustige Blätter', Germany, 1907. Printed by Hollerbaum and Schmidt. E.616-1915

Poster for a satirical magazine.

189. Lucian Bernhard. 'Stiller', Germany, 1907-8. E.928-1966

Poster for Stiller shoes.

During the 1920s and 1930s the professional graphic designer gradually emerged in Germany. From 1928, Otto Arpke (plate 190), for example, had his own studio with ten employees, and from 1928 was professor of commercial art in Munich and Berlin. Considerable impetus was given by the Modernist teachings of the Bauhaus. By the late 1930s however the impact of National Socialism was evident, and heroic realism became the acceptable style (plate 192).

Social change after World War I in Britain, as elsewhere, was profound. Increased production and expanding markets led to an ever greater need for advertising. The International Advertising Convention, held in 1924, established a new code of ethics, and was seen as 'the commencement of the effective organisation of British Advertising'.[24] American techniques such as behavioural psychology and market research were widely disseminated, although not universally accepted by British advertisers until the 1930s.[25] Nevertheless, five main US agencies were based in London, and one, J. Walter Thompson, expanded enormously in the 1920s. UK advertising expenditure rose from an estimated £31 million in 1920 to £59 million in 1938.

190. Otto Arpke. 'IPA Internationale Pelzfach-Ausstellung' (International Fur Exhibition), Germany, 1930. E.1332-1931

191. Ludwig Hohlwein. 'Marco-Polo-Tee', Germany, 1910. E.361-1921

Poster for a brand of tea.

192. **L. Heinemann. 'Germany, the Land of Music', Germany, c. 1938.** E.144-1961

In poster advertising, many of the techniques devised in the previous decade persisted – for example the use of humorous brand characters who became family favourites. Now, psychology and research confirmed the rapid impact of images and the value of the association of ideas. In 1920 the International Advertising Exhibition at White City included a 'Pageant of Publicity', a procession through the streets of London of such brand characters as Bubbles, the Kodak Girl and the Michelin Man: the message was 'Advertising Benefits the Buyer' (plate 193). S.H. Benson in particular invented further brand characters, such as the Rowntree's Cocoa-Nibs children. These,

193. Frederick Charles Herrick.
'Underground to Wood Lane:
International Advertising Exhibition
At The White City', UK, 1920.
E.455-1921

and a very British type of humour (for example, plate 201), distinguished Benson's work. A brand character was generally linked to a slogan devised by copywriters. In *BOVRIL Prevents that sinking feeling* (1920; see plate 222, chapter 6) the copy accompanying H.H. Harris's pyjama-clad man was devised by Oswald Green, who used the phrase a 'sinking feeling' from a free Bovril booklet (1890) which advised golfers to keep well nourished when playing. The slogan and the pyjama man were to crop up regularly in the next 20 years.

The copywriters at Benson's were called the Literary Department until 1939, and a number were writers, working in advertising temporarily, such as Dorothy L. Sayers, who based Pym's Publicity in her novel *Murder Must Advertise* (1931) on her experience at Benson's. Others were professionals, such as Oswald Green, and a new generation of Oxbridge graduates, like Robert Bevan who joined Benson's in 1923.

Benson's artists were either in-house, freelance or working for printers. Tom Purvis designed a number of posters for Bovril, such as *Bovril Keeps You Going* (1915); the artwork was the actual size of the 16-sheet poster and painted in oils on canvas. He may have been freelance or commissioned via the printers, Avenue Press, for whom he then designed part time. John Gilroy worked in-house. He had studied at the Royal College of Art, where he began designing posters and teaching part time after the war; one day's work at Benson's was worth a week's salary in teaching. In 1929 he began on the Guinness campaigns with the copywriter Robert Bevan and art director Dicky Richards. His Guinness characters included the anthropomorphic pint (from 1933) and the famous girder man (1934) illustrating '*Guinness for Strength*'. They were followed by the zoo-keeper series (from 1935; plate 194), devised after a visit to Bertram Mills' Circus with its performing sea lion. He depicted himself as the zoo-keeper. The series continued with new animals, drawn from life at Regent's Park Zoo, up until the 1950s. Gilroy generally drew his designs to 30 ins, not full scale as was normal practice, and restricted himself to five or six colours, instead of ten or more, and the background was always white to emphasize the figures. The posters were 'reminder advertising' that 'Guinness is good for you' and focused on good humour.

W.S. Crawford's was another leading London agency but, unlike Benson's, its advertising revealed a greater awareness of the Modernist movement in Europe. William Crawford's dynamic and forceful personality is conveyed in his booklet for prospective advertising men and women, *How to Succeed in Advertising* (1931):

> Advertising is a great force when it is used for the good of the people – the common man and the common woman. He, the ordinary man, is the focal point of all our endeavours. It is he who makes history. It is he, who by buying, creates trade and work and wealth.

194. John Gilroy. 'Keep Smiling', UK, 1936. E.131-1973

'My Goodness My Guinness' (sea lion), first issued 1935 and adapted for World War II. E.129-1973

'My Goodness My Guinness' (ostrich), 1936. E.152-1973

'My Goodness My Guinness' (pelican), c. 1939. E.132-1973

John Gilroy was art director at S.H. Benson

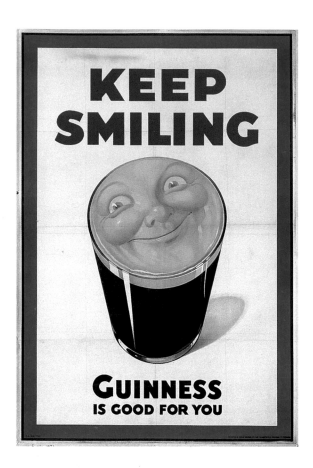

Crawford studied methods in the USA and realized the importance of research, including consumer research, and behavioural psychology. He believed that advertising was for the young and energetic, those with a fresh outlook, including women who could identify with the important female consumer.

Ashley Havinden joined Crawford's in 1921 as a junior trainee layout man; within two years he was an art director and in 1929 a member of the Board. Instead of working in the Studio, Havinden was allowed to form a team with the young account executive Margaret Sangster and, in 1924, the copywriter G. H. Saxon Mills. They endorsed the ideas of the Bauhaus, such as the use of asymmetry and white space as part of a dynamic composition: Havinden felt this offered a new freedom and a break from traditional layouts.[26] His first opportunity came with the account of the Chrysler Corporation; in order to emphasize speed and performance, he used an asymmetrical layout and got rid of all extraneous detail, including the company name-block. In 1927 the team devised a campaign for ENO's Fruit Salt. The imagery used in both poster and press advertisements depicted three horsemen whose lancers carried banners bearing the copy (plate 195). The asymmetrical layout created a dynamic yet unified design, and the sense of movement suggested the beneficial effect of the product on health.

Following such successful campaigns, Chrysler put Crawford in charge of its European advertising and the firm opened offices in Germany and Paris. Although they were soon forced to close because of the American Depression and the rise of Nazism in Germany, Crawford maintained links with France and Germany. He employed

195. Ashley Havinden. 'First Thing Every Morning Renew Your Health With Eno's "Fruit Salt"', UK, 1927. CIRC 456-1971

Havinden was art director at W.S. Crawford Ltd.

Jean Carlu and Cassandre, among others. These links influenced his own artists, such as Havinden and E. McKnight Kauffer, who worked part time for Crawford 1927-29. During this period Kauffer's style moved away from 'Jazz age and Archaism' to a more Modernist idiom, with greater use of photomontage. He stood out from other British commercial artists in his working practices and professional outlook; he designed standing up at his German adjustable architect's desk and used expensive artists' materials and the flexible rulers and set squares soon associated with the professional designer; the rest of the studio worked at tables with poster paints and shiny white hot-pressed boards.[27]

196. Hans Schleger (centre), Terence Prentis (left) and Tony Page (right) discussing a campaign, probably in Crawford's Berlin office, 1928.

This shows how designers' working methods in the 1920s differed from those of poster artists in the 1890s (see plate 177), in particular the impact of German modernist design practice.

Kauffer was seen as a leader of the new profession. He arrived from America in 1914 and was in Britain until the outbreak of World War II. He generally worked freelance, occasionally taking up short-term, part-time posts, as with Crawford's. He produced about 250 posters as well as paintings and a wide variety of design work. He was a committee member of a number of professional bodies such as the Society of Industrial Artists (founded 1930); in 1936 the RSA made him the first Honorary Designer for Industry. His statement of 1938 indicates his attitude to advertising: 'The artist in advertising is a new kind of being ... it is his business constantly to correct values, to establish new ones, to stimulate advertising and help to make it worthy of the civilisation that needs it'.[28] Paul Nash in 1935 stated that Kauffer was 'responsible above anyone else for the change in attitude towards commercial art in this country'.[29]

Frank Pick was responsible from 1908 for the London Underground's publicity for trains, trams and buses. He began by commissioning posters through the printers; thus many pre-1920 posters were unsigned. Initially posters aimed to encourage commuter travel on the new lines to the suburbs, then they began to promote off-peak travel – visits to the theatre in the evenings and into fresh country air at the weekends (see plate 229, chapter 6). In the 1920s, Pick defined the purpose of his advertising as:

> the establishment of good will and good understanding between the passengers and the companies .... To create a feeling of restlessness, a distaste for the immediate surroundings, to revive that desire for change, which all inherit from their barbarous ancestors ...[30]

By the 1920s Pick was commissioning artists directly and London Transport had become an important patron, particularly of young artists (plate 197). He bought twice as many designs as he could use, his main criterion being the Design for Industry Association's 'fitness for purpose'. Over 40 posters were commissioned a year, and 1,000 copies of each were printed. After Pick's retirement in 1940, Nikolaus Pevsner described him as 'the greatest patron of the arts whom this century has so far produced in England, and indeed the ideal patron of the age'.[31]

Pick's work inspired other clients. The railways were reorganized in 1921 into four main companies: London & North Eastern Railway (LNER), Great Western (GWR), London Midland & Scottish (LMS) and Southern; each had its own advertising manager and a different approach to advertising. In 1923 LMS launched its main poster campaign, under the guidance of the painter Norman Wilkinson. It consisted of the oil paintings of 18 Royal Academicians. Although designed as posters, they were essentially reproductions of oil paintings which were displayed on special boards on station platforms. At about the same time the manager of LNER, William Teasdale and his successor Cecil Daindridge, commissioned a large number of commercial artists and RAs working in different styles to create much more extensive and exciting poster campaigns. They focused on seaside resorts, inland and inter-continental attractions and 'reminder advertising' promoting the main routes, such as King's Cross to Scotland. Between 1926 and 1932 they also contracted five commercial artists to work exclusively for them: Austin Cooper, Frank Mason, Frank Newbould, Tom Purvis and Fred Taylor. The last, arguably the most popular with his depictions of historic towns and cities, was paid considerably

197. Vera Willoughby. 'General Joy',

UK, 1928. E.940-1928

Poster for the London General
Omnibus Co.

more than the others. Yet Tom Purvis's series were the most widely praised by the critics. *The Observer* wrote (17 March 1929): 'He understands the value of elimination and of rendering any subject in its simplest forms and bare essentials. His effective flat patterns explain the design in a flash' (plate 198). His second 'East Coast Joys' series (1931), a set of six which could be shown separately or together in a single composition, had great impact on the hoardings.

Southern Rail used posters extensively in the 1930s on completion of the final electrification of the lines. The slogan 'Southern Electric' was used, and artists generally emphasized the sense of speed, portraying the railway as modern and progressive. In contrast, the Great Western concentrated on other forms of advertising, although, in 1933, it did produce a famous set of posters by McKnight Kauffer depicting Devon and Cornwall.

In the 1920s, Shell advertised extensively through the British branch of the American advertising agent Lord & Thomas, through the press and some posters. Heeding the protests of SCAPA (The Society for Checking the Abuses of Public Advertising) against poster hoardings and obtrusive signs along the roadside, Shell began attaching posters to the sides and backs of lorries. In 1932 Jack Beddington became publicity director of the amalgamated Shell-Mex and BP Ltd, although posters advertised Shell and BP separately. A man of strong ideas and

198. Tom Purvis. 'East Coast by L.N.E.R.', UK, 1925. E.744-1925

inspired by Frank Pick, he first employed Stuart Advertising to produce high-quality humorous advertisements by Rex Whistler and John Reynolds, but commissioned the lorry bills himself. Shell's name was now linked with the pleasure of motoring, and more generally with the pleasures of nature and of art. One of its most extensive series depicted British landmarks, with such slogans as 'See Britain First on Shell' or 'Everywhere You Go You Can be Sure of Shell'. Another popular campaign claimed that a wide range of people, from photographers to scientists, used Shell: for example 'You Can be Sure of Shell – Footballers Prefer Shell' by Paul Nash (plate 199).

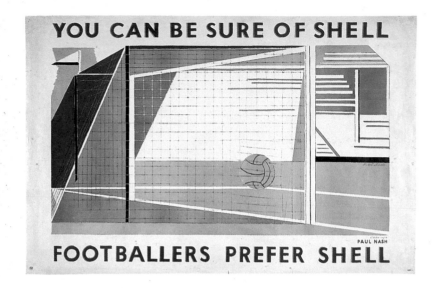

200. Edward McKnight Kauffer. 'BP
Ethyl Controls Horse-Power', UK,
1933. CIRC 317-1971

The slogan 'You Can be Sure of Shell' aimed to promote good will towards the company and assure the motorist that Shell was available throughout Britain. The lorry bills were changed every few weeks, so many artists were involved. They included established artists such as Vanessa Bell, Tristram Hillier and Graham Sutherland (see plate 230, chapter 6), young artists working in a traditional British landscape idiom, specialist poster artists such as Tom Purvis, Hans Schleger and McKnight Kauffer, as well as such artists as Paul Nash who were anxious to close the gap between fine artists and artists working in design and industry. In the 1930s, Kauffer's more Modernist work was confined to BP; he used photomontage, dynamic rectangles and asymmetrical lettering to emphasize power and movement. In *BP Ethyl Controls Horse-Power* he combined his own night photograph of the statues from the Place de la Concorde with a flash of lightning against a black background to highlight the technical virtues of anti-knock fuel and horse-power (plate 200). Beddington's use of artists and emphasis on landscape for Shell campaigns was part of a carefully targeted scheme to win the support of the primarily middle-class customer, who not only appreciated art but, in this period, was being rallied by action groups such as CPRE (Council for the Preservation of Rural England) and SCAPA to ban unsightly advertising in the countryside.

The successful publicity of the railways, London Transport and Shell encouraged the British government to use posters. The Empire Marketing Board was set up in 1926 under the chairmanship of Sir Stephen Tallents to promote the sale of Empire produce in the UK and

Did you MACLEAN your teeth to-day Daisy ?

It's a cert, Gert.

201. Anonymous. 'Did you Maclean your teeth to-day Daisy? It's a cert, Gert', UK, c. 1938. E.124-1973

Poster advertising toothpaste and featuring the comedy act of Elsie and Doris Waters.

encourage Empire trade (see plate 100, chapter 3). William Crawford and Frank Pick were brought in to advise, but after a brief period of intense commissioning, the EMB was disbanded. Tallents went to the Post Office, where he again used some of the best poster artists, a policy that continued until well after World War II (plate 202), and the government had a pool of artists ready for its propaganda during World War II. All these prestigious sources of work boosted the professional status of the commercial artist.

In Japan, in the nineteenth century, posters had been either coloured woodcuts or painted on cloth or paper, and it was not until the early twentieth century that full colour lithography became a practical option. At that time Japanese department stores were among the most extensive users of advertising, and their posters were portraits of beautiful Japanese women often in traditional costume. In the 1920s and 1930s, however, the West had a radical impact on Japanese

202. Hans Schleger. 'Think Ahead — write instead', UK, 1945. E.534-1985

Poster issued by the General Post Office.

posters. A number of designers travelled to Europe and brought back examples of graphics, as well as descriptions of the organization of the profession in Europe and the USA. These trips were often followed by exhibitions and publications, and thus Japanese artists became familiar with Dada, Russian Constructivism and the Bauhaus. Hisui Sugiura's work for Mitsukoshi Department store shows him moving from realistic Bijin-ga to Matisse-like depictions of women and integrated typography. Gihachiro Okuyama, in his series of posters for the Nikke clothing store throughout the 1930s, reflects the impact of German Expressionism and Constructivism: his nervous

203. Gihachiro Okuyama.

'Nikke', Japan, c. 1935.

E.184-1935

Poster for a clothing shop.

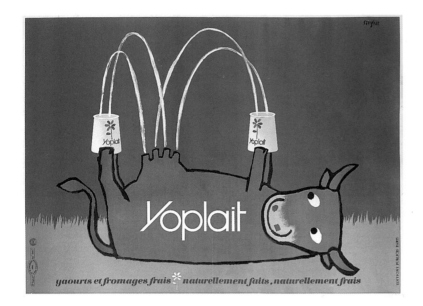

204. Raymond Savignac. 'Yoplait',

France, 1967. E.598-1981

Poster advertising a brand of

yoghourt.

205. Herbert Leupin. 'Pause. Trink Coca

Cola', Switzerland, c. 1954. E.627-1981

pen showed the influence of George Grosz, which alongside Japanese woodblock tradition was used to create dynamic compositions of abstract figures and lettering, which was no longer confined to a straight vertical (plate 203). The European Modernist style was deemed especially suitable for such new products as record players and cars.

In the 25 years after World War II the poster was radically transformed. Autographic artwork was gradually replaced by photography. The commercial artist became the graphic designer, and most commercial posters were designed by creative teams within advertising agencies. A crucial factor in this change was the advent of commercial television advertising in the 1950s. Television became the primary advertising medium, thereby lowering the status of posters within campaigns and leading to numerous posters which were simply photographic stills from commercials.

During the war commercial advertising was much reduced and hoardings were commandeered by the government. Poster artists either enlisted or worked on propaganda, except in occupied Europe. Rationing and paper shortages

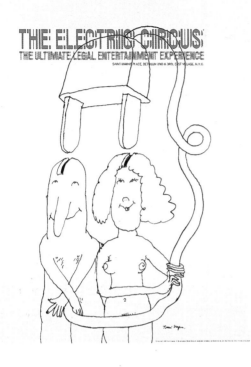

meant that commercial posters did not reappear until the end of the 1940s, when those that made most impact focused on humour. Raymond Savignac was seen as the master of the 'visual gag', as in his Yoplait poster (plate 204). His career was launched in 1949 with Montsavon soap. This is made from milk and so he depicted the bar of soap being formed from the udders of an amused purple cow. Commissions from all over Europe followed, well into the 1960s. Another prolific designer was Herbert Leupin in Switzerland, who conveyed his humour by his cartoonist style of drawing, often juxtaposed with photomontage and innovative use of typography (plate 205). Illustrated humorous posters continued to be popular into the 1960s, but were not widespread. In many cases they were designed by illustrators and caricaturists (plate 206) or for newspapers by their own staff (plate 207).

The American Push Pin Studios, founded in 1954, were famous in the 1950s and 1960s in the USA and Europe. The founding members were the illustrators Seymour Chwast and Milton Glaser but they were joined at various times by others. Their work, characterized by freedom from graphic conventions and a willingness to experiment, often incorporates imagery from the history of art and graphics. This approach was combined with individualistic drawing styles, such as Milton Glaser's use of delicate line and watercolour washes to create almost surreal spaces (plate 208).

During the war the British government provided many freelance commercial artists who had set up in the 1930s with opportunities to design official posters. Abram Games disliked the anonymity and lack of total responsibility for a design in the work of a studio, so he set up on his own in 1935. He won commissions from Shell, London Transport and the Post Office in the 1930s,

206. Tomi Ungerer. 'The Electric Circus', reissue of a poster advertising a rock palace, first issued USA 1969. E.426-1973

207. Charles Santore. 'Bring 'em up short', quote Newsweek, USA, 1966. E.320-1973

206

208. Milton Glaser.

'From Poppy With Love',

USA, 1967. CIRC 225-1972

Poster advertising

Poppy Records.

but established his reputation during the war. He designed recruitment posters and was the only Official War Poster Designer. Other designers working for the Ministry of Information include F.H.K. Henrion, Milner Gray and Hans Schleger.

After the war, Games continued to receive many commissions. His personal maxim was 'maximum meaning; minimum means'. His poster for the prestigious Orient Line, publicizing cruises to Australia, is an almost surreal interpretation that closely binds the image and lettering (plate 209). Perhaps more typically however, his commercial posters carried their messages through

humour. He continued to produce posters until the 1980s, but he was aware that his type of work had become marginalized. In his essay *Over My Shoulder* (1960), he bemoans the increasing power of motivation research, the consequential loss of initiative for the poster artist and 'the end of truly creative design'. Games and a few other British poster designers, such as Tom Eckersley, did maintain their high reputations but were no longer part of mainstream commercial advertising, which was dominated by advertising agencies.

Other wartime poster artists, in particular the émigré designers F.H.K. Henrion and Hans Schleger (Zéró), began to see themselves as graphic designers. They formed design studios and took on new areas of work. Henrion, who described posters as 'the most glamorous, most artistic' medium for a designer ('You could sign a poster'), and who had built up a considerable reputation during the war, was one of the first to foresee their displacement by television. In 1949, he set up Studio H and began working on house styles for companies. The movement towards working in studios meant that larger projects could be undertaken. Furthermore, young graphic designers found that corporate identity work for prestigious clients enhanced their professional reputations.

209. Abram Games. 'Orient Line to Australia', UK, 1951-52. E.197-1952
Poster advertising Orient Line passenger cruises.

A few large European companies had commissioned corporate identity schemes from designers since early in the century, for example Peter Behrens for AEG (1907), but new schemes were commissioned in the 1950s in particular by the Container Corporation of America (manufacturers of paperboard containers and cartons) and Olivetti. After the Depression of the early 1930s, the owner and president of CCA, Walter Paepcke, decided that the company needed a distinctive visual corporate image. Advised by his recently appointed art director, Egbert Jacobson, the agency N.W. Ayer & Son and his wife Nina, Paepcke was persuaded that the leading exponents of Modernist design, Herbert Bayer and Herbert Matter among others, should design the advertisements. The final series, called 'Great Ideas of Western Man', which ran from 1950 to 1980, was the most ambitious, controversial and long lasting. It grew out of Paepcke's involvement with Chicago Great Books Club, organized by Chicago University president Robert Hutches and philosophy professor Mortimer Adler. Paepcke employed Adler to choose quotations, which were then matched with work by contemporary artists, including Herbert Bayer, René Magritte and Ben Shahn. The success of these campaigns was reflected in rising sales and in the perception of the company as a prestigious business with unique advertising and strong cultural commitments, initiated by the personal interests of its founder (plate 210). Curators even held exhibitions of the work in their museums. The example of the CCA led other companies (Dole Pineapple, De Beers Diamonds and the American Tobacco Company) to follow its example.

Adriano Olivetti, son of the Italian Olivetti company's founder, set up the Advertising and Development Office in Milan in 1931. He gathered together painters, graphic designers, poets and architects, but employed many as freelance consultants so that they remained in touch with the art scene. He encouraged them to experiment in design as well as to link the company with contemporary cultural trends. The very distinctive Olivetti graphics appeared in the late 1940s and 1950s when the painter Giovanni Pintori designed a remarkable series of posters. In some he used collage, bright colours and witty graphic devices on plain white backgrounds (plate 211), and in others he used conceptual photography. Since the 1930s Adriano Olivetti's schemes had expanded to embrace modern architecture for new factories and staff facilities, as well as publishing, particularly magazines, on the arts and social sciences. All these activities gave Olivetti world-wide recognition, and inspired many other companies, in particular IBM. The Museum of Modern Art in New York exhibited some of the typewriters and posters in 1952. After Adriano Olivetti's death the cultural activities continued, while the company adapted itself to the electronic age. In 1969 Ettore Sotsass designed the Valentine portable typewriter specifically for the youth market. The posters depicted the machine being used outdoors, such as on the beach, as well as

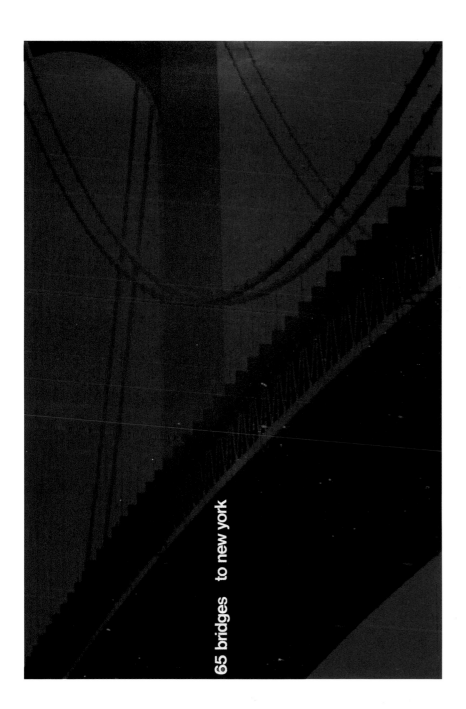

210. Tomoko Miho. '65 bridges to new york', USA, 1968. E.420-1973

Poster for the Container Corporation of America.

211. Giovanni Pintori. 'Olivetti Lexicon', Italy, 1953. CIRC 634-1965

in private domestic spaces (plate 212). Another key poster campaign was entitled 'Save Our Planet', a series of six posters by such famous artists as Georgia O'Keefe, Roy Lichtenstein and Alexander Calder, part of a UNESCO ecological campaign in 1971 and a useful public relations exercise for the company.

During the 1950s, a number of outstanding graphic designers emerged in Japan, including Yusaku Kamekura. They aimed to establish design as a profession in Japan and to win international recognition for their work. Kamekura abandoned Japanese traditions to achieve a more universally recognizable abstract language. A key industrial client was Nippon Kogaku, manufacturer of Nikon cameras, and in his earliest posters for Nikon Kamekura achieved his own individual style. In 1957, for the Nikon SP camera, he used Western typography as though it were composed of abstract forms (plate 213), and for the company he employed a limited range of bright colours on a black background. His work won numerous awards, and following its success he founded (with Hiromu Hara and Ryuichi Yamashiro) the Japan Design Centre to encourage industrial clients, such as Asahi Breweries and Toshiba Electric, to use leading graphic designers working in the Centre. It had limited success because of the low standard of printing technology until the early 1960s. From then on, large commercial clients, led by Shiseido and Suntory as well as the department stores, began making extensive use of posters, in particular colour photographic posters.

In the 1950s and 1960s American advertising changed. 'New Advertising', or the 'Creative Revolution', affected both the appearance of advertisements and also the structure of agencies. The 'father' of 'New Advertising' was William

212. Tadaaki Kanasashi. 'Study And Love', Japan, c. 1975. E.1528-1979

Poster for the Valentine typewriter issued by Olivetti Corporation of Japan.

Bernbach, co-founder of the agency Doyle Dane Bernbach in 1949. His key campaign, for Volkswagen, began in the late 1950s. The VW advertisements, through the use of ironic humour, drew attention to a flaw in the product and then emphasized its many good points, such as engineering and economy. The caption 'Think Small' accompanied a small black and white photograph of the car in a large white space (see plate 223, chapter 6). The design characteristics making the advertisements stand out were: short, disarming headline; simple black and white photograph of the product, with no unnecessary settings, and further copy confined to the bottom of the page.

DDB pioneered the use of creative teams where copywriters and art directors were involved in discussions with the client from the beginning. Bernbach believed intuition, provocation and humour led to effective advertising, in contrast to other agencies in the 1950s where market research and demographics dominated thinking. Within most agencies, account executives were superior to copywriters and art directors, and this led to much mediocre, safe advertising. Following Bernbach's example, agencies began to restructure, the status of the creative teams increased and creative directors set up their own agencies. Gradually the old Ivy League network in advertising was broken, and increasing numbers of Jewish, Greek, Irish and Italian copywriters and art directors were employed. Both in the large agencies and in the new 'boutiques', or small agencies, the creative teams provided a fresh outlook and ideas; they also impressed clients that they could reach a wide section of the population (plate 214). Some of the smaller agencies were set up by those who had worked at DDB, such as George Lois, who after a year formed the innovative Papert, Koenig, Lois.

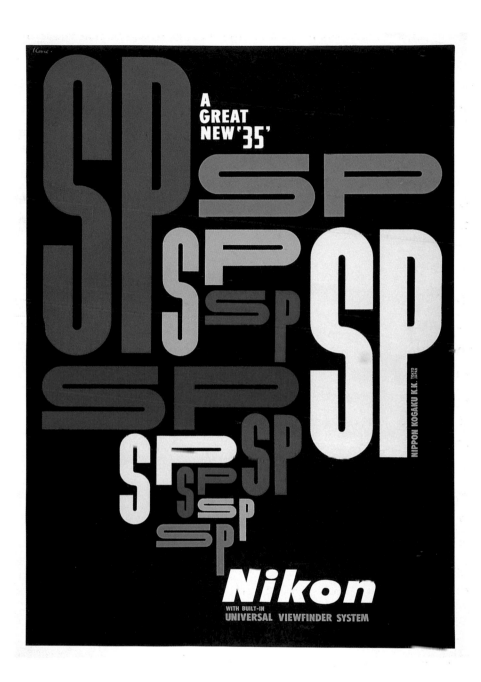

213. Yusaku Kamekura. 'A Great New "35" SP Nikon', Japan, 1957. E.760-1963

Poster advertising a Nikon camera.

Bernbach, however, was not the only influence; in the same period David Ogilvy had established Ogilvy & Mather in New York and developed a reputation based on very different principles, primarily research. Using the findings of men such as Dr George Gallup, he formulated various 'rules' as the key to successful advertising, most famously 'people don't buy from clowns'.[32] He also preferred press to poster advertising, believing in the greater efficacy of the word, but for posters, for example those for the Schweppes campaign in the 1950s and '60s, he stated that research showed photographic or realistic illustration to be more effective than the more 'artistic' work of artists such as Savignac and Cassandre; art directors should confine themselves to not more than three elements in a design – a silhouette against a white background and minimal copy – so that the whole poster could be absorbed by the passer-by in five seconds.[33] By this time, the role of photography generally had changed, and now art directors worked mainly with photographers rather than illustrators, and were more in control of the visual image.

The changes however came gradually. In the mid-1960s DDB opened a London office and trained local staff. Advertising had expanded and a number of small advertising agencies and groups responded by offering specialist services, for example Minale Tattersfield. A London Designers and Art Directors Association was set up, based on the American model (founded in 1920) with annual exhibitions and publications, to recognize individual professional status.

A small number of graphic designers used autographic techniques as well as photography in their posters. Bob Gill, an American who joined Charles Hobson Grey (a subsidiary of the American agency Grey's) and then in 1962 became part of the design group Fletcher Forbes and Gill, was one. He differentiated between his work and that of the English poster artists by the fact that he worked to the same concept of the

214. Doyle Dane Bernbach (New York): art director: William Taubin; copywriter: Judy Protas. 'You don't have to be Jewish to love Levy's real Jewish Rye', USA, 1967. E.307-1973

'idea' as Bill Bernbach, producing simple, apposite, witty designs. This type of work, however, did not represent all poster advertising. Many mediocre posters were simply enlarged colour photographs. Ashley Havinden wrote in *The Times* in 1963:

> The creativity of the draftsman and of the poster artist have been sadly amputated. Photography is used in too many English advertisements today. Graphic design and the art of the poster as we know it seem to have entirely disappeared from the billboards in favour of enlarged photographs. Advertising these days does not appeal to the intuition of unconscious depths but to surface rationality tending to cupidity.

By the 1970s creative teams were the norm, and colour photography was being taken in new directions. Collett Dickenson Pearce (CDP) had been early aware of the changes in the USA, and in the early 1960s had established a reputation as a 'creative' agency through its use of such leading fashion photographers as Terence Donovan. Many of its campaigns were inspired by the design and photography used in innovative magazines, such as *About Town*, *Queen* and *Nova*. CDP expanded advertising photography to new lengths in 1977 when it began its Benson & Hedges campaigns, which continue today.

CDP had had the Gallaher account since 1963 and in 1965 launched the 'Pure Gold' campaign in which Benson & Hedges were equated with gold bullion bars. During the 1960s and 1970s in the UK, government restrictions were placed on cigarette advertising: no advertising on television; each packet and all promotional material to include government health warnings; scenes not to show cigarettes contributing to social or business success, depict young people or use celebrities, or associate cigarettes with nature. CDP devised the campaign based on the surreal photograph, inspired by Magritte, and the client allowed them an open brief. The campaign relied on a high level of visual literacy, as there was no overt message, and Alan Waldie, the art director, insisted on having the best photographers, such as Brian Duffy, Adrian Flowers and David Montgomery. Some advertisements were straightforward visual jokes, such as the image of the pyramids (see plate 227, chapter 6), while others required a second glance. In order to keep up these innovative ideas a number of teams worked on the campaign at the same time. By the 1980s no intact packets were shown, and the only copy was the government health warning. Now photography alone communicated the message, creating a sense of intrigue: viewers sought to solve the mystery and once they succeeded the product was remembered more clearly. The campaigns resulted in increased sales, as well as numerous awards for innovative advertising.

Photography has remained the main medium for posters, but the types of images have changed. In 1971, Levi's distributed an image of a nude female back (plate 215), reflecting the sexual liberation of the late 1960s and early 1970s and a period when denim jeans were synonymous with youth and rebellion. By the 1980s, following the growth of the women's movement, such images were not publicly acceptable. In 1984 research by Levi's agency, Bartle Bogle and Hegarty, showed that teenagers in the 1980s revered the America of the 1950s, in particular the

216. Bartle Bogle Hegarty (London): creative

team: Victoria Fallon and Steve Hudson;

photographer: Nick Knight. 'Levi's', UK, 1996.

E.875-1997

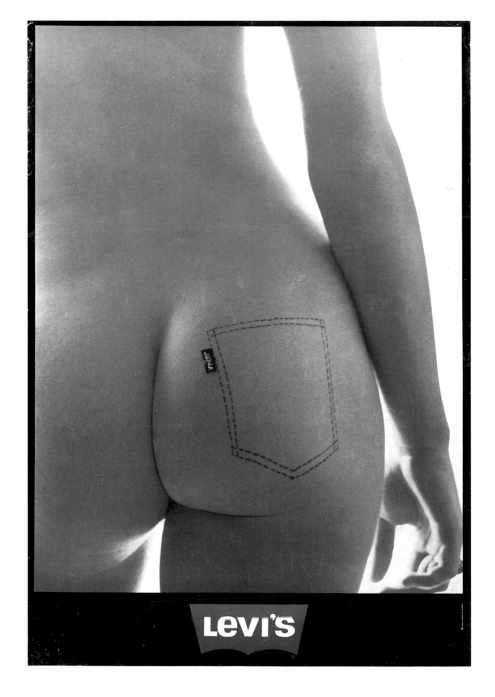

215. Ida van Bladel. 'Levi's', Belgium, 1973.

E.1546-1979

rebellious sex icons James Dean and Elvis Presley, as well as the clothes and collectables. The 'Classic America' campaign was launched by the 'Laundrette' commercial of 1985 which showed a well-muscled youth stripping down to his underpants; point-of-sale posters showing the star, Nick Kamen, were stolen from shops. The latest campaign has taken this theme further: those who had worn Levi's in the 1940s and 1950s and who still looked good in jeans were photographed by fashion photographer Nick Knight (plate 216). This marked a remarkable breakthrough in the ageist attitude of advertising towards fashion.

Advertising boomed in the 1980s, but many large companies over expanded and were hit by recession in the early 1990s. By 1993 the UK had an advertising expenditure of £9.5 billion; but in that year 62 per cent was spent on press, approximately 30 per cent on television and only a minute 4 per cent on posters and outdoor advertising. In the USA only 1 per cent of advertising expenditure was spent on posters. When commercial clients do decide to focus on posters, however, there are often very specific and interesting reasons.

Since the mid-1980s, The Body Shop has run over 20 issue-led poster campaigns, from those on the environment, such as *Stop the Burning* (Brazilian rainforests; plate 217) to those on Human Rights for Amnesty International. The owner of this toiletries and cosmetic company, Anita Roddick, estimated that around 2 million people went into the 400 shops every week, while

217. Jon Crossland. 'Stop the Burning', UK, 1990. E.3074-1991

Poster issued by **The Body Shop** plc to heighten public awareness of rainforest destruction.

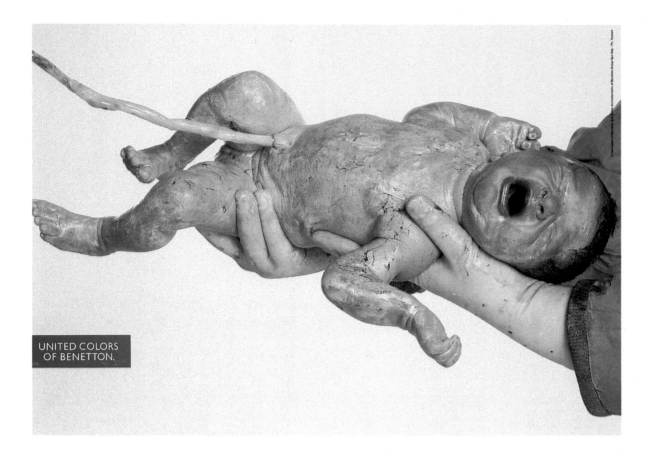

UNITED COLORS
OF BENETTON.

218. Benetton Creative Team: concept
and photography: Oliviero Toscani.
'United Colors of Benetton. Giusy',
Italy, 1991. E.2208-1997

219. Simons Palmer Denton Clemmow
& Johnson (London): art director:
Paul Shearer; copy director: Rob
Jack. Eric Cantona: 'I have worked
hard to improve English football. Now
it must be destroyed', UK, 1996.
E.884-1997

Poster for Nike sportswear.

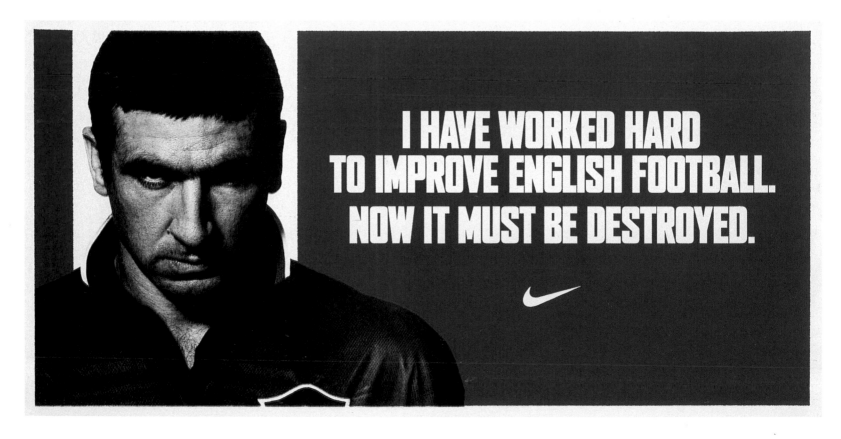

a further 10 million passed by their windows. Apart from publicizing the views of the founders, the poster campaign raised the profile of the company, led to media attention and increased sales. Similarly the clothing retailer, Benetton, has also used 'global problems' in its posters since the early 1990s, but this time to promote global fashion. In 1996 it had over 7,000 shops in 120 countries. The 'global issues' chosen to be represented under the slogan 'United Colors of Benetton' have been highly controversial. The poster of the new-born baby (plate 218) was quickly withdrawn in the USA and the UK, but perhaps the most controversial was the depiction of the dying AIDS activist David Kirby (see plate 232, chapter 6). Although Kirby's family gave permission for the advertisement, many felt the association of such a tragic image with the sale of jumpers was distasteful. Both owners of these commercial companies have described their aims in similar terms. The Body Shop stated: 'Poster campaigns in Body Shop windows are the most public forum the company possess for education and agitation',[34] while Toscani of Benetton stated: '... we touch on themes that unite the whole world. Advertising is the richest and most powerful form of communication in the world. We need to have images that will make people think.'[35]

Some companies with limited advertising budgets choose the economical option of posters (the 'Wonderbra' campaign – see plate 234, chapter 6 – is an example), but other companies specifically want to target people in the street, the best example being the Nike sportswear campaigns. The American agency Weiden & Kennedy targeted young people and used the 'cool' image of the street, which was so much a part of hip hop culture. Initial posters in New York used graffiti-like images and copy in the language of street talk. The British market is seen to need a slightly different campaign, but the agency Simons Palmer Denton Clemmow & Johnson still concentrate on posters with 'attitude' (plate 219).

In Japan posters are a prestigious form of advertising. Printing quality is extremely high (some are even silk-screened in limited editions), and both illustrations and photography are used. Consumer manufacturers, such as Shiseido Cosmetics and the drinks manufacturer Suntory and department stores, employ posters extensively. They are generally designed to be intriguing, even poetic, and to appeal more to the senses than to reason. Thus the poster by Makoto Saito for a Buddhist home altar shop depicts a photograph of a purple blue leg bone in an open white space. The simple text translates as: 'I am the future of the ancestor' (plate 220). Even his posters for the stores Parco and Garo confine their names to a small corner. In many examples there is therefore only a narrow divide between art and commercial graphics. Similarly advertising and graphic design are not seen as mutually exclusive, as in Europe. Designers and art directors can work freelance or as part of a team, such as in the two leading agencies, Dentsu and Hakuhodo.

Since the 1980s there has been much debate about the globalization of advertising, following the prediction of Marshall McLuhan in 1964 that the developments of mass media would create a 'global village', a shared global culture.[36] Key developments in the 1980s and 1990s in cross-border media have been satellite television and the Internet. Global marketing and communications services groups have formed international networks and include some of the largest advertising agencies.

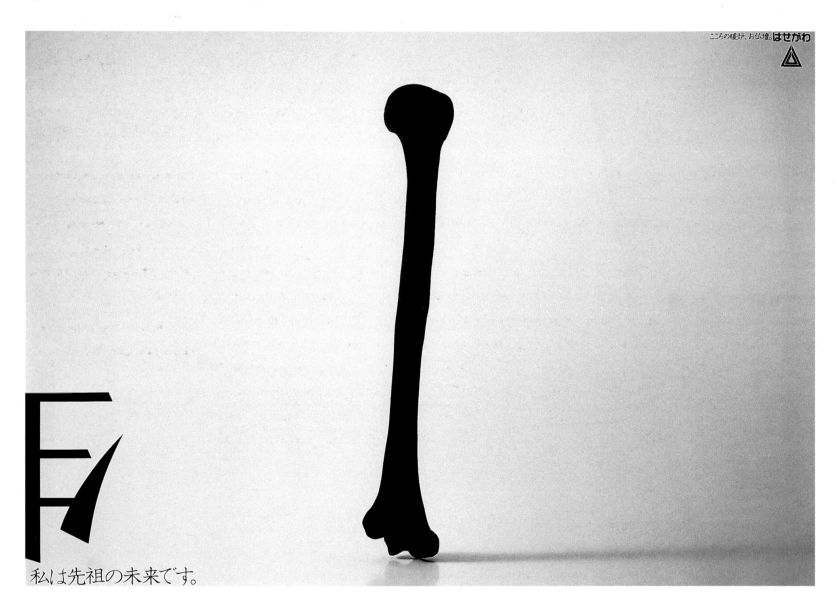

220. Makoto Saito. Hasegawa, Japan, 1985. E.2211-1997

Poster advertising a Buddhist home altar shop.

Yet few campaigns are in fact global, as national differences remain an important factor. Some areas are, however, moving this way: the youth market, for example, has some homogeneity in its interest in sport, rock music and teen lifestyle. Hollywood's dissemination of American popular culture internationally has been powerful. Levi's, for example, has run some European campaigns in Latin America and Asia. To be international, campaigns tend to focus on strong visual imagery, showing little copy, as with Benetton's images which deliberately avoid depicting their product because of different national fashions and seasons. The reception of these images is however culturally specific. Arab countries banned the image of the children sticking out their tongues, as it is considered pornographic to expose internal organs; the nun kissing the priest was banned in Italy; and the black woman suckling a white baby was seen, in the USA, to revive the racist stereotype of the black nanny: but the same campaigns won advertising prizes in other parts of the world. Global advertising is, however, possible (plate 221), and for many agencies will shape the form of the poster in the future.

221. Lowe Howard-Spink (London):
art director: Brian Campbell;
photographer: Mike Parsons;
copywriter: Paul Fallar.
'Smirnoff. The Other Side', UK, 1994.
E.2216-1997

Poster from a global campaign for
Smirnoff Vodka.

6 SELLING THE PRODUCT

JOHN HEGARTY

John Hegarty (born 1944) is Creative Director and Chairman of the advertising agency Bartle Bogle Hegarty Ltd. Having studied Graphic Design at the London College of Printing, he was Junior Art Director at Benton & Bowles, 1965-66, then Art Director at John Collings & Partners, 1966-67. In 1967 he joined the Cramer Saatchi consultancy, which in 1970 became Saatchi & Saatchi, where he was a founding shareholder and Deputy Creative Director, 1971-73. He was a founding partner and Creative Director of TBWA, London, 1973-82.

One of the most acclaimed Art Directors in the UK, John Hegarty includes among his credits 'Launderette' for Levi's and 'Vorsprung Durch Technik' for Audi. In 1994 he won the Design and Art Direction President's Award for outstanding achievements in the advertising industry, and he is a major spokesman for his profession. Here, in conversation with Margaret Timmers and Ruth Walton in January 1997, he discusses some famous poster campaigns and wider issues of advertising.

'*Guinness is Good for You*', *Bovril Prevents that Sinking Feeling* (plate 222) and *Persil Washes Whiter* are 'messages' that exist in our collective memory. They show the power of the poster to talk to a mass audience in a way that is both accessible and memorable, using the most public and ubiquitous form of advertising media. The ability of the poster to sell a product remains as strong today as ever. It is even having a second coming. In the first half of the twentieth century, along with newspapers and periodicals, it was a dominant force in commercial advertising. And although it went into a decline with the advent of commercial television, and much later commercial radio, its ability to reach a broad national audience is once again crucial in a world of increasingly fragmented electronic media.

My interest in posters was originally stimulated by Doyle Dane Bernbach's American campaign in the late 1950s for the Volkswagen Beetle, an incredibly successful and influential campaign which ran in the USA on posters, in print and on television and established the Beetle as the cult car of the time. At that date, after World War II, Volkswagen was still shaky and struggling to re-group. America was in the throes of thinking 'big', and here was a small motor car, rear engine, noisy, not much luggage space – how on earth could it be sold in America? It was DDB, under the creative guidance of Bill Bernbach, that produced an inventive campaign (plate 223) and turned the Beetle into a phenomenon, with huge sales – re-establishing Volkswagen as a major motor car manufacturer.

When I saw this campaign – so intelligent, witty, clever without being élitist, so involving yet not excluding – it was like a window in a darkened room being opened, or a light switch being thrown. I thought that this was what I would like to do. That is how I got into advertising back in the Sixties. At that time, most people going into advertising were artists more interested in painting, or were writers who were really trying to write a book, but who would knock out a bit of copy to keep paying the bills; Fay Weldon who worked as a

222. H.H. Harris. 'Bovril Prevents that sinking feeling', UK, 1920. Produced by S.H. Benson. E.39-1973

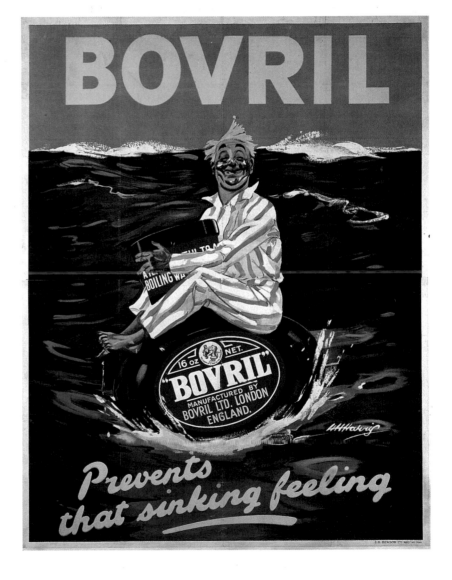

Think small.

Our little car isn't so much of a novelty any more.
A couple of dozen college kids don't try to squeeze inside it.
The guy at the gas station doesn't ask where the gas goes.
Nobody even stares at our shape.
In fact, some people who drive our little flivver don't even think 32 miles to the gallon is going any great guns.
Or using five pints of oil instead of five quarts.
Or never needing anti-freeze.
Or racking up 40,000 miles on a set of tires.
That's because once you get used to some of our economies, you don't even think about them any more.
Except when you squeeze into a small parking spot. Or renew your small insurance. Or pay a small repair bill. Or trade in your old VW for a new one.
Think it over.

223, *left* **Doyle Dane Bernbach (New York): art director: Helmut Krone; copywriter: Julian Koenig. Press advertisement from the 'Think Small' campaign, USA, 1960. Client: Volkswagen of America.**

copywriter at Mather & Crowther in the 1950s was an example. As a profession, advertising was not considered serious. But through the 1960s and 1970s it was realized that pop art – the popular arts – was a great instigator of what is happening in the world. And poster advertising is an art form that speaks to everybody, a wonderful medium in full view of the public, which involves everyone in its creativity.

In order to sell, advertising must convert as well as confirm. In my view the 'overheard conversation' is almost as important as the direct address. The power of poster advertising rests in its ability not only to talk to targeted consumers, but also to influence the casual bystander, thereby enhancing the value of a product in the eyes of a wider public. It is important to establish a simple issue that the brand should communicate, and then relentlessly to pursue that issue wherever the advertising appears. Much advertising fails, not because it has not got something interesting to say, but because it fails to simplify its message, thus confusing the public.

The 1982 UK campaign for 'Black Levi's' (plate 225), was to promote the concept of black denim. Naturally it had to be done in a stylish and fashionable way to attract the right audience, people who were young, streetwise and fashion conscious. Posters were chosen, first because they were the fastest way, with selected sites, to reach this fairly elusive clientele. The style magazines of today were not being published back in the early 1980s, and television was too expensive. Also, because posters are such a public medium, it was possible through them to make that fashion statement to a very wide audience.

224. Mather & Crowther (London): art director: Ruth Gill; copywriter: Francis Ogilvy; photography: Len Fulford. 'Go to work on an egg', UK, c. 1957. Client: The British Egg Marketing Board.

225. Bartle Bogle Hegarty (London): art director: John Hegarty; copywriter: Barbara Noakes; photgrapher Alan Brooking. 'Black Levi's', UK, 1982. Client: Levi Strauss.

"I never read The Economist."

Management trainee. Aged 42.

It was an interesting brief, and the final concept was a simple but dramatic exposition of the value of black: a flock of white sheep heading in one direction with a single black sheep in their midst heading the other way, with the line 'Black Levi's. When the world zigs, zag'. Initially, Levi's were unsure about this approach; they worried that it was too subtle and that there was no picture of the jeans. But eventually they decided it was challenging, and that the product did not have to be shown to make the point. Because the poster made viewers think, it forced them to complete the circle of logic and therefore became a much more powerful piece of communication. It did not try to spoon-feed the idea to its audience; it simply dramatized the point Levi's were trying to communicate.

A poster makes its impact out of the juxtaposition of words and images in some shape or form. But the important thing is to simplify the message. Blaise Pascal wrote to one of his correspondents (1657), 'I have made this letter longer than usual, only because I have not had the time to make it shorter'. The poster is denied the luxury of long, elegant headlines and extensive copy, so it must make its point fast and powerfully, and, by reduction, create a message that is both memorable and compelling. The more an idea is distilled, the more forceful it becomes; it is part of the fascination and strange allure of the poster that it can say so much by using so little. Especially nowadays, as we are increasingly bombarded with messages, this skill becomes ever more relevant. It is an essential factor in the art of communication.

226. Abbott Mead Vickers BBDO: art director: Ron Brown; copywriter: David Abbott. ' "I Never Read The Economist". Management Trainee. Aged 42', UK, 1988. Client: The Economist. E.2149-1997

Take the advertisement for *The Economist* (1988): "'*I never read* The Economist". *Management Trainee, Aged 42*' (plate 226): in eight words and a number, the poster defines the magazine, and creates for it a competitive edge. You are told what it does, that it is for business people, that it is aspirational, that it has clever ideas, and that smart people who are successful or on the way up read it. The boldness and apparent anarchy of the slogan grab your attention and make you think. Again the circle of communication between creator and observer must be completed.

Coded messages can be an extremely effective way of reaching your public. In Saatchi & Saatchi's poster launching *The Independent* (1986), the phrase 'It is. Are you?' identified the target audience. If you understood the enigma, then perhaps you should be reading the newspaper. It was an unusual example of making the poster work in a tangential way, of seeking an audience who would identify with it, and therefore with the product. Because those who found it a bit too clever would reject it, in a sense it created a kind of club of people who were in the know. The conundrum was the challenge.

In the long-running UK campaign for Benson & Hedges cigarettes, the viewer is enticed into working out the puzzle of the gold box (plate 227). Why is it there, and what does it mean? This works on the theory that the more you are forced to use your imagination, the more you will remember. A powerful message is one that opens out inside your head, not one that is laid out, ready-made before you. Ironically, the only words on the Benson & Hedges posters tell you not to smoke!

Another powerful method of getting people to identify with the product is through humour; it binds people together, makes the unacceptable acceptable, makes you listen more attentively. And if you are really listening, there is a chance that you might be learning and remembering. The adult literacy poster (1964) for the Chicago Board of Education, '*I quit school when I were sixteen*' is witty and pithy, and immediately makes you think. In UK advertising especially, irony is important. The British think they have the ability to mock themselves; this implies inner security, and a sense of belonging. Irony succeeded in the 'Heineken. Refreshes the parts other beers cannot reach' campaign (plate 228), and in the previously mentioned *Economist* advertisement.

Capturing the true desires and ambitions of the public has always been an important factor in selling a product; and posters provide a chronicle of the changes and developments in urban society. The early London Underground posters (from 1908) played on the longing for green pastures and a rural escape from the city (plate 229). Similarly, in the 1930s, Shell tapped the aspirations of the newly mobile public, when it advertised the delights of the countryside, yet reassured motorists of Shell's fuel presence everywhere (plate 230). The graphic artists created images of wish fulfilment, and they had an invisible finger on the pulse of the nation.

227. **Collett Dickenson Pearce & Partners (London): art director: Neil Godfrey; copywriter: Tony Brignull; photography: Jimmy Wormser. 'Benson & Hedges Special Filter', UK, 1977. Printer's proof. Client: Gallaher Ltd. E.1884-1990**

228. **Collett Dickenson Pearce & Partners (London): art director: Alan Waldie; illustrator: Mike Terry. 'Heineken. Refreshes the parts other beers cannot reach.' UK, 1976. Printer's proof. Client: Whitbread & Co. plc. E.365-1982**

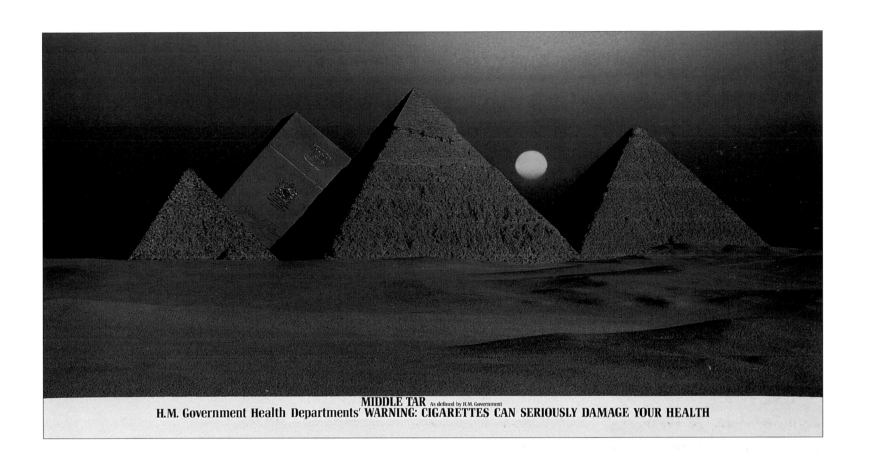

MIDDLE TAR As defined by H.M. Government
H.M. Government Health Departments' WARNING: CIGARETTES CAN SERIOUSLY DAMAGE YOUR HEALTH

Heineken. Refreshes the parts other beers cannot reach.

The recent (1991) Bartle Bogle Hegarty Häagen-Dazs campaign (plate 231), was ultimately selling pleasure rather that just a luxury ice-cream. The initial research revealed that people described eating that brand of ice-cream as a sensual, almost sexual, experience. Just as wearing perfume is not about stopping smells but is about feeling good and being alluring, so Häagen-Dazs was promoted on its sensuous appeal, thus creating a completely new sector for the ice-cream market, one that would choose the ice-cream because it was advertised as sexy and pleasurable.

Creative processes attempt to adjust the viewer's perspectives in some way, either attitudinal or visual. One of the advantages of the poster can be its sheer size and scale. If you have a large 48-sheet poster, with a large pea on it, you will look at that pea as you have never looked at a pea before, in the way Pop Art took very mundane objects and blew them up hugely. When a painting of a tin of Campbell's Soup was put on exhibition, you were made to look at it and wonder what a can of soup was doing in a gallery; it made you think. A poster can also present something and alter the way you look at it, make you look again and re-assess it. The idea of placing an object in an outrageous way was part of advertising before surrealism became an art movement.

231. Bartle Bogle Hegarty (London): art director: Rooney Carruthers; copywriter: Larry Barker; photographer: Jeanloup Sieff. 'It is the intense flavour of the finest ingredients combined with fresh cream that is essentially Häagen-Dazs', UK, 1991. Printer's proof. Client: Grand Metropolitan Foods Ltd. E.874-1997

Shock tactics provide another common means of persuasion, although causing outrage can be counter-productive. Benetton's campaigns have created great controversy. Some people find the images they use frightening, or feel they should not be shown, and others, like me, perhaps are worried about the ethics of what they are doing. Does Benetton really believe in and support the issues and causes they promote, such as AIDS (plate 232) and the environment? In my view, the images themselves are not affronting – for example, the picture of a baby being born is simply truthful: a newly born baby does look like that, covered in blood (see plate 218). We should not be offended by normal everyday things, because that simply creates ignorance in society.

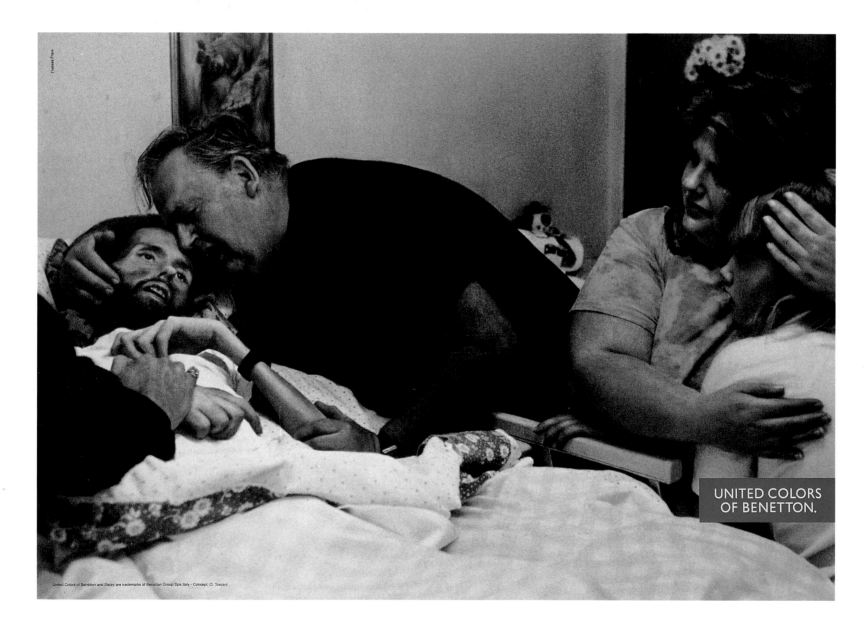

UNITED COLORS OF BENETTON.

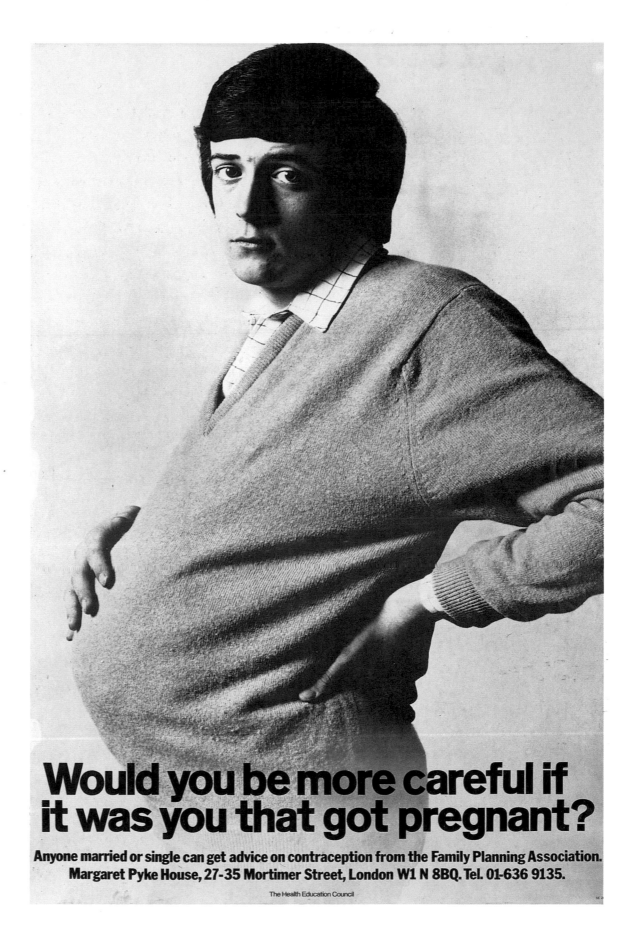

Would you be more careful if it was you that got pregnant?

Anyone married or single can get advice on contraception from the Family Planning Association. Margaret Pyke House, 27-35 Mortimer Street, London W1 N 8BQ. Tel. 01-636 9135.

The Health Education Council

232. Benetton Creative Team: concept: Oliviero Toscani. 'United Colors of Benetton', Italy, 1991. Based on a photograph by Therese Frare entitled 'Final Moment', 1990. Client: Benetton Group Spa. E.2207-1997

Therese Frare, an American photographer, took the original photograph as part of a series documenting the work and life of AIDS activist David Kirby.

233. Cramer Saatchi (London): art director: Bill Atherton; copywriter: Jeremy Sinclair; photographer: Alan Brooking. 'Would you be more careful if it was you that got pregnant?' UK, 1969. Client: The Health Education Council. E.755-1997

But what one generation finds shocking, the next generation finds perfectly acceptable. For example, the pregnant man ('*Would you be more careful if it was you that got pregnant?*'; plate 233) devised by Cramer Saatchi (the forerunner to the agency Saatchi & Saatchi) for the UK Health Education Council in 1969 was considered fairly shocking, even offensive, at the time. But taste is such a blurred issue, and the question was whether the message justified the means: that poster was making a very powerful point. A sophisticated public frequently sees through the advertiser's tactics, and determines not to be manipulated by them. In response, the advertiser can intensify the shock, causing controversy and debate, but occasionally can go too far so that the campaign backfires.

A poster is trying to create an impact. When you walk down the street a thousand images hit you: a red bus, a new yellow car, a shop window, a house painted a strange colour, someone with a funny hat on .... It is in the power of the poster's creator to bite through this visual clutter and break into people's consciousness. It is exciting to be given the opportunity to say something on a 48-sheet poster, pasted up in a main city thoroughfare or throughout the country, to a potentially huge audience. The poster is the people's art, making statements in the public domain and in a medium that is accessible to all.

It was striking that the UK 1994 Wonderbra campaign was on posters – a good example of Marshall McLuhan's theory that 'the medium is the message'. It was a very simple advertisment, unusual because underwear publicity had previously been largely confined to women's magazines. Here however it was up on a huge scale, and the medium was being used provocatively, challenging with slogans like 'Hello Boys' (plate 234) and 'Or are you just pleased to see me?' Words normally only said in private were being said in public, and the target audience was forced to respond.

Another device to gain the viewer's attention is to use the poster's physical location in an inventive way, for instance to play off the clichés of the surrounding posters or even physically to alter the site that has been bought. In the UK in 1992 the Prudential bought pairs of sites and put a spoof travel poster, 'Holiday 92°', in half of the 96-sheet space, emphasizing the adjacent Prudential advertisement captioned 'I want to be in the other poster'. Then there are three-dimensional posters, like the famous one for Araldite where a real car was glued to the hoarding with the caption 'It also sticks handles to teapots'. Recently, some posters have used sounds and smells as gimmicks to gain attention. But there is a danger in getting too gimmicky: people remember the gimmick, not the message. It is best to remember that a hoarding is a space bounded by four pieces of wood, in which you have to distil a complex message down to a simple thought that is both powerful and motivating.

In my view, posters have once again become a truly broadcast medium. Electronic media are becoming ever more fragmented, with each commercial channel focusing on specific target audiences, but the poster remains a constant medium. It can conduct a nationwide campaign, address broad audiences across society, and its great glory and value remain that it can speak to us all, in public, in a language we understand, with few barriers to entry.

234. TBWA: art director and copywriter: Nigel Rose; photographer: Ellen von Unwerth. 'Hello Boys. The One and Only Wonderbra', UK, 1994. Client: Playtex. E.872-1997

EPILOGUE

HOW POSTERS HAVE CHANGED THE LANDSCAPE

CHARLES NEWTON

Posters are an essential ingredient of Modernity.[1] From the end of the eighteenth century, the modern world, as we see it now, sprang up like a fast-growing plant rooted in the fertile soil of new industry and commerce, replacing forms of life that had endured for millennia. The poster flourished in parallel both with the expanding needs of mass propaganda, and with the necessity to sell more and more consumer goods. At first composed of the printed word, and illustrated (if at all) with small black and white images, by the end of the nineteenth century the poster was the medium for a vast range of iconography, increasingly brilliant in colour, like the packaging of the goods it often advertised.

The inner landscape of the imagination and the outer landscape of the environment were subject to a stream of completely new kinds of image competing for attention. Huge colour prints, once rare and remarkable, became through posters commonplace elements in the sight and memory of every citizen. They changed the perception of the world by thrusting forward pictures, sometimes tinged with fantasy, sometimes composed of it, ineluctably creating a store of mental images in everyone. This was inevitable, given the vast resources poured into their production and display. Modern posters are deliberately designed to appeal to the intellect and the emotions of as great an audience as possible, and from the beginning their copywriters, artists and designers showed immense skill and creativity.

'The fact that poster and other advertising images invade the unconscious was exploited by the founders of Dada and Surrealism, George Grosz and John Heartfield in 1916 (or according to another account, Raoul Hausmann and Hannah Höch in 1918), who claimed to have started with absurd collages of advertisements.[2]

Human beings, particularly urban dwellers, constantly need colour and fantasy. City streets were always a kaleidoscopic show, even in the ancient world. Roman cities, for example, were not

the pure white, cool, classical, icing-sugar assemblage of the architectural historian's fantasy, but the setting for a riot of brilliantly polychrome sculptures on temples and public buildings, whose walls were often disfigured by dense and scabrous graffiti. So although colour posters are modern, they slot into a pre-existing pattern of urban landscape, meeting the human need to bring life and colour to the city street. We might imagine that eighteenth-century London was a city of grace and elegance, now that the surviving buildings have been cleaned and 'heritagized', but that would be to forget the forest of painted signboards and large three-dimensional signs that adorned the bustling streets. A

235. Anonymous. 'Astley's Advertising Cart', UK, c. 1830. Watercolour. British Museum, London, 1880/11/13/5408

multiplicity of vigorous images roughly made for the purpose of trade advertisement jostled and competed for attention in the smoky air, often to bizarre effect. Addison, writing in *The Spectator* in 1710, noted: 'Our streets are filled with blue boars, black swans, and red lions, not to mention flying pigs, and hogs in armour, with many creatures more extraordinary than any in the deserts of Africa'. If the language were modernized slightly, this could be a description of the *outré* images produced by some of the more creative advertising agencies nowadays.

Yet with the advent of Modernity, the look of these streets has changed, partly because of the modern poster. The London signs seen by Addison, and admired (some even painted) by Hogarth, were in the eighteenth century perceived as quaint. The modern poster which came after was not quaint, but something newer, unprecedented, and *raw*. By the middle of the nineteenth century cities everywhere were in a proto-Modernistic chaos of building and rebuilding and posters flourished. Paris, the very cradle of Modernity, had wide boulevards ruthlessly driven through its crowded medieval and Renaissance arrondissements at the command of Baron Haussmann. The modern city (and the perception of it) changed at alarming speed.

In Paris and London, as the old buildings were demolished, rough hoardings would mushroom around the building sites. On them would appear, just as rapidly, a bewildering array of posters, stuck on by a new race of *afficheurs* (or bill-stickers as they were less romantically known in England). After the hoardings came down the *afficheurs* would seek new places to carry out their work – often clandestinely. There was never enough space for the commercial expression that was needed. In Paris the defiant words 'Défense d'afficher' were sometimes even carved into the stonework of the buildings in the hope that this would deter the irresistible commercial forces behind illegal fly-posting. The famous *vespasiennes*,[3] or circular cast-iron street urinals, were found to be perfectly adapted for poster sites. They typify the pragmatic approach of the new advertisers, desperate for wall space.

Since the introduction of printing to Europe, bills had always been posted on walls, including official proclamations, advertisements, unofficial and even illegal or subversive statements. The images at first were monochrome, crude woodcuts, and never large. The pace of increasing change was accelerated by the French Revolution:

> Every morning in Paris forty bill stickers would paste the city with news of battles won or lost; edicts of the King and the government; public festivities to mark some auspicious event; timely indications about the transport of ordure or the removal of graves. At moments of crisis they would be defaced or (illegally) supplanted by notices parodying government orders or pillorying ministers.[4]

236. Rue Descartes, viewed from the rue Mouffetard, Paris 5e. France, c. 1870-4. Photographed by Charles Marville. Bibliothèque Historique de la Ville de Paris.

237. Poster-covered hoardings screening building work in the Strand, London, 1900-01.

238. Petr Chytrý. 'Václavské náměstí, PRAHA, listopad 1989' ('Wensceslas Square, Prague, November 1989'), Czechoslovakia E.117-1991

Detail of a poster illustrating scenes in Wenceslas Square during the Velvet Revolution, showing posters illegally displayed on the base of the Wenceslas monument.

239. Music-hall posters on the Thames Coffee

Shop, Cheyne Walk, London, 1865

(see chapter 1, p.28). Anonymous photograph.

Chelsea Library, L/2798

In the following century, railway cuttings and embankments caused livid scars in the landscape, bringing the new commercial ethos to every town of any size, and creating completely new cities *en route*. The commerce, and the commercial art that it generated, needed, and enforced, a modern form of expression. Steam power and colour lithography provided this means, and by 1870 it was possible to produce and distribute huge rapidly made images in large quantities. As successive waves of construction moved out from city centres, so the poster flowed wherever the railways, roads

and tendrils of speculative building reached, and insinuated itself into the open countryside.

In the UK, among other institutions The Countryside Commission and The Council for the Preservation of Rural England (CPRE) looked askance at the attempts by the big advertising agencies to cover the countryside with hoardings along the ribbon development of the new arterial

240. Fifth Avenue and 98th Street,

New York, USA, 1913.

Photograph from *The Mayor's*

Billboard Advertising Commission.

roads. Country dwellers, particularly those who had recently fled the city, bitterly opposed any new poster hoarding sites that threatened their particular locality. This struggle continues to this day. By the 1920s planning was certainly needed, as the improved technologies of colour printing were exploited by advertising agencies to reach new and previously inaccessible customers with their publicity. American advertising, which provided the model, provoked Ogden Nash's verse:

> I think that I shall never see
>
> A billboard lovely as a tree.
>
> Perhaps, unless the billboards fall,
>
> I'll never see a tree at all.[5]

It was the automobile that ultimately threatened the landscape of America, as it

> became a more and more powerful machine, and speeds increased, the small winding roads which were such convenient points of display were by-passed by the straight, wide ribbons which cut through the open country side. The billboard was developed and became a primary poster display device. Billboards were placed strategically within the vision of the occupants of the automobiles speeding past them.[6]

Frank Pick, in charge of London Transport design and advertising, was also a leading member of the CPRE. In preparation for an article on advertising, he had noted in 1923 that in America standard large posters were 26 ft wide by 10 ft high, a result, he thought, of the creation of the Ford car. Car drivers needed a wider poster to give themselves time to register what was on display. 'Initially it seems exaggerated like most American things – but it is thought applied to a problem – with thought comes reform.'[7]

241. 'A Tree of Knowledge, Salford, Oxfordshire', UK, 1937. Photographed by John Piper. Ph. 270 1997

The free-for-all in Britain prompted such harsh comments as those in *The Observer* of 21 June 1931:

> The act of 1925 gives local authorities considerable powers of control .... The best advertisers have ceased to scream across moors and bellow in a bluebell wood, but those who insist on ... 'mad dog publicity' can at least be notified by post card that this is the way to avert custom and not to find it ...

The 'best advertisers' included Shell, who decided in the 1930s to support the Campaign for the Preservation of Rural England by placing their posters on the backs and sides of lorries rather than on roadside sites. The debate was an acknowledgment of the dominating impact of the unfettered poster. With many other forms of advertising there is a choice, but 'Poster advertising is widely regarded as the only true mass form of advertising which can reach entire populations, including those who refuse to let other media, like television, into their homes'.[8]

Posters arouse conflicting feelings. While many people, most of the time, welcome the splash of colour, the appeal to the emotions, the exotic places, the glamour brought to things, products and places ordinarily thought of as mundane, there are and were dissenting voices. Since posters deliberately appeal directly to the emotions, the responses they provoke range from pleasure, nostalgia and amusement, to rage and despair at the inanity of their messages and their impact on the familiar scene, whether in the city or in the countryside.

Early posters were not all by talented artists with high-quality images printed in subtle and glorious colour. The majority were mundane in design and content. In the 1920s Oliver St John Gogarty (poet, writer, surgeon and the model for Buck Mulligan in James Joyce's *Ulysses*) took a jaundiced view from the railway carriage as he travelled from Liverpool, and glanced at the posters by the way: 'Liverpool to London, judging by advertisements for food, sauces, soups, purgatives, and hygienic porcelain, is an intestinal tract'.[9]

In James Joyce's Dublin, posters are part of the landscape and fabric of modern life, inspiring new thoughts and surges of feeling; there is some censure, but mostly amusement or recalled pleasure. To the knowledgeable eye of the advertising agent Bloom in *Ulysses*, various poster images occur and re-occur as he wanders the city. There is the leitmotif of a theatre poster showing 'A charming soubrette, the great Marie Kendall, with dauby cheeks and lifted skirt, [who] smiled daubily from her poster ...'. And erotic imagery as 'Wise Bloom eyed on the door a poster, a swaying mermaid smoking mid nice waves. Smoke mermaids, coolest whiff of all. Hair streaming: lovelorn. For some man. For Raoul.'[10]

Dorothy L. Sayers took a sceptical look at the advertising industry in *Murder Must Advertise*, a detective novel based on her experiences working as a successful copywriter for Benson's:

> Not on the wealthy, who buy only what they want when they want it, was the vast superstructure of industry built up, but on those who ... could be bullied or wheedled into spending their few hardly won shillings on whatever might give them, if only for a moment, a leisured and luxurious illusion. Phantasmagoria – a city of dreadful day, of crude shapes and colours piled Babel-like in a heaven of harsh cobalt and rocking over a void of bankruptcy – a Cloud Cuckooland... [11]

George Orwell's wartime diaries reveal a disillusionment with modern advertising, but acknowledge the power of the poster: 'Always, as I walk through the Underground stations, sickened by the advertisements, the silly staring faces and strident colours, the general frantic

242. Jean de Paleologu ('PAL'). 'Whitworth Cycles', France, before 1896. E.270-1921

243. St James's Park Underground station with posters *in situ*, 1948. The names 'St James Park' and 'St James's Park' appear simultaneously in different parts of the station. The London Transport Museum, U40346

244. Political poster on a wall in
Teheran, Persia, 1956. Photographed
by the American Edward R. Miller,
Ph.156-1967

245. 'Appel, 1950', France.
Photographed by Otto Steinert.
Ph.308-1985

struggle to induce people to waste labour and material by consuming useless luxuries or harmful drugs ...'[12] Orwell did not disapprove of all posters however: he knew how powerful they were in the service of propaganda. His earlier participation in the Spanish Civil War prompted him to note how the wartime Ministry of Information was failing its public: '... A striking thing is the absence of any propaganda posters of a general kind, dealing with the struggle against Fascism, etc. If only some one would show the MOI the posters used in the Spanish war, even the Franco ones for that matter'.[13]

Following the London Blitz, posters found another habitat on the first signs of reconstruction. To the generation that grew up after the bombing and conflagration, the sight of rosebay willowherb or fireweed growing through the rubble in the ruined cellars, surrounded by a high poster-clad fence, was the City of London's most melancholy image.

Posters are so much a part of our collective unconscious that they have become a metaphor for memory itself: they are, as it were, brilliantly coloured fantasies, clean and new at first, then decaying, fading away in the strong light of a new day, or patched and peeled, sheet after sheet building up into layers of card, like layers of meaning. As the Czech writer Bohumil Hrabal wrote of the process of memory:

> I was emptying out of myself drawers and boxes full of old bills and useless letters and postcards, as if fragments of tattered poster were blowing out of my mouth, posters pasted one on top of the other, so that when you rip them away you create nonsense signs, where soccer matches blend into concerts or where art exhibits get mixed up with brass band tattoos .... [14]

Some images can even become fossils, when the process of renewal and destruction is overtaken by events, as at the abandoned London Underground stations where the posters are sealed in a time capsule, still in place above the ghostly platforms.

246. Advertising posters on buses, Threadneedle Street, London, c. 1922.

Love and hate for the unsettling and impermanent alternate. Posters contribute to the restlessness of Modernity, both in the landscape of the city and in the landscape of the mind. In some people, they can give rise to feelings of alienation. It is difficult to be rooted in a place if the imagination is continuously stimulated by unsettling and bizarre images, infinitely brighter and more enticing than the grey streets that surround the hoardings. Paradoxically, the skills of the best artists and draughtsmen gave an impossible glamour to a place or product in a town which would never see it in reality. In heavy industrial areas in the 1930s, only in a poster would you experience exotic palm trees and the shining sands of the Pacific. Real life, as most people struggled to endure it, and the dream world of the imagination were contrasted and characterized as early as 1929 as 'The pain of living and the drug of dreams'.[15]

Posters encapsulate the ambivalence felt by human beings about the modern world. They are a mix of fantasy and reality, sometimes seductive and sometimes repellent, depending on the mood of the observer. What cannot be denied is that the poster has become irredeemably, for better or worse, part of our ever-changing landscape.

247. 'Air Power 1979', USA, 1982. Photographed by Robert W. Fichter. Hand-coloured gelatin-silver print. Ph.121-1984

The old-fashioned billboard poster, set in a car lot, is recruiting for the ultra high-tech **US Air Force. This is** paralleled by the photographer's use of crude hand colouring and toy rubber stamps to subvert the pretensions of his own high-quality photographic print. Thus the image and its subject-matter are filled with Post-modern ironies.

NOTES AND BIBLIOGRAPHIES

Introduction

NOTES

1. John Ruskin, letter 21 (September 1872) in *Fors Clavigera: Letters to the workmen and labourers of Great Britain (The Works of John Ruskin). Library Edition*, E. T. Cook and A. Wedderburn (eds) (London, George Allen, 39 vols, 1903-12), vol. XXVII, 1907, p. 355.
2. Roger Marx, Preface to *Les Maîtres de l'Affiche* (Paris, 1899), vol. IV, pp. I-IV.
3. *L'Estampe et l'Affiche* (Paris, 1899), vol. 3, pp. 69-72 and 114-116.
4. René Grohnert, 'Hans Sachs – der Plakatfreund', in *Kunst Kommerz Visionen: Deutsche Plakate 1888-1933*, an exhibition catalogue of the Deutsches Historisches Museum, Berlin, 1992.
5. Martin Hardie was Assistant Keeper (1914-21) and Keeper (1921-35) of the Museum's Department of Engraving, Illustration and Design (precursor of the Department of Prints, Drawings and Paintings).
6. Hardie and Sabin (1920), pp. 4-5.
7. V&A Archive: Nominal File (hereunder referred to as VANF): London Underground Electric Railways. Letter from Frank Pick to Cecil Harcourt Smith, 1 June 1909.
8. Ibid. Letter from Cecil Harcourt Smith to Frank Pick, 12 June 1909.
9. Ibid. Letter from Frank Pick to Cecil Harcourt Smith, 24 October 1911.
10. Bella (ed.)(1894), pp. 7-12.
11. VANF: Mrs Agnes Clarke. Letter from Martin Hardie to the Director, Cecil Harcourt Smith, 31 January 1921.
12. VANF: Shell-Mex Co. Ltd. Letter from Eric Maclagan to Jack Beddington, 5 July 1938.
13. VANF: London & North Eastern Railway. Letter from W. M. Teasdale to Martin Hardie, 14 August 1925.
14. Constantine (1986), p. 1.
15. Harold F. Hutchison. 'A Poster Tradition', *Art For All* (1949), p. 20.
16. Brian Reade (1913-89) joined the V&A in 1936, and was Deputy Keeper in the Department of Prints and Drawings (1958-73). He organized both the successful *Art Nouveau Designs and Posters by Alphonse Mucha* (1963) and *Aubrey Beardsley* (1966) exhibitions at the V&A. His standard monograph *Beardsley* (London, Studio Vista) was published 1967, revised 1987.

BIBLIOGRAPHY

Bella, Edward (ed.), *A Collection of Posters. The Illustrated Catalogue of the First Exhibition* (London, Royal Aquarium, 1894)

Constantine, Stephen, *Buy & Build. The Advertising Posters of the Empire Marketing Board* (London, HMSO, 1986)

L'Estampe et l'Affiche (Paris, L'Estampe et l'Affiche, 3 vols, 1897-99)

Hardie, Martin, and Sabin, A. K., *War Posters issued by Belligerent and Neutral Nations, 1914-19* (London, A. & C. Black Ltd, 1920)

Jones, Sydney R. (text), and Holme, C.G. (ed.), 'Posters and their designers', *The Studio*, Special Number (Autumn 1924)

London Transport Executive, *Art For All* (London, Art and Technics Ltd, 1949)

Maîtres de l'Affiche, Les (Paris, Chaix, 5 vols, 1896-1900)

Plakat: Mitteilungen des Vereins der Plakatfreunde, Das (Berlin, Max Schildberger, 12 vols, 1910-21)

PART I: PLEASURE AND LEISURE

1 Posters for Performance

NOTES

1. Marks (1896), p. 232.
2. 'Fine Art Gossip', *The Athenaeum*, 27 October 1894, no. 3496, p. 576.
3. Campbell (1990), p. 15.
4. Marks (1896), p. 232.
5. Smith (1863), p. 63.
6. Price (1913), p. 21.
7. Francis Jourdain. Quoted in Huisman and Dortu (1964), p. 91.
8. Guilbert (1929), p. 75.
9. Ibid., p. 80.
10. Dudley Hardy. Quoted in 'Dudley Hardy and His Posters' by 'Idler', *The Poster*, December 1899, p. 188.
11. Kauffer (1924), p. x.
12. Hiatt (1895), p. 220.
13. Campbell (1990), p. 84.
14. Marion H. Spielmann, 'Posters and poster designing in England', *Scribner's Magazine*, New York, July 1895, vol. xviii, p. 46.
15. *Windsor Magazine* (1933), p. 340.
16. *Comoedia Illustré*, 1911. Quoted in translation in Steegmuller (1986), p. 79.
17. Quoted in conversation with Maurice Denis, 7 June 1981; see Ades (1984), p. 77.
18. Jan Sawka in conversation with the author, April 1997.
19. Grushkin (1987), p. 71.
20. Ibid., p. 73.
21. Ibid., p. 73.
22. Victor Moscoso. Quoted in 'Bill posters will be stoned', *Mojo*, June 1997, p. 16.
23. Michael English in conversation with the author, April 1997.
24. Neville (1995), p. 96.
25. Holger Matthies in conversation with the author, April 1997.
26. Bob King of Dewynters in conversation with the author, May 1997.
27. Jamie Reid in Reid and Savage (1987), p. 57.
28. Naylor (1990), p. 379.

2 Posters for Art's Sake

NOTES

1. Susan Sontag, 'Posters: advertisement, art, political artifact, commodity' in Stermer (1970).
2. See my essay, 'Function and Abstraction in Poster Design' in Ades (1984).
3. Roger Marx, preface to vol. III (1898) of *Les Maîtres de l'Affiche, Masters of the Poster 1896-1900* (London, Academy Editions, 1977), transl. Bernard Jacobson, p. 14.
4. Roger Marx, preface to vol. II (1897), ibid., p. 12.
5. Ibid., p. 13.
6. Roger Marx, preface to vol. I (1896), ibid., p. 11.
7. Maurice Talmeyr, 'L'Age de l'Affiche', *Revue de deux mondes*, 137, September 1896, pp. 208-09, quoted in Varnedoe and Gopnik (1991), p. 236.
8. Joris-Karl Huysmans, *Le Voltaire*, Paris, 17 May 1879, quoted in Hillier (1969), p. 33.
9. Wyndham Lewis, Introduction to the catalogue for the first Vorticist Exhibition, Doré Galleries, London, 1915.
10. Fernand Léger, 'Contemporary Achievements in Painting' (1914) in Fernand Léger, *Functions of Painting* (London, Thames & Hudson, 1973), p. 12.
11. El Lissitzky, 'Exhibitions in Berlin', *Veshch*, 3, Berlin, 1922, quoted in Ades (1984), p. 29.
12. F.T. Marinetti, 'War, the World's Only Hygiene', quoted in Ades, ibid.
13. Fry (1926), p. 19.
14. Barr (1936), p. 24. This original edition was produced as a catalogue to accompany an exhibition at the Museum of Modern Art. For a more detailed discussion see Ades (1984), pp. 23-24.
15. Abdy (1969), p. 164..

16. See Dominique Marechal, *Brugge Stedelijke Musea: Collectie Frank Brangwyn Catalogus* (Bruges, Stedelijke Musea, 1987), pp. 26-30.
17. See Banham (1960), p. 72.
18. Ibid., p. 73.
19. Roger Fry, Introduction, *Second Post-Impressionist Exhibition* catalogue, Grafton Galleries, London, 1912, p. 20.
20. See Fischer Fine Art Bomberg catalogues for 1973 and 1988 (no. 23).
21. C.R.W. Nevinson, *Paint and Prejudice* (London, 1937), p. 125.
22. C.R.W. Nevinson, preface to catalogue *Pictures by Nevinson*, Leicester Galleries, London, 1919.
23. El Lissitzky, 'Proun, Not World Visions BUT – World Reality', De Stijl 1922, transl. Sophie Lissitzky-Küppers, *El Lissitzky : Life, Letters, Text* (London, Thames & Hudson, 1968), p. 343.
24. Richard Hamilton with John McHale, quoted in Richard Morphet 'Commentary' for the catalogue for the exhibition, *Richard Hamilton*, Tate Gallery, London, 1970, p. 30; exhibition toured to Stedelijk van Abbemuseum, Eindhoven and Kunsthalle, Bern, both 1970.
25. Richard Hamilton, catalogue introduction, *Slip it to me*, Hanover Gallery, London, 1964.
26. Seymour Chwast, statement in Naylor, ed., (1990), p. 107.
27. Barnicoat, in Naylor (1972), p. 107-8.
28. See for example his poster for the Exhibition of Soviet Art, Zurich, 1929, in Ades, *Photomontage*, p. 62, or Ladislav Sutnar's poster for an exhibition of modern trade in Brno, Czechoslovakia, 1929, see Ades (1984), p. 142.
29. The Guerrilla Girls, *Confessions of the Guerrilla Girls* (London, HarperCollins, 1995).

BIBLIOGRAPHY for Part I: Pleasure and Leisure

Abdy, Jane, *The French Poster* (London, Studio Vista, 1969)
Ades, Dawn, *The 20th-century Poster: Design of the Avant-Garde* (New York, Abbeville Press, 1984)
    Photomontage (London, Thames & Hudson, 1976; revised ed. 1986)
Banham, Rayner, *Theory and Design in the First Machine Age* (London, Architectural Press, 1960)
Barnicoat, John, *Posters* (London, Thames & Hudson, 1972; reprinted 1994)
Barr, Alfred, *Cubism and Abstract Art* (New York, The Museum of Modern Art, 1936)
Bazarov, Konstantin, 'Diaghilev and the radical years of Modern art', *Art and Artists* (London, Hansom Books, 1966-86), July 1975, vol. 10, no.4
Bella, Edward (ed.), *A Collection of Posters. The Illustrated Catalogue of the First Exhibition* (London, Royal Aquarium, 1894)
Bernhardt, Sarah, *My Double Life. The Memoirs of Sarah Bernhardt* (London, Peter Owen, 1977)
Black, Clementina, *Frederick Walker* (London and New York, Duckworth, 1902)
Bojko, Szymon, *New Graphic Design in Revolutionary Russia* (London, Lund Humphries, 1972)
Bouret, Jean, *Toulouse-Lautrec* (London, Thames & Hudson, 1964)
Campbell, Colin, *The Beggarstaff Posters: The Work of James Pryde and William Nicholson* (London, Barrie & Jenkins, 1990)
Cate, Phillip Dennis, and Gill, Susan, *Théophile Alexandre Steinlen* (Salt Lake City, Gibbs M. Smith, 1982)
Dydo, Krzysztof, *Polish Film Posters. 100th Anniversary of the Cinema in Poland* (Krakow, Krzysztof Dydo, 1996)
Fry, Roger, *Art and Commerce* (London, Hogarth Essays, 1926)
Grushkin, Paul, *The Art of Rock* (New York, Abbeville Press, 1987)
Guilbert, Yvette, *The Song of My Life* (London, Harrap, 1929)
Haill, Catherine, *Theatre Posters* (London, HMSO, 1983)
Hiatt, Charles, *Picture Posters* (London, George Bell & Sons, 1895)
Hillier, Bevis, *Posters* (London, Weidenfeld & Nicholson, 1969)

Hoole, John, and Sato, Tomoko (eds), *Alphonse Mucha* (London, Lund Humphries, in association with the Barbican Art Gallery, 1993)

Huisman, P., and Dortu, M.G., *Lautrec by Lautrec* (London, Macmillan, 1964)

Kauffer, E. McKnight, *The Art of the Poster* (London, Cecil Palmer, 1924)

Lambourne, Lionel, *The Aesthetic Movement* (London, Phaidon, 1996)

Maindron, Ernest, *Les Affiches Illustrées 1886-1895* (Paris, Librairie Artistique, 1896)

Maîtres de l'Affiche, Les (Paris, Chaix, 5 vols, 1895-1900)

Marks, J.G., *The Life and Letters of Frederick Walker* (London and New York, Macmillan, 1896)

Muriand, Raoul, *Les Folies Bergère* (Sèvres, Editions La Sirène, 1994)

Naylor, C. (ed.), *Contemporary Designers*, 2nd edn (Chicago and London, St James Press, 1990)

Neville, Richard, *Hippie Hippie Shake* (London, Bloomsbury, 1995)

Pessis, Jacques, and Crepineau, Jacques, *Les Folies Bergère* (Rennes, Fixot, 1990)

Price, Charles Matlock, *Posters: A Critical Study of the Development of Poster Design in Continental Europe, England and America*
    (New York, George W. Bricka, 1913)

Reid, Jamie, and Savage, Jon, *Up They rise: The Incomplete Works of Jamie Reid* (London, Faber, 1987)

Rennert, Jack (ed.), *The Poster Art of Tomi Ungerer* (Zürich, Diogenes, 1971)

Selling Dreams: British and American film Posters 1890-1976 (Welsh Arts Council Exhibition Catalogue, 1977)

Smith, William, *Advertise. How? When? Where?* (London, Routledge, Warne and Routledge, 1863)

Steegmuller, Francis, *Cocteau* (London, Constable, 1986)

Stermer, Dugald, *The Art of Revolution: 96 Posters from Cuba* (London, Pall Mall Press, 1970)

Twyman, Michael, *Printing 1770-1970* (London, Eyre & Spottiswoode, 1970)

Varnedoe, Kirk, and Gopnik, Adam, *High and Low: Modern Art and Popular Culture* (New York, Museum of Modern Art, 1991)

PART II: PROTEST AND PROPAGANDA

3 The Propaganda Poster

NOTES

1. Eric Hobsbawm, *Echoes of the Marseillaise* (London, Verso, 1989), pp. 2-23.

2. Polychromatic lithographs had been available since 1817.

3. *Punch*, 13 October 1888, pp. 170-71.

4. Eric Hobsbawm, 'Mass Producing Traditions: Europe, 1987-1914' in E. Hobsbawm and T. Ranger (eds), *The Invention of Tradition* (Cambridge, CUP, 1983).

5. A connection between Christianity and the sword was made in other reflections on the affair. The Dreyfusard periodical *Le Sifflet* published a cartoon which showed a cross rising on the horizon before which a crowd genuflected. The caption asked the rhetorical question 'Est-ce une Croix ou un Sabre?' (10 March 1898).

6. See L. Tickner, *The Spectacle of Women. Imagery of the Suffrage Campaign 1907-14* (London, Chatto and Windus, 1987).

7. George Bernard Shaw cited by Tickner, ibid., p. 159.

8. Hardie and Sabin (1920), p. 8.

9. L. Davidoff and C. Hall, *Family Fortunes. Men and Women of the English Middle Class 1780-1850* (London, Hutchinson, 1987), *passim*.

10. See M.L. Sanders and P. Taylor, *British Propaganda during the First World War* (London, Macmillan, 1982), pp. 141-50.

11. See S. Baker, 'Describing images of the national self. Popular accounts of the construction of pictorial identity in the First World War poster', *Oxford Art Journal*, 13:2 (1990), pp. 24-30.

12. Curtis (1980), p. 48.

13. C. Asquith, *Diaries 1915-1918* (London, Hutchinson, 1968), p. 17. Ironically, the rather literary and sometimes convoluted speeches of her father-in-law, Prime Minister Asquith, were quoted at length in PRC posters.

14. G. Orwell, 'My Country Right or Left' (1940) in *The Collected Essays, Journalism and Letters of George Orwell*, vol. 1 (London, Secker & Warburg, 1968), p. 537.

15. Lambert (1938), p. 152.

16. R. Kenney (Foreign Office minute dated 19 February 1932) quoted by P.M. Taylor, *The Projection of Britain* (Cambridge, CUP, 1981), p. 5.

17. See Constantine (1986).

18. A. Rodchenko, 'Foto-montazh' in *LEF*, no. 4, 1924, p. 41, quoted in C. Lodder, *Russian Constructivism* (New Haven and London, Yale, 1981), p. 187.

19. See D. Welch (ed.), *Nazi Propaganda: The Power and the Limitations* (London, Croom Helm, 1983) and D. Welch, *The Third Reich: Politics and Propaganda* (London, Routledge, 1993).

20. *The Times*, cited by L. MacLaine, *Ministry of Morale* (London, George Allen & Unwin, 1979), p. 31.

21. R. Minns, *Bombers and Mash* (London, Virago, 1980), p. 187.

22. A. Marwick (ed.), *Total War and Social Change* (London, Macmillan, 1988), p. xvi.

23. See Anon., 'War Propaganda from Soviet Russia' in *Art and Industry*, May 1945, pp. 130-38.

24. R. Willet, *The Americanisation of Germany 1945-1949* (London, Routledge, 1989), p. 2.

25. Atelier Populaire (1969).

26. I. Orosz in Sylvestrová (1992), p. 11.

27. E. Bell, 'Politicians take a Pasting' in *The Observer*, 8 March 1992, p. 37.

▣ Four in Focus

NOTES
BRANGWYN

1. Minna Lewinson, 'Artists Mobilize for World War' in *The Poster*, Chicago, June 1917, p. 24.
2. Frederic Haskin, 'War Brings Advance in Poster Art' in *The Poster*, Chicago, May 1918, p. 83.
3. Hardie and Sabin (1920), p. 13.
4. William de Belleroche, *Brangwyn Talks* (London, Chapman & Hall, 1944; limited edition), p. 7.
5. R. Brangwyn, *Brangwyn* (London, William Kimber, 1978), p. 173. Rodney Brangwyn received this information from Kenneth Center, Brangwyn's assistant for many years. Author's conversation with Rodney Brangwyn, 30 April 1997.
6. Will Dyson was an official war artist for the Australian government. His violent war cartoons published in the British press reflected his own experiences in the trenches.
7. Letter dated 27 May 1918 from H. Holford Bottomley, Head of Special Publicity for the National War Savings Committee, to Lieut. Charles ffoulkes, Imperial War Museum. File ref. Art Dept, Brangwyn, 366/8.
8. Reginald G. Praill, undated (after 1938) typescript account of Brangwyn's posters held at The Jointure.
9. Rickards (1968), p. 14.
10. Ibid., p. 23.
11. Author's conversation with Rodney Brangwyn, 30 April 1997.
12. R.G. Praill, undated typescript, op. cit.
13. P. Macer-Wright, *The Study of a Genius at Close Quarters* (London and Melbourne, Hutchinson, 1940), p. 95.
14. W. de Belleroche, *Brangwyn's Pilgrimage* (London, Chapman & Hall, 1948), p. 80.

FOUGASSE

15. Founded in 1937 by Tom Harrisson, Charles Madge and Humphrey Jennings to create a study of the everyday lives of ordinary people in Britain, Mass-Observation was co-opted by the government during World War II to report, through interviews and overheard conversations, on various aspects of the population's reactions to the current situation. Extracts from the Mass-Observation Report *Government Posters in War Time* are copyright the Trustees of the Mass-Observation Archive at the University of Sussex and are reproduced by permission of the Curtis Brown Group Ltd, London.
16. M-O, FR2 (1939), p. 75.
17. The wording was criticised for not mentioning the navy and amended in the published version.
18. M-O, FR2 (1939), p. 45.
19. Ibid., p. 127.
20. Ed. with an introduction by Bevis Hillier, *Fougasse* (London, Elm Tree Books, 1977), p. 15.
21. Fougasse, *The Good-Tempered Pencil* (London, 1956), p. 76.

22. Fougasse (1946), p. 14.
23. Ibid., pp. 43-48.
24. The government's anti-rumour campaign generated in summer 1940 by the fear of spies and fifth columnists is discussed by Ian McLaine in his book *Ministry of Morale* (London, Allen & Unwin, 1979).
25. John Gloag, *Commercial and State Propaganda in War-Time*, in Mercer and Lovat Fraser (1941), p. 21.
26. Quoted by Ernest O. Hauser in 'The British Think It's Funny', *Saturday Evening Post*, 28 January 1950, p. 27.

I WANT OUT

27. 'Unmasking the Pentagon', *Newsweek*, 8 March 1971, p. 74.
28. Philip Dougherty, 'Advertising: Plan Seeks to Unsell the War', *The New York Times*, 23 March 1971, p. 60.
29. Ibid. For a full account of the campaign see Mitchell Hall, 'Unsell the War: Vietnam and Antiwar Advertising', *The Historian* (Allentown, Pa.), vol. 58, autumn 1995, pp. 69-86.
30. Conversation 15 May 1997 with Larry Dunst, originator of *I Want OUT*.
31. The poster was reissued by Darien House Inc., New York. The V&A's impression of the poster, gift of the publisher, is from this reissue.
32. *United States Statutes at Large Containing the Laws and Concurrent Resolutions Enacted During the First Session of the Eighty-Seventh Congress of the United States of America 1961 and Reorganization Plans, Amendment to the Constitution, and Proclamations*, vol. 75 (Washington, United States Government Printing Office, 1961), p. 966.
33. Maymie R. Krythe, *What So Proudly We Hail* (New York, Evanston and London, Harper & Row, 1969), p. 49.
34. Hal Morgan, *Symbols of America* (New York, Penguin Books, 1987), p. 21.
35. Letter to the author 4 March 1997 from James Fraser, author of *The American Billboard: 100 Years* (New York, Harry N. Abrams Inc., 1991).
36. Susan E. Meyer, *James Montgomery Flagg* (New York, Watson-Guptill, 1974), p. 37.
37. Hall (1995), op. cit., p. 74.
38. *Newsweek*, 3 May 1971, pp. 24-25.
39. McCormich in Martin (1996), p. 27.

'56.10.23

40. Author's conversation with the artist, 1 March 1997.
41. Ibid.
42. Ibid.
43. Ibid.
44. K. Bakos, in *Posters by PÓCS* (Hungary, Zrinyi Publishing, 1990), p. 8.
45. Author's conversation with the artist, 1 March 1997.
46. István Orosz, 'The Age of the Poster' in Sylvestrová and Bartelt (1992), p. 12.

BIBLIOGRAPHY for Part II: Protest and Propaganda

Atelier Populaire, *Mai 1968: Posters from the Revolution, Paris May 1968* (London, Dobson Books, 1969)

Balfour, M., *Propaganda in War 1939-1945. Organisations, Policies and Publics in Britain and Germany* (London, Routledge, Kegan Paul, 1979)

Constantine, S., *Buy & Build: The Advertising Posters of the Empire Marketing Board* (London, HMSO, 1986)

Curtis, B., 'Posters as Visual Propaganda in the Great War', *Block*, 12 (1980), p. 48

Evans, D., and Gohl, S., *Photomontage: A Political Weapon* (London, Fraser, 1986)

Fougasse, *A School of Purposes: A Selection of Fougasse Posters, 1939-1945*, introduced by A.P. Herbert (London, Methuen, 1946)

Hardie, M., and Sabin, A.K., *War Posters issued by Belligerent and Neutral Nations 1914-19* (London, A. & C. Black, 1920)

Haste, C., *Keep the Home Fires Burning; Propaganda in the First World War* (London, Allen Lane, 1977)

Hayward Gallery, London (exh. cat.) *Art and Power: Images of the 1930s* (1995)

Jobling, P., and Crowley, D., *Graphic Design. Reproduction and Representation since 1800* (Manchester University Press, 1996)

Jowett, G.S., and O'Donnell, V., *Propaganda and Persuasion* (London, Sage, 1992)

Lambert, R.S., *Propaganda* (London, Nelson, 1938)

Landsberger, S., *Chinese Propaganda Posters: From Revolution to Modernisation* (Amsterdam, Pepin Press, 1995)

McLaine, I., *Ministry of Morale* (London, Allen & Unwin, 1979)

McQuiston, L., *Graphic Agitation: Social and Political Graphics since the Sixties* (London, Phaidon, 1993)

Martin, Susan (ed.), *Decade of Protest: Political Posters from the United States, Viet Nam, Cuba, 1965-1975* (Santa Monica, Smart Art Press, 1996)

Mercer, F.A., and Lovat Fraser, Grace (eds), *Modern Publicity in War* (London and New York, Studio Publications, 1941)

M-O FR2, *Government Posters in War Time* (October 1939)

Rees, L., *Selling Politics* (London, BBC Books, 1992)

Rhodes, A., *Propaganda. The Art of Persuasion in World War II* (New York and London, Angus & Robertson, 1976)

Rickards, M., *The Rise and Fall of the Poster* (Newton Abbot, David & Charles, 1971)

— *Posters of the First World War* (London, Adams & Mackay, 1968)

Sylvestrová, M., and Bartelt, D., *Art as Activist: Revolutionary Posters from Central and Eastern Europe* (London, Thames & Hudson, 1992)

Tisa, J., *The Palette and the Flame: Posters of the Spanish Civil War* (London, Collet's, 1980)

White, S., *The Bolshevik Poster* (New Haven and London, Yale University Press, 1988)

PART III: COMMERCE AND COMMUNICATION

5 Commercial Advertising

NOTES

1. This text attempts to place the V&A's collection of posters within the history of commercial advertising: the collection, although large, is not comprehensive, and this is reflected in this survey.

2. For example Camille Mauclair, *Jules Chéret* (Paris, 1930); E. Maindron, *Les Affiches illustrée 1886-1895* (1896); R. Marx (ed.), *Les Maîtres d'Affiche* (Chaix, 1896-1900); C. Hiatt, *Picture Posters* (1895); André Mellerio, *La Lithographie originale en couleurs* (1898); Henri Beraldi, *Les Graveurs du XIX siècle* (1886).

3. Bradford Collins, 'Poster as Art: J. Chéret and the Struggle for the Equality of the Arts in late 19th-century France', *Design Issues* (spring 1985), vol. II, no. 1, p. 50.

4. Cate and Hitchings (1978).

5. See note 2 above.

6. Bella (1894), pp. 10-11.

7. For example W.P. Frith, 'Artistic Advertising', *The Magazine of Art* (1889), pp. 421-27.

8. Millais' reactions are not known. His son, J.G. Millais, published his account in his *Life and Letters of Sir John Everett Millais* (London,

Methuen, 1899), p. 189. According to T.J. Barratt's letter to *The Times*, 17 November 1899, p. 14, Millais described it as 'magnificent' and even said: 'I will paint as many pictures for advertisements as you like to give me commissions for ...'. Charles Deschamps' letter to *The Times*, 23 November 1899, p. 15, quoted Millais as saying, 'It is an admirable reproduction and is a credit to Messrs. Pears, and to my picture, which is a good one'.

9. See note 7.

10. *Pall Mall Gazette*, 14 June 1884, pp. 19-20.

11. A.E. Johnson, *Dudley Hardy, R.I., R.M.S.* (London, 1909), p. 39.

12. W.S. Rogers, 'W.S. Rogers on his poster work', *The Poster*, November 1899, p. 98.

13. S.H. Benson, *Wisdom in Advertising* (London, 1901); *Force in Advertising* (London, 1904); *Facts for Advertisers* (London, 1905); and *Five Fingers of an Advertising Organisation* (London, 1911-12).

14. S.H. Benson, *Advertising Equipment in S.H. Benson Ltd* (London, c. 1912-14).

15. Quoted in Strasser (1989), p. 93.

16. H.C. Bunner, 'American Posters Past and Present', *The Modern Poster* (New York, Charles Scribner's Sons, 1895), p. 78.
17. *Bradley: His Book* (May 1896).
18. M. Bogart, *Advertising and the Borders of Art* (Chicago and London, University of Chicago Press, 1995), p. 87.
19. Presbrey (1929), pp. 384-85.
20. resbrey (1929), p. 528.
21. M. Bogart, *Advertising and the Borders of Art* (Chicago and London, 1995), p. 118.
22. *La Revue de L'Union de L'Affiche Française* (December 1926) quoted in Mouron (1985), p. 15.
23. *L'Art International d'Aujourd'hui* (1929) quoted in Mouron (1985), p. 48.
24. President of the Advertising Association, 1928.
25. Percy Bradshaw, 'Art and Advertising' (London, 1925), p. 86; Turner (1952), chapter 7.

26. Frostick (1970), Prologue.
27. Haworth-Booth (1979), p. 49.
28. E. McKnight Kauffer, 'Art and advertising, the designer and the public', *Journal of the Society of Arts* (1938), vol. 87, pp. 51-70.
29. Quoted in Green (1990), p. 141.
30. *Commercial Art*, April 1927, p. 137.
31. *Architectural Review* (1942).
32. David Ogilvy, *Confessions of an Advertising Man* (London, Pan, 1963), p. 116.
33. Ibid., chapter 7.
34. *Body Shop Annual Report* (1989), p. 7.
35. L. Baker, 'Taking advertising to its limits', *The Guardian*, 22 July 1991, p. 29.
36. Marshall McLuhan, *Understanding the Media: The Extensions of Man* (New York, McGraw Hill, 1964).

BIBLIOGRAPHY for Part III: Commerce and Communication

Bella, Edward (ed.), *A Collection of Posters. The Illustrated Catalogue of the First Exhibition* (London, Royal Aquarium, 1894)

Brandt, F., *American Posters: Designed to Sell* (Virginia Museum of Fine Arts, 1994)

Broido, Lucy, *The Posters of Jules Chéret* (New York, Dover, 1982)

Block, Jane, *Hommage to Brussels: The Art of Belgian Posters 1895-1915* (New Jersey, The Jane Voorhees Zimmerli Art Museum, 1992)

Campbell, Colin, *The Beggarstaff Posters* (London, Barrie & Jenkins, 1990)

Cate, Philip, and Hitchings, S.H., *The Colour Revolution: Colour Lithography in France 1890-1900* (Santa Barbara and Salt Lake City, Peregrine Smith, 1978)

Cole, B., and Durack, R., *Railway Posters 1923-1947* (London, Laurence King, 1992)

Dempsey, Mike (ed.), *Early Advertising Art from A. & F. Pears Ltd.* (London, Fontana, 1978)

Dobrow, L., *When Advertising Tried Harder: The Sixties* (New York, Friendly Press, 1984)

Friedman, Mildred, et al., *Graphic Design in America* (Minneapolis, Walker Art Center, 1989)

Frostick, M., *Advertising and the Motor Car* (London and New York, Lund Humphries, 1970)

Games, Abram, *Over My Shoulder* (London, 1960)

Green, Oliver, *Underground Art* (London, Studio Vista, 1990)

Haworth-Booth, Mark, *E. McKnight Kauffer* (London, Gordon Fraser, 1979)

Hewitt, John, *The Commercial Art of Tom Purvis* (Manchester Metropolitan University Press, 1996)

Hindley, D. and G., *Advertising in Victorian England 1837-1901* (London, Wayland, 1992)

Kinross, Robin, 'From Commercial Art to Plain Commercial', *Blueprint*, April 1988, pp. 105-12

Marchand, Roland, *Advertising the American Dream* (Berkeley, University of California Press, 1985)

Margolin, Victor, *American Poster Renaissance* (New York, Watson-Guptill, 1975)

Meggs, Philip, *A History of Graphic Design* (New York, Viking, 1985)

Mouron, Henri, *Cassandre* (London, Thames & Hudson, 1985)

Murgatroyd, Keith, *Modern Graphics* (London, Studio Vista, 1969)

Nevitt, T.R., *Advertising in Britain* (London, Heinemann, 1982)

Pigott, S., *OBM* (London, Ogilvy Benson & Mather, 1975)

Presbrey, F., *The History and Development of Advertising* (New York, Doubleday, Doran, 1929)

Rennert, Jack, and Weill, A., *Alphonse Mucha* (Boston, G.K. Hall, 1984)

Strasser, Susan, *Satisfaction Guaranteed* (New York, Pantheon, 1989)

Sumitomo, Kazuko, et al., *Posters – Japan 1800s-1980s* (Nagoya, The Bank of Nagoya, 1989)

Thornton, Richard S., *Japanese Graphic Design* (London, Lawrence King, 1991)

Turner, E.S., *The Shocking History of Advertising* (Harmondsworth, Penguin, 1952)

Varnedoe, Kirk, and Copnik, Adam, *High and Low: Modern Art and Popular Culture* (New York, Museum of Modern Art, 1991)

Weill, Alain, *The Poster* (London, Sotheby's Publications, 1985)

Epilogue: How Posters Have Changed The Landscape

NOTES

1. Marshall Berman proposes definitions for Modernity in *All that is Solid melts into Air: The Experience of Modernity* (New York, Simon & Schuster, 1982).
2. Hans Richter, *Dada, Art and Anti-Art* (London, Thames & Hudson, 1965), p. 117.
3. Named after the Roman Emperor Vespasian who notoriously imposed a tax on the collection of urine for the cloth-fulling trade. See Suetonius, *The Twelve Caesars*.
4. Simon Schama, *Citizens: A Chronicle of the French Revolution* (London, Viking, 1989), vol. IV, p. 181.
5. Ogden Nash, 'Song of the Open Road', *Happy Days* (London, John Lane, 1936).
6. Edgar Breitenbach and Margaret Coswell, *The American Poster* (New York, The American Federation of Arts, 1967), p. 52.
7. Frank Pick, typescript in Frank Pick file, London Transport Museum Archives, Covent Garden, London.
8. John Trimbos, 'Hoarding up positive benefit for outdoor advertisements', *Planning*, 16 August 1996.
9. Oliver St John Gogarty, *As I was going down Sackville Street* (London, Rich & Cowan, 1937), chap. III.
10. James Joyce, *Ulysses* (London, The Bodley Head, 1960), pp. 326, 339.
11. Dorothy L. Sayers, *Murder Must Advertise* (London, Gollancz, 1931), chap. XI.
12. George Orwell, *Collected Essays*, vol. 2, 'Wartime Diary' (London, Penguin), 14 June 1940 entry.
13. Ibid., 27 June 1940.
14. Bohumil Hrabal, *I served the King of England*, transl. Paul Wilson (London, Picador, 1990), p. 221.
15. T.S. Eliot, 'Animula', *Ariel Poems*, No. 23 [single sheet] (London, Faber & Faber, 1929).

ILLUSTRATION ACKNOWLEDGEMENTS

Introduction

Plate

2. Courtesy of the London Transport Museum
3. Photograph courtesy of the Shell Art Collection at The National Motor Museum, Beaulieu
4. Museum of London, no. 29-166
5. © News Team International Limited, Birmingham
6. Courtesy BMP DDB Limited
9. Courtesy of the London Transport Museum
10. Courtesy of Curatorial Assistance and the E.O. Hoppé Trust
11. © ADAGP, Paris and DACS, London, 1997

1 Posters for Performance

15. The Tate Gallery, London, no. 2080
16. Mary Evans Picture Library
20. © ADAGP, Paris and DACS, London 1997
26. © ADAGP, Paris and DACS, London 1997
29. Courtesy of Aerofilms of Borehamwood
31. Reproduced by permission of Elizabeth Banks
33. © ADAGP, Paris and DACS, London 1997
35. Courtesy of Rosemary Meredith
36. Courtesy of Charmian Varley
38. © DACS 1997
40. © ADAGP Paris and DACS, London 1997
41 and 42. Courtesy of International Olympic Committee
43. © Bubbles Incorporated S.A. 1997
45. © Edward Bawden. All rights reserved DACS
47. Courtesy of Hubert Hilscher
48. Courtesy of Jan Sawka.
49. Wes Wilson © 1967 Bill Graham Enterprises
50. Courtesy of Michael English
51. Toppan Picture Library
52. Courtesy of Martin Sharp

55. © Robert Rauschenberg/VAGA, New York/DACS, London 1997
56. Courtesy of Per Arnoldi
57. Courtesy Twentieth Century Fox
58. Courtesy of Holger Matthies
59. Courtesy of International Olympic Committee
60. Courtesy of Boris Bucán
61. V&A
62. Courtesy of the ENO/Anthony Crickmay
64. Reproduced by courtesy of Warner Brothers

2 Posters for Art's Sake

65. © Roy Lichtenstein/DACS 1998
66. Courtesy La Biennale di Venezia
72. © DACS 1998
74. © Casa Ricordi Historical Archive
75. © 1978 The Duncan Grant Estate
76. © DACS 1997
77. © Dinora Davies-Rees and Juliet Lamont
79. © Anne C. Patterson
81. Courtesy of Richard Hamilton
82. UFA Productions
84. © 1967 Neon Rose
85. © Mednarodni Graficni Likovni Center
86. Courtesy of Seymour Chwast
87. © Guerrilla Girls

3 The Propaganda Poster

88. Hulton Getty Picture Library
89. © DACS 1997
91. National Museum of Labour History
92. Courtesy of Bob Cramp
101. Courtesy Ministerio de Educación y Cultura, Archivo Histórico Nacional, Sección Guerra Civil, Cartel No. 481
106. © DACS 1997
110. Courtesy of Patrick Braddell
111. Courtesy of the American Cancer Society
116. Private collection
121. © Campaign for Nuclear Disarmament
122. Courtesy of the Estate of Paul Peter Piech
123. © Danny Lyon and Edwynn Houk Gallery, NYC

124. © Ben Shahn/VAGA, New York/DACS, London 1997.
127. © Usine-Université-Union
128. © Martin Walker and Bernadette Brittain
129. Courtesy of Pen Dalton
130. © Robert Rauschenberg/VAGA, New York/DACS, London 1997
131. Courtesy of David Bailey
133. Courtesy of Gran Fury/Avram Finkelstein

4 Four in Focus

136 and 137. Courtesy of the London Transport Museum
140. Private collection.
154. Courtesy of Larry Dunst
156. Imperial War Museum cat. no. 2747
157. Imperial War Museum cat. no. 2734
158. Imperial War Museum cat. no. 2524
159 to 161. © DACS 1997

5 Commercial Advertising

164 to 166. © ADAGP, Paris and DACS, London 1997
170. © Casa Ricordi Historical Archive
174. © ADAGP, Paris and DACS, London 1997
176. Reproduced by permission of Elizabeth Banks
178. Courtesy of Skegness Town Council
179. Courtesy of CPC Ltd
182. © Maxfield Parrish/VAGA, New York/DACS, London 1997
185. © A.C. Fincken and B.R.Fincken
186 and 187. © ADAGP, Paris and DACS, London 1997
191. © DACS 1997
192. Courtesy of Deutsche Bahn
194 © Guinness Brewing Worldwide Ltd
196. Reproduced with kind permission of Pat Schleger
197. Courtesy of the London Transport Museum
198. The National Railway Museum
199. Courtesy of the Shell Art Collection at the National Motor Museum, Beaulieu
200. Courtesy of Shell Mex and B.P. Advertising Archive

202. Courtesy of the Post Office
203. Courtesy of Yoshito Okuyama
204. © DACS 1997
205. © Herbert Leupin
206. Courtesy of Tomi Ungerer
207. Courtesy of Newsweek
208. © The Estate of Abram Games
209. Courtesy of Milton Glaser
210. © DACS 1997
211 and 212. Courtesy of Olivetti Spa
213. Courtesy of Yusaku Kamekura
215 and 216 Courtesy of Levi Strauss & Co
217. Courtesy of the Bodyshop
218. © Oliviero Toscani/United Colors of Benetton
219. Courtesy of Nike
220. Courtesy of Makoto Saito
221. Courtesy of Lowe Howard-Spink

6 Selling the Product

222. Courtesy of CPC Ltd
223. Courtesy of Volkswagon of America
224. Courtesy of Mather & Crowther
225. Courtesy of Alan Brooking
226. Courtesy of The Economist/Abbot Mead Vickers, BBDO Ltd
227. Courtesy of Jimmy Wormser
228. Courtesy of Heineken/Lowe-Howard Spink
229. Courtesy of the London Transport Museum
230. Courtesy of the Shell Art Collection at the National Motor Museum, Beaulieu
231. Courtesy of Häagen-Dazs
232. © Oliviero Toscani/United Colors of Benetton
233. Courtesy of Alan Brooking
234. Courtesy of Playtex

Epilogue

235. The British Museum
236. Bibliothèque Historique de la Ville de Paris
237. Hulton Getty Picture Library
239. Courtesy of Chelsea Library, L/2798
243. Courtesy of the London Transport Museum
245. © Stefan Steinert
246. Hulton Getty Picture Library

INDEX